SUPERMAN'S EYES

Six true and sordid stories
about big city cops.

Bluebird Publishing Co.
St. Louis, MO 63144
www.Bluebirdbookpub.com

Table of Contents:

PROLOGUE

When I first met the famous movie star, Christopher Reeve, I was a beat cop at Union Station, the historical refurbished luxurious old train station that was now a mall with a four star hotel built inside of it.

There was a room built especially for him, a room for someone who was severely injured and unable to fend for himself in anyway.

As luck would have it, it was raining in St. Louis and cold. I spent most of my time inside the old building. I was a thirty year veteran of the cop business, and I knew how to schmooze a free meal or a place to be comfortable. Entitlement is one of the first lessons learned in the cop/crook game of survival.

The radio dispatcher gave me an assignment to meet an ambulance in the front of the station. When a cop is advised to meet anyone or anything, it usually means trouble for the cop. We are all leery of such an assignment. Most times it is another cop trying to dump his problem call on you, or a supervisor who is drunk, has wrecked his car, and expects you to be his savior and write him out of his dilemma.

I cautiously walked outside into the weather and looked for an ambulance. I found it; it was big and fancy, customized for someone important, I noted. The driver asked me if I would direct him as he backed up the ramp at the east side of the building.

I replied with a "sure" as the driver blocked traffic on Eighteenth Street then started backing over the sidewalk and onto the ramp leading to the second floor of the hotel.

I did my cop thing and walked backwards alongside the ambulance motioning, with my hands for the driver to follow me, nodding and loudly saying "okay" as the vehicle crept upward its backing alarm sounding obnoxiously.

I was walking next to a large window, and I could see out of my peripheral vision a man sitting in a wheel chair, his head erect, white scarf around his neck with a tube. He was watching me, studying me, and I waved to him and smiled. It's what cops learn to do over time. Deep down inside of us we come to realize that we are mini-celebrities in our own right. People are naturally curious about us.

I recognized him and had a flashback about his accident. I had read somewhere that Mr. Reeve had been frequenting a hospital in this city.

It had been several years since he was injured, and I was certain his life had been a living hell. St. Louis is noted for many things, having a plethora of hospitals is one of them.

We have one hospital that takes up a square mile of prime city real estate, and it has other hospitals surrounding it. I always thought this St. Louis medical facility thing was extreme, given the dwindling population of the region.

Square mile hospital has an international reputation and patients come from the far corners of the earth with extreme medical problems.

But we are a region of extremes. We have extreme cold, heat, rain, floods. We have extreme wealth and poverty, charity and crime. For folks like Mr. Reeve, we have extreme pain and misery.

In the article I read about him, the square mile hospital was preparing him for stem cell research to repair his shattered spine. The only problem was a politician had to allow stem cell research to be used for medical purposes. It had to be a bill, voted on, and passed by congress and signed by the president.

Mr. Reeve was in a holding pattern. It was the hook, the sound of the other shoe dropping, the final payment into the Ponzi scheme. It was false hope and the coup de grace for this once perfect human specimen of muscle and bone.

The fancy vehicle came to a stop, and I stood there wondering what else I could do for the driver. No one moved so I continued to stand, and wait, another thing cops are used to doing.

Finally, an attractive lady exited the van and walked into the hotel. The driver got out and asked me to stay where I was until Mr. Reeve was taken inside. I nodded in compliance and held my ground next to the window while Mr. Reeve stared at me.

I felt for an instant that in actuality he wasn't watching me but just the traffic and the cityscape. I adjusted my location so he could get a better view of the street. It upset him; I could sense it, another cop trait, so I moved back into his view.

His blue eyes were penetrating my soul, and I was beginning to feel his pain and misery. I remembered his accident, thrown by a horse while competing in an equestrian event. His neck or spine was severed and there was not much hope for him ever being ambulatory.

He was strong and handsome and smart before his accident. He had a beautiful wife and a cute kid and he lived an enviable life.

He had taken a chance by climbing onto a spirited horse and going the limit with it. It balked and he will pay the price forever. I thought about it.

We all take chances. I thought about the dozens of doors I had kicked in doing search warrants. The scores of madmen I had faced in the darkness of the cop job, the hundreds of hand to hand combat confrontations I had experienced in my lifetime. I flashbacked to a time when I rode an English motorcycle, lying down on it, and going 120 MPH. I had tempted fate most of my life, and so far I had gotten away with it.

Had I been killed kicking in a door during a search warrant, fist fighting with a madman or recklessly riding a motorcycle, I doubt my demise would be deemed an accident.

I came to the realization that my extravagantly dangerous exploits were different from the famous movie star, Christopher Reeve; and in retrospect, cops don't hold much credence in accidents. Usually, bad things happen for a reason.

Few humans can figure out what a horse is going to do. If you are on it and it decides to bolt, stop, or jump, you either hang on or get thrown.

As I stood before him with the cold rain running off of my hat brim, I became self-conscious. I wondered why he was staring so intently at me. I wondered if he suspected I was a mall security guard. I turned my body so he could read my badge, St. Louis Metropolitan Police Department was emblazoned on it.

I was always proud of the badge and I wore it proudly. I refused to get lumpy in my old age. Lumpy cops in uniform are the brunt of bad jokes. I was 5'11, 190 and solid. I worked out three days a week, and I still looked like a Marine.

I could see his eyes reading the badge, then my name tag. They darted back up to my face. Was he envious of me? That had to be it. The man who "had it all" was envious of the old beat-cop, but only because I was on my feet, free and still spirited. He could see that.

I wondered if he thought I was a failure. I didn't have rank. I was long of tooth for a cop, and I was standing in the rain acting like a servant for him. He continued to stare.

"I have stories that would make your hair curl, Mr. Reeve," I muttered to myself. I wished I could tell him some of them. The attractive lady came to the back of the ambulance and opened the door. She and the ambulance driver whisked him away while I stood guard for them. "I have stories," I softly said as I walked into the station.

A couple of months whizzed by. It was still cold in St. Louis but it wasn't raining. I got the same radio assignment to meet an ambulance driver at Eighteenth and Market.

We went through the same routine, the driver backing, me walking, and motioning next to the window. Mr. Reeve was watching me more intently this time than the last. The ambulance stopped. The driver and the attractive woman got out and walked into the hotel. I stood my post next to the window, posing for the movie star to watch me. But he wanted more this trip.

He motioned with his eyes for me to come to the rear of the ambulance. I did. I turned the handle and pulled the big door open. He was dressed warmly; cardigan sweater and the always present silk scarf around his neck.

He wanted to converse. He had remembered my name from my name tag on my jacket. "Richards, right?" he said clearly.

"Yes, sir," I replied.

"I want to thank you for helping us get the ambulance up the ramp," he said.

I wasn't speechless, but I didn't know how to respond to his statement. It's what cops do, we try to help people, but I didn't wish to tell him that. It would have been redundant. He knew what cops do, so I said, "You are welcome."

I stood my ground as I viewed him. Atrophy had destroyed him, he was skin and bones. I felt sad for him for he was once solid muscle, an athlete to be admired. He spoke well, but he had to draw on the oxygen tube almost after every sentence.

"You've been doing this for a very long time, haven't you?" he asked.

"Being a cop? Yes, I've been doing it for over thirty years, but I wasn't always in uniform walking a beat," I replied.

"Were you in an investigative assignment?" he asked.

I paused before answering. I didn't know what he wanted. Was he bored? Was he interested in me as a human being? If so, why? Some people desire to have cops as friends. Was he one of them? If so, why not Los Angeles cops? What kind of friendship could I offer him? I've only seen him twice, briefly.

"Yes," I replied. "I've just about done it all: organized crime, drugs, homicide, fugitive. Now I'm walking a beat in a mall. Strange what cards life deals you."

He paused this time. "I bet you have many stories," he said after drawing on the tube. I would love to hear some of them. The next time I come to St. Louis will you tell me some of them?" It was as if he had read my mind.

I nodded. He seemed upbeat. I had read in the St. Louis newspaper that the scientists at square mile hospital were still experimenting with stem cell research, and that the United States Senate had written a bill that would make the treatment legal.

The news article stated the treatment consisted of pluripotent stem cells derived from human embryos or fetal tissue destined to be part of the gonads.

The attractive woman, (Dana Reeve), came out of the hotel, and with the help of the ambulance driver maneuvered the wheelchair on-to the hoist and lowered it to the pavement. Without a word to me they wheeled Mr. Reeve into the hotel. I never saw him again.

Winters slowly rolled into summers. I was now an old bicycle cop riding around downtown St. Louis with a group of cops in their twenties. It was a fun job.

I read in the newspaper that Christopher Reeve had died. The stem cell senate bill languished, then was passed.

In July of 2006 I read in the newspaper that President George W. Bush vetoed the senate bill allowing stem cell research and treatment. It was too late for Chris Reeve, anyway.

I wondered if the treatment was ever an actual reality or if some-one at square mile hospital was bleeding the Reeve family for all that they had. I had heard he was broke and was getting assistance from celebrity friends

President Bush explained his veto saying the bill would support the taking of innocent lives in the hope of finding medical benefits for others.

Hope was the definitive word in that statement. It was all Chris Reeve had, besides millions of dollars. He died without either. His wife died shortly thereafter.

'THE MISTAKE'

Story one:

The City of St. Louis, Missouri is roughly sixty two square miles of flat land, oval in shape, lying in a large bend of the Mississippi River with nineteen miles of river front.

The population is about 320,000 (2010 census), forty six percent white, forty eight percent black and the rest assorted races. There are 5,157 persons per square mile.

There are nine police districts in the city. Each district is swamped with police calls for service and each district is unusual in and of itself, concerning crime categories: rape, robbery, larceny, murder.

St. Louis is well known for its bizarre criminals. Most cops in the trenches brag about their districts as being the worst for crime, or the busiest, or the weirdest, but only one is referred to as the bloodiest. That is the "Bloody Ninth Police District."

It was in the summer of 1970 when I came to the Ninth District, fresh out of the police academy, the Marine Corps before that, and the streets of the Metro East prior to that. I was worldly, but I didn't give that impression. The old cops looked at me like I was a babe in the woods.

It did not take me long to figure the cops out. They take most things at face value and they believe almost anything they hear, especially if it's negative. They mostly think of themselves as members of a big close-knit family, but that is far from the truth. They subconsciously seek out things and people to be suspicious of. It is a true form of competition.

If given the opportunity, they trash their fellow colleagues behind their backs to the extent of slander. When in the presence of their coworkers they shake hands, hug and pat each other on the back.

The police academy was a hoot, as far as work was concerned. The city paid us to sit in a classroom for sixteen weeks being preached to about things we, as a group, already knew.

My class was full of guys just looking for a paycheck. Nobody cared about crime or social problems. It was just a few short years after the dawning of the Age of Aquarius, free love, beards and dope, and the dropout society.

Cops were referred to as "pigs." The police department was hurting for officers. The personnel office advertised in the local newspapers for applicants. Part of the advertisement was the fact that military veterans could get "on the job training" pay for becoming a cop, and that the city would pay for all of the veterans' college if he or she chose to go.

It was a deal too good to pass up. Many of the guys in my class were veterans of the Viet Nam War, recently discharged and suspicious of anything bureaucratic. The academy was fun because of that fact. The veterans didn't care about anything. The cop instructors didn't know how to react to their insolence, so the cop recruits mostly strutted through the procedure carrying bad attitudes.

The bottom line was the city needed bodies to place uniforms on and to patrol the city streets. We were the bodies. The mission of the police academy was to train us, get us onto the streets and let the district commanders deal with us.

A police instructor once told our class, "You are the biggest group of losers I have ever seen." Having just been released from the military, we as a group were accustomed to verbal abuse. As far as we were concerned, he was the loser. Most of us were certain we would do a short time as cops, get a degree and land a big-time federal law enforcement position. The joke was on us.

Being a cop in a city like St. Louis subconsciously grows on you. You begin to feel special. The job takes over your every thought, on and off duty.

There are times when you miss being at work with your other loser associates. You miss making decisions for poor, black folk who daily seek and expect your help. When you are on the street you are "the man;" you have that feeling and no one can override you or your decision.

The "loser" comment by the academy instructor haunted me as the years passed. I knew he was correct in his assumption. Anyone who does this job for a long period of time is in fact somewhat of a loser. He's a hooked loser plying the trade he learned through osmosis.

Being a big city cop can't be taught in a classroom. You learn procedure, law and some tidy tidbits of survival training, but being a slave to a police radio in a black city must be experienced hands-on in order to be learned correctly. Combat veterans already know how to survive.

I often wondered what ever happened to the academy instructor who referred to us as "losers." I catalogued him in my psyche. He was next to a Marine Corps instructor who lived in the jungles of Okinawa, training jungle war tactics to guys like me and another loser group I was assigned to.

The Marine in question lived in a tent. He had no contact with the outside world, no women, no good wholesome food, just him and all of the beer he could consume, supplied by the United States Government. It was cheap pay for a lifetime of servitude.

My Marine Corps group was required to go through an intense jungle warfare class. Our instructor was a lot like the instructor in the academy. We referred to them as "lifers."

We looked down on lifers. They were the establishment. We were just passing through because the government told us we had an obligation to our country. We, as a group, understood the obligation to our country, but we didn't understand our obligation to him, a "lifer".

The Marine Corps jungle instructor advised us on one, fine, hot, bug-infested morning that if he was assigned to our group he would disembowel himself. It's typical establishment "lifer" mentality. Do or die.

I often wondered if the lifer Marine ever killed himself. He obviously had the thought to do himself in. He had the time to ponder it, and obviously he had pondered his demise.

He was in a tent in a jungle, alone with his knife and gun and an over-abundance of government beer. After two weeks of his badgering, we returned to our base near civilization, but like the academy instructor, I never forgot him or his plight.

I swore to myself that I would never become a "lifer" in the police department. But it was a different set of circumstances in the cop job compared to the Marine Corps job.

A Marine Corps lifer usually gets promoted a couple of times. He allows himself to be brainwashed because he wants to be a combat robot. It is offensive to the casual observer, us "losers," because we know that someday we are going to be discharged, go back to our parent's home, resume our love affair with our sexy girlfriends, fire up our old hot-rods and resume our dream life as casual observers.

But as any rational man knows, your parents don't want you in their home. Your girlfriend has married your best friend, and your dad has sold your hot-rod.

You are trained as a military man and you don't wish to admit it. It is all you can do, so you become a big-city cop.

In the police department the lifer/loser psychology is different. We are all lifers and we are all losers. After years of deep thinking riding around the ghetto of the Ninth District, being a casual observer and a slave to the police radio it came to me like an epiphany. The Marine Corps instructor and the academy instructor were correct in their assumptions.

I was lucky to be assigned to the Ninth District. It was in the center of the town, had restaurants, nice neighborhoods, lovely women to gawk at, millionaires and their mansions, poor folks, and their ghettos and government housing.

I had field training in the Seventh District. The cop recruits get to go to a district and ride with the cops there. You aren't allowed to choose a district you wish to go to. I arrived at the seventh, a district situated at the far western edge of the city for a Saturday evening ride-along.

I was placed in a car with two cops, probably only five years my senior. There was a place for the cops to park their personal vehicles across the street from the station house at Union & Page. It was a hideous old building. It was like a giant old house, three stories with a cupola on top. At night it looked like a haunted house.

One of the cops I was riding with had some civilian clothing hanging in his personal car. A cop caught a street creature breaking into the cop's car to steal his civies. He called the cop I was with on the radio and asked him to meet him at the station.

The thief was handcuffed to a large wooden chair in the detective bureau on the third floor of the dilapidated building. The cop's civilian clothing was hanging nearby within view.

I could see that the thief had been roughed up by the arresting cops. The cops made a big-play out of the arrest. They were badgering the thief, telling him he should have never stolen from a cop. The thief was slapped several times but did not cop-a-plea or beg for mercy.

A well-worn yellow pages phone book with black tape around it was brought in to the fray. They beat the thief with the book. They beat him on top of his head and on the sides, carefully not touching his face.

The thief was nearing unconsciousness. I looked around the room. I was in a torture chamber viewing a torture of another human being. It was something I thought I would never be a part of. I kept hearing the chants of protesters from around the world. "No justice, no peace."

I took a quick look at the cop's clothing. It was a cheap shirt and a cheaper pair of jeans. Probably worth ten dollars. "Let the punishment fit the crime;" the chants were haunting me.

They finally stopped beating the street creature. He was booked for "Stealing" and conveyed downtown. I wondered if he had learned his lesson. The experience was kind of like a furious dad beating his child. The child isn't supposed to hate his dad for beating him. Should the street creature not hate the cops for beating him? The cop game was confusing at the outset.

After graduating from the academy I was assigned to the Ninth District. I was elated that I didn't get assigned to the seventh.

Harry Lee was the Captain of the Ninth District. I reported to him with my new uniform on, stood before his desk as he visually inspected me and gave me the usual pep talk. "Do your job, get along with the supervisors, don't call in sick, answer your radio, and don't shit where you eat. Dismissed!"

I had heard of Harry Lee. He was a military man, an officer in the Army Reserves. People who met him did not forget him. He was talkative, selling himself constantly but in an intelligent manner. He was an intelligent man and charismatic when he wished to be.

I fell into the routine quickly. Being a cop was fun. It became tedious when I forced myself to enroll in the junior college. It was where the money was, for being a cop in the City of St. Louis didn't pay much.

The ninth was an "old boys" club. It seemed like most of the cops had become cops in the fifties and early sixties. There were cliques in each of the watches. Guys on "A" platoon didn't associate with guys on "C" platoon.

The old cops played pranks on the new cops. At the beginning of a watch an old cop tossed an M-80 firecracker at me. It exploded at knee level busting open my flesh and tearing my cop trousers. It was a big laugh for the observers. I had to go to the emergency room and have it stitched up.

Each platoon had its own niche. Some watches were burners. If there was a house where criminals were insolent to the patrol cops, their house would mysteriously burn. It was folklore. I figured the cops made this stuff up to bolster their image among themselves.

I had a partner for a while named Patrolman Robert. His partner had gone to the desk which meant he fielded and screened the telephone calls to the watch commander. He was also the booking officer and made cash bonds for arrested subjects.

We had just gotten the first of the new cop cars, a Chevy with a big engine. I was chasing a stolen car one night and Patrolman Robert leaned out the window and started shooting at it.

We were driving through alleys and side streets, and it was in the middle of the night. It was a fun pursuit. I asked Patrolman Robert if we were supposed to shoot at stolen cars and he said, "Yes."

We were frequently called to the station house to transport prisoners to the downtown holdover. Patrolman Robert's old partner would be the one giving us the paper work. His name was Patrolman Warren. I could sense some animosity between them.

Patrolman Warren was a nervous guy, and he was intoxicated most of the time. He was always red faced, and he would shake uncontrollably. When the shaking started, he would run back to the holdover for a few minutes then come back in better condition, smelling like a fresh beer.

I asked Patrolman Robert about the obvious tension between them. He told me that he and Patrolman Warren were the best of friends, and that during their shift they always had a case of cold beer stashed in a vacant lot in their area.

He said things were fine for a year or so. They drank a little beer between radio calls, and then Patrolman Warren started drinking heavily while on duty. He became real nervous about getting fired or brought up on charges, and he didn't want to be scrutinized.

Patrolman Robert didn't care about anything. His wife had a good paying job, and the cop job was just a good time for him.

Patrolman Robert and Patrolman Warren were on a domestic disturbance call in the ghetto, which is mostly what cops do. The boyfriend had left the scene and Patrolman Warren was talking to the caller, a lady approximately forty years of age.

The house was a rehab with new fixtures, and there was a young lady living in the house. Patrolman Robert took her to another room to get her statement. The ploy is just for show. Nobody cares about poor ghetto residents and their domestic problems. The young lady and Patrolman Robert apparently had some chemistry.

Patrolman Warren came in to the room and observed the young lady bent over with Patrolman Robert laboring over her. That was the end of their friendship. Patrolman Warren requested desk duty.

I pondered Patrolman Robert's story. I wanted to categorize it as cop folklore. But cops and ghetto residents had a strange relationship. If it was true, then Patrolman Robert was insane.

Patrolman Robert got divorced. He retired after twenty- nine years and died shortly thereafter.

The Chief of Police, Eugene Camp, had gone to college and graduated with a degree in business. He was making $35,000 a year. We, the young cops, thought of him as wealthy. New cops were making about $6500, and we were in combat almost every night. The "on the job training" money the veteran's administration gave me for attending college classes, and my wife's meager bank employee salary helped us to live a good life.

Cops in St. Louis were working poor. All city employees were. Cops dealt directly and continually with black people. There was a section of the Ninth District referred to as "the hole." It was a slum in the north-eastern quadrant of the district, bordering North Jefferson, directly across the street from the infamous Pruitt Igoe high- rise government housing. It and the" hole" neighborhood held about 45,000 non-working, government subsidized black folks.

Pruitt Igoe was the dream housing project that was going to solve all of the slum housing problems in the city, much like heroin was the dream drug that was going to cure morphine addiction in Europe.

There were intense slums in and around the downtown merchant area of the city. Mill Creek, or Mill Creek Valley was a slum that had been established by migrating southern blacks at the end of the civil war. It was at the south-west central portion and ran as far as Union Station to the east and as far as St. Louis University to the west.

It was 465 acres and consisted of 5,600 slum dwellings, most without indoor plumbing. There were 20,000 poor black residents living there. In 1959, the city, with the backing of the N.A.A.C.P. and ten million dollars of bond and government money began the demolition of Mill Creek Valley.

Many of those Mill Creek residents moved to Pruitt Igoe. Laclede

Town, a community of trendy townhouses, was built at the northern edge of what was once Mill Creek Valley, but poor blacks didn't move in to it. It was a bohemian mixture of students and artists. It was all subsidized by the fed.

It took twenty years, but Laclede Town was demolished and sold off to St. Louis University and big business. It was on prime real estate, positioned between rail yards and interstate highways and in the central part of the City of St. Louis. Poor people were still scrambling for a place to live.

But it seemed that most city residents were subsidized to some extent. There was federal grant money available to big city police departments. Most of our police cars had hundreds of thousands of miles on them. The suspensions on them were shot and the cars bottomed out when going to calls. There was the word "POLICE" stenciled on both front doors and little taxi cab type radios on the dash. They stunk from old blood, vomit, and urine. More new cars started showing up in the districts, Chevy's with big engines and modern police radios.

There were federal grants for overtime projects, street patrols on foot, new uniforms, and weapons. Many of the cops were subsidized, either through on the job training through the Veterans Administration, like me, or through food stamps if they had an abundance of dependents. The whole region was living off of the fed.

Richard Nixon was the president at that time; J.Edgar Hoover was the head of the FBI. Many of the poor blacks could identify with the cops who contained, and detained them, twenty four hours a day. They didn't work and were poor. We worked and were poor. Corralling the poor blacks was the primary job of the district cops. "Control the black masses" were the buzz words of the street cop. In reality, they were controlling us.

Pruitt Igoe was in the Fourth District, but the residents, when they got their government welfare checks at the first of the month wandered into the Ninth District to shop. The white merchants on Easton Ave, later changed to Dr. Martin Luther King Boulevard, welcomed the instant cash. They over-charged them for their purchases, short changed them, sold them tainted meat and old vegetables, substandard clothing and an over-abundance of whiskey, beer, wine and cigarettes.

The problem arose toward the middle of the month when the poor ghetto and high-rise residents didn't have any government cash to spend. They would come in begging, or stealing or threatening the merchants. The merchants didn't live anywhere near the Ninth District. They were mostly West County residents, politically connected and wealthy.

Some wanted Captain Harry Lee to put more cops in their neighborhoods, but not at the first of the month. I observed a merchant charge into Harry Lee's office and make demands on him for more cops around his store. They felt they owned the city cops no matter what his rank was. The merchant told Harry he was going to get a gun and start shooting the blacks who came into his store and threatened him.

Harry nonchalantly stood from his desk, went to a closet behind his desk and came out with a Thompson sub-machine gun. He laid it on his desk and said, "Here, use this, kill as many of those Maryland Farmers as you can and see where that gets you."

The merchant quickly walked out. Harry laughed. He was a showman, and he knew how to read people. He allowed me to examine the weapon. I had been a machine gunner in the Marine Corps, and I knew guns, but Harry Lee knew that fact. He knew his men and their backgrounds.

The Ninth District was allowed to have such firepower because of the Black Liberators, a local street gang. Before I came to the ninth the gang cruised by the district station and shot it up. It was a big deal at the time, although no one was injured.

Shortly after that someone tossed a fire bomb through a front window. It landed on concrete and did little damage.

A team of FBI agents investigated both incidents. After several months they strolled into Harry Lee's office and advised him there was a contract on his life by the Black Liberators street gang henchman.

Harry was pragmatic to a fault. Gossip was not his style, and he had been in law enforcement long enough to take what the FBI said with a grain of salt.

The fed will feed information to anybody who is available just to get a reaction. They probably wanted Harry Lee to give the order to his detectives to kill the person who had presumably placed the contract on him.

Harry could have picked up the phone and told one of five or six men in his bureau that he wanted someone eliminated. It would have happened. His detectives respected him, revered him. He was their charismatic leader.

That reaction would have been the beginning of anarchy. Harry's detectives wanted only to do his bidding. Locking up and beating criminals was the way Harry wanted it in the past, but threatening their mentor and idol with death was a new ballgame.

The FBI agents probably had Harry's office and telephone bugged. They wanted a reaction to their carefully planted information. They were setting him up. Harry was too intelligent to believe anything they said to him or about him. In this street game of criminal and cop, there was a gray area about who was the "good guy" and who was the criminal.

But FBI agents always underestimate their quarry. They are so sold on themselves and their station in life that they are certain they can manipulate a lowly city cop into doing their dirty work for them.

Harry Lee wasn't your typical city police commander. He was worldly and not likely to play federal law enforcement games. He laughed the threat off. The agents wandered out of his office.

The reason the shooting and the fire-bombing of the station was such a big deal was that it was obvious the blacks who had been trounced on for so long in this city and many other cities were beginning to fight back, and that it was an organized fight, not one black guy and three cops, but a handful of armed black guys and a district station.

It was common knowledge on the street that if you wised off to a cop, or even slightly resisted arrest you would be taken into the Ninth District station and beaten, while you were handcuffed.

After the beatings, the detectives would march the suspect before the oncoming cops at their roll call. It was like waving a raw T-bone steak in front of a pack of wolves. The detectives would read the charges, "striking a police officer," "wounding an officer," etc. It wasn't good for police community relations.

The district station was wide open. The neighboring street people had access to the whole station. They wandered the halls, used our toilets, drank from our water cooler, and panhandled for change.

Occasionally they would wander in just to pick a fight with a cop. That never ended well for them. It was as if they wanted to be tortured and abused. It seemed that for every crime they committed they either got caught in the act or left something incriminating at the scene. Or they would be snitched on.

If a street creature was a nice guy, the watch commander would allow him to wash our personal vehicles in the cop garage. There was a car wash area there that was hardly ever used. The cops would pay $5.00 to have their cars washed. It never ended well. The car washing gave the washer a little cash and the chance to drink while he was washing. Quality went down. Arguments went up. Fist fights occurred. We were one big dysfunctional family.

Burglary was a big concern in the district. Businesses were burglarized nightly. The creatures would climb onto the roof and hit the roof with an axe. It only took one swipe with an axe, and then they would silently peel the roofing away and gain access to the inside. The businessman would open his doors in the morning, and he would be wiped out. It became open season on burglars.

If a cop shot a burglar he would receive praise from his supervisor and the respect of his peers. Many of the cops would telephone their dads to brag about the shootings. It was always an open phone call. Anyone within earshot could hear what was said. When the cop would hang up, he'd convey the message from his dad. It was always the same, "I hope you killed the bastard."

The Zulu 1200 was another name for the Black Liberators street gang. They had a club house at Easton and Leffingwell. There was a mural on the east wall of the building. The mural took up the whole side of the building. There were paintings of black leaders: Malcolm X, Muhammed Ali, Dr. Martin Luther King, Elijah Muhammed, and some local black politicians.

There was a caption: "UP YOU MIGHTY RACE." Harry Lee would call his detectives into his office and say, "I think there is a medical emergency at Easton & Leffingwell. Go in there and make sure everyone is okay."

The detectives would converge on the Zulu 1200's, looking for anything incriminating. If there was someone there they didn't know they would identify him and document that he was there.

Charles Koen, an activist from Cairo, Illinois, was identified. He arrived in St. Louis in 1968 and formed the Black Liberator street gang from the Zulu 1200.

That was when the station was shot up and the fire bomb was

tossed through the front window. Harry Lee ordered his detectives to bring the occupants of the Zulu 1200 clubhouse into the station. The shooting of the station house and the fire-bombing was the last straw for him.

The detectives brought in four or five gang members, including Charles Koen. There is always a threatening look or an insolent word tossed around in such confrontations. A fight ensued, a big fight. Cops were running back to the bureau to help the detectives. The Black Liberators lost the battle. They were beaten almost to death. They had fingers broken, heads broken, arms and legs broken. The detective bureau offices were covered in blood.

Shortly thereafter the Zulu 1200 clubhouse mysteriously burned. There were so many police cars blocking the fire trucks that it was a complete loss.

The 'UP YOU MIGHTY RACE" mural was still there, blaring. Harry Lee gave the command for some of his detectives to toss white paint on the mural. It remained in that condition until the building was torn down.

The street gang moved out of state, to Cairo, Illinois shortly after the beating at the station. A news team went there to interview them. They were video-taped in their beaten condition: turbans and casts. Harry Lee won the battle.

Charles Koen continued his activist role in Cairo. He had access to government grants and formed the United Front, a social services agency. The building housing the United Front burned, and Koen attempted to claim insurance funds. He was tried and convicted of embezzlement, misapplication of Federal Program Funds, theft of public money, false statements, arson, and mail fraud.

He was sentenced to twelve years imprisonment, ordered to pay $636,000 in restitution, and $5,000 in penalties. But he had a following. Koen was honored with a tribute on an album by jazz drummer Max Roach.

Harry Lee continued to woo his constituents. He was a frequent flyer at several restaurants in the Ninth District. He loved going into the El Sarape Tex Mex Restaurant.

The restaurant was operated by the Leos family. The owner Joseph Leos Sr. respected cops. He would never allow a cop to pay for a meal in his restaurant. He thought of city cops as personal friends.

The tex mex was excellent at El Sarape. I frequented the restaurant. Most Ninth District cops ate there. Joseph Sr. passed away and Joseph Jr. handled the bar area. He loved cops as much as his dad.

Harry Lee made it a point to sit at the bar and feed Joe Jr. cop stories. Joe fed him free booze in return. Joe Leos revered Harry Lee more than any other human being on this earth, except maybe his children.

But there was a problem with the restaurant. They gave away their fortune, not only to cops, but to anyone who they felt was their friend. They gave their fine tex mex food away to a bunch of Gringos. It was sad to watch.

It was a family venture. For years the family lived above the restaurant at 3500 Olive. They didn't need much to sustain themselves.

Cops from all over the city started frequenting the restaurant. It was no longer a Ninth District secret. It wouldn't be long and it would have to close.

Joe Jr. assisted his son, Mike Leos to be hired by the city police department. He was proud of Mike. A city police officer was held in high esteem in the Leos family. He is a good cop, professional, and caring.

The restaurant hung on and turned into a cop hangout for free burritos. Some cops drank there after hours, but mostly it was a free food paradise.

Harry Lee put the word out for the out of district guys to stay away from El Sarape. Some stayed away, most didn't.   The Ninth District cops were embarrassed about the out of district cops taking over. Many stopped going in for lunch or dinner. It hurt Joe's feelings that his old friends stopped coming in.

A commander called Mike Leos on the radio and ordered him to telephone him at the command post. Mike respected the ranking cops. He called and he was instructed to go by his dad's restaurant and bring back some tex mex to the command post.

Mike took down the order as the commander read it off. It was a big order; Big enough for several people. Mike called out of service and drove to the restaurant. He got the food and quickly conveyed it to the command post.

Mike was expecting accolades for obtaining the free food for the commander. The commander took the food out of the bags, inspected it and then said, "The order is not correct. You screwed up my order." The commander was red faced and angry. Mike turned and walked away from the spoiled cop commander. Entitlements and power will corrupt anyone.

The business was stripped like a piranha pig carcass. Commanders were bringing their friends into the place. At closing they would go to the back room and walk out with cases of booze. It soon closed.

There were cops on the street who shouldn't have been in the business. One such cop was a retread from the federal government. Most cops yearned to be on the federal payroll, but it took a degree, and it took the ability to pass the stringent written test. Few cops were good test takers.

The test for the Treasury Department was basically a math test: calculus, algebra, time and motion questions. If a cop could pass the test, he was given the job as a Treasury Agent even if he did not have a degree.

The cop in question was intelligent but not street savvy. He was naïve to the basic principles of one on one confrontation, the interview, the pat down, and the street vernacular.

He didn't understand his adversary. But he passed the treasury exam and was hired by Alcohol Tobacco and Firearms. He was gone for a couple of years and then returned to the police department.

The cop made a routine vehicle stop on north Vandeventer in broad daylight in the winter of 1970. The driver sat in his dilapidated old car and waited for the cop to approach his window.

As was often the case, the driver didn't have a driver's license, or a job, and the vehicle wasn't issued to anyone. It was a salvage vehicle, purchased by him from a junk yard. It was hideous, but it was transportation for him and his fifteen year-old pregnant girlfriend to bop around in the ghetto.

The cop approached the driver's window and the confrontation began. The driver was pulled out of the vehicle and forced to assume the position at the front of the police car and eventually laid over the hood.

The driver didn't appreciate being violated by the fat cop in front of his girlfriend, and he told the cop that fact. The cop reverted back to his Treasury Agent days, pulled his huge, nickel plated six inch barreled Colt Python .357 revolver and stuck it in the driver's face.

Feds can and do stick their handguns in people's faces. It is what they are noted for. A fed can actually kill almost anyone and get away with it. It is part of their job; killing for the United States of America. They feel they are "Superman," but this cop was no Christopher Reeve.

They all think they are hired assassins and they dream of being given the secret mission to kill someone, a bad guy or a good guy, it doesn't matter as long as they fulfill their mission.

The cop weighed in at about 250 pounds. Willie, the driver went about 130 soaking wet. The fight began over control of the Python. Willie knew that he wasn't likely to be shot in broad daylight on north Vandeventer. If it was dark out then maybe he would have but not in front of witnesses. Cops aren't licensed to kill, not legally anyway.

Willie grabbed the gun and spun the fat cop around, placing him backwards on the hood of the cop car. The cop started firing the Python, the bullets shattering the windshield and going through the hood and into the engine compartment of the cop car.

The cop managed to push the skinny ghetto rider off of him, and they continued to fight for control of the Python while standing on the sidewalk. Someone called the Ninth District, and a radio call came out that a cop was fighting with a Negro male on north Vandeventer. I was the lucky cop who got the call.

As Willie and the fat cop tussled, Willie's six-month pregnant fifteen-year-old-girlfriend climbed out of the car, found a wine bottle in the gutter and smashed it against the cop's head. End of fight. Willie and his girlfriend were now the proud owners of a Colt .357, nickel plated, six-inch magnum. They jumped into their wreck of a car and sped away.

There was a hospital for blacks (Homer G. Phillips) and there was a hospital for whites (City Hospital number one) and there was a hospital for cops (Deaconess) which is where the cop was whisked away to.

He told us his tearful story before he left in the back of a paddy wagon. We didn't have ambulances in those days. The area sergeant called for the district detectives. They showed up, heard the story, and identified the assailant. They knew him and where he and his girlfriend lived.

Willie and his girlfriend were in the station handcuffed to a chair in the detective bureau before the fat cop could get stitches in his head.

Harry Lee, whose office was connected to the detective bureau office by a short hallway, wandered in and told the detectives to take the pregnant fifteen year old home. Harry then walked back to his office.

Willie had chosen the wrong time to fight with a city cop. The cops were against the wall with insolent, scofflaw, black ghetto residents. One of the detectives hit Willie with his right fist, in the face rendering him unconscious. Some of the detectives were amused by this. They made a game out of the punishment. Someone had the idea to wake him up and then take turns knocking him out.

They brought Willie around and then knocked him unconscious several times while Harry Lee sat in his office and read police reports. Ultimately, Willie went to prison for assaulting a police officer. The fat cop quit shortly after the incident. He became a private detective for a while then faded away. His claim to fame was that he was a great test taker.

Even though the Black Liberators had run off to Cairo, Illinois, the desk officer at the station would get anonymous telephone calls stating the Black Liberators were going to shoot the station house up again.

The watch commander would call cops in off of the street, place a couple on the roof of the station with shot guns, a cooler of beer and a pizza, waiting for the carnage to begin. I had been on the roof. It was a break in the routine of wrestling and fist fighting drunk black guys.

While this cop/crook stuff was going on, I was attending college on my own time. It was a liberal arts education, completely different from my job description, and my classmates weren't in the cop trade.

Most of them were young men and women who just wanted to better themselves. They knew nothing about what a cop does in a big city, even though many of them grew up there. The contrast was mind boggling. I would go from liberal student to head busting ghetto cop in the same day.

And the irony of the whole scenario was that the police were slaves to the slick businessmen just like the poor black citizens were. And to add insult to injury, we were servants to the ghetto blacks.

This wasn't just happening in the Ninth District. It was occurring in the fourth, fifth, sixth, seventh and eighth police districts, anywhere there were housing projects or slums to rent with government cash. The first, second and third districts were supporting the entire city, except for the downtown merchants.

It was obvious this experiment in human housing was a failure. The government invented the 235 loan, a loan for poor people to buy their own homes. The far north part of the city was targeted (Walnut Park) neat little brick homes surrounded by parks and cemeteries. Real estate agents were advised to steer the blacks leaving the projects toward this neighborhood.

In the mind of the government, the white residents had lived in the neighborhood long enough. The houses were mostly impeccable and would make good residences for the ghetto dwellers. The whites were forced out and mostly moved out of the city and into trendy North County.

After several years, the Walnut Park neighborhood turned into the same type of ghetto the blacks had been fleeing, and the government stepped up to the plate again with more 235 loans, no money down. The government makes part of the payment for the buyer if he or she can't make their payments, and hardly anyone was ever turned down for a home loan.

It was time for the government to target another community. The fed targeted Spanish Lake in North County. Realtors were steering poor blacks to North County by the thousands. The theory behind this graphic plan was to do anything that it took to keep ghetto blacks out of south St. Louis, the bastion of the tax base for the city. It didn't work.

Many of the ghetto kids had joined the military in the sixties and were starting to return home. They had been in the Viet Nam War, fought with dignity and naturally expected to be treated with respect when they returned to the streets of St. Louis.

Their expectations were short sighted. Nothing had changed in ghettos of the city. I had had the same expectations when I returned home from the service. It is dog eat dog no matter what color you are.

There was a heroin craze in the city. Most of the people we stopped on the street or came into contact with were heroin addicts. A large percentage of these addicts were veterans returning from Viet Nam.

There was a Veterans' Administration Hospital at Grand and Enright in the Ninth District. It had always been a sleepy kind of a place where old vets came after making appointments to see a doctor for an ailment. It was now bombarded with insane, addicted, and violent neighborhood vets demanding services far beyond the hospital's ability to perform. There was no emergency room for trauma facilities, and the emergency room the hospital used was mostly for sick vets brought into the hospital for triage and treatment.

The ghetto vets were there daily for overdoses, injuries, mental issues. The hospital beefed up its security staff with neighborhood security guards and locked the hospital down after regular business hours.

The neighborhood vets would try coming through the front door, and if it was locked, they would break the glass doors down and enter, demanding treatment. The security guards had no pity on the doped-up vets. They had grown up under the same circumstances and were capable of being as violent as the patients.

We received calls to the hospital for disturbances on a daily basis on all three watches. By the time we arrived, there would be broken glass and busted heads. The guards took their positions seriously. When someone broke in they reacted as if their posts were being overrun by Viet Cong, for most of them were vets themselves.

There was carnage in the Veterans Administration Hospital on North Grand, and we, the cops, had to clean up their messes for them. Many were cut from breaking the glass door. All of them had gashes in their heads from the guards' nightsticks. The hospital staff refused to treat the wounded vets. "Take them to Homer G. Phillips," they would say.

We would request a paddy wagon, strap them to a stretcher while they were now fighting us, and convey them to the city-owned hospital. The fed apparently examined this problem and decided it was caused by drug abuse in South East Asia while the vets were serving their country, and a new approach to curing addiction had to be developed.

A methadone clinic was built at the rear of the hospital on Spring at Enright. Another irony of big government: the heroin addicts were using methadone to keep from going through withdrawal from heroin.

They were now addicted to two drugs, one from Asia (heroin) and the new and improved government drug, methadone. It seemed there was a pattern in the irony. Now the majority of poor citizens in the region were dependent on the fed for something.

It seemed that most neighborhoods had a corner confectionary or grocery store in it, maybe more than one. They sold the basics: canned goods, stale bread, cigarettes, and booze. Small business administration loans provided the capital for these enterprises.

There was always a new Caddy parked at the curb in front of them. The first thing the recipient of government funds did was buy a new flashy car and then stocked his business with what was left over.

The latest trend for the ghetto boys was to rob the little stores. But they weren't interested in just robbing them; it seemed they always had to show their displeasure with the system by shooting the person working behind the counter. Most times it ended with a homicide.

In the fall of 1970 I received a radio assignment to a little grocery store in the Central West End at Taylor and Maryland, a nice neighborhood, fashionable and safe. People could walk the streets and feel safe. The call was for a shooting. I was real fresh as a cop but I knew what to expect when the call came out.

I walked inside the little store and there was a guy lying on the floor clutching his gut. He was shot badly. I called for the paddy wagon, and a supervisor showed up to assist me along with another officer.

We placed the guy on a stretcher and carted him to the paddy wagon. I slid in next to him and a young female slid in across from me on the bench type seat. The cruiser driver, a turnkey, which is a guy who drives the paddy wagon, works in the jail, or works the desk in the district stations, headed for City Hospital number one, for the victim was white.

Turnkeys are licensed to carry firearms and are almost cops, but they don't work the street in a police officer capacity. They assist cops. I heard the sergeant at the scene tell the wagon driver via radio to head for Deaconess Hospital. I wondered why but didn't ask any questions.

On the way the wounded guy pulls out a thirty-eight Colt revolver and hands it to me. He then hands me his badge and identification card. I read the card: Paul Kramer, Turnkey City of St. Louis, Missouri.

He was wearing an expensive wristwatch and had a couple of large diamond rings on each hand. He removed the watch and rings and handed them to the young female passenger. He then reached into his front pocket and pulled out a huge wad of cash. He gave the cash to the young female. She quickly stuffed the valuables and cash into her purse.

We arrived at the hospital. The Police Department surgeon, Dr. James F. Cooper was arriving at about the same time. We carried Paul Kramer into the emergency room, placed him in an examination room, and waited out in the hallway. If he died, homicide would take the case over, and I wouldn't have anything else to with it except give a statement. I figured he was going to die. Gut shot victims don't usually live. I had seen it before.

Dr. Cooper went inside and started working on him. "He's full of food," I heard him say. They had to remove the food from his belly in order to proceed. We waited in the hallway with some other cops who knew Paul Kramer.

Lieutenant James Hackett, Eighth district watch commander, arrived on the scene. He later attained the rank of Lt. Colonel and remained on the department until his sixty-fifth birthday, mandatory retirement age.

Paul Kramer died. Homicide showed up and took charge of the case. There was small talk among the cops who knew Paul. He always had a lot of cash on him. He was a big time gambler and he worked the door (was security) for gangster card games.

He was a hustler, a respectable title for people in law enforcement in those days. And again irony played into the tragedy; Paul was on sick leave, and was working at his brother's grocery store when he was shot by the robbers.

Just maybe, if he hadn't been on sick leave he would have shot the robbers who shot him. He hesitated, a fatal mistake for anyone carrying a sidearm and a badge.

In his mind, maybe he said to himself, "It's just a robbery. They won't get much and they will be out of the store with a mere pittance and I'll be able to keep my badge and gun and continue my life of guarding gangster card games under the protection of the St. Louis Metropolitan Police Department."

But Paul didn't factor in heroin addiction or the hatred of business owners by the ghetto populace. They had enough. They were becoming organized and they could kill without remorse. It was another learning experience for me, but not for Paul Kramer.

A couple of weeks passed. I was riding with a cop who had once been a fireman. He was a laid back guy, and he knew the city way of life. He had lived on the Hill (Italian part of town) for his entire life. His brother was a state representative, which meant he was destined for promotion for as long as his brother was in politics.

The supervisors bent over backwards to appease this guy because of his brother's stature. He was such a nice guy it embarrassed him, but he knew the system and all he had to do is get some time on the street and he would be sitting at a desk downtown with a city view for the rest of his career.

We were sitting in a police car eating pizza and drinking soda. It was at the scene of a fire. A house was burning and we had to block the street. The fire was so intense the smoke was coming through the bricks which must have been two feet thick.

He felt obligated to school me. "See how that smoke is coming through those bricks."

"Yeah," I replied.

"Don't ever run into a burning house thinking you can hold your breath to rescue someone. The smoke will penetrate your skin. It will go right through your body and kill you." Before I could answer him, the watch commander, Lieutenant Bob Scheetz, got on the air and asked for our location. We told him and he pulled up alongside of us. He told me to get into his car. I complied.

We headed north. I didn't ask any questions. I figured we were going to Homer G. Phillips Hospital. There was always a hospital detail there, and since I was a new guy, I got most of them. Besides, I had grown to know Bob Scheetz quickly. He had been my watch commander from the beginning of my stint in the Ninth District.

He was stressed to the max; nine kids, trying to survive on a cop's salary, even though he was a lieutenant, he was still working poor. Having a flock of children just made it worse. His nick name (behind his back) was Der Fuehrer.

Lieutenant Scheetz, at times would act like he wanted to be your dad or your big brother. He would turn on the charm and make you think that being a "working poor" policeman in a socialistic land locked community, without a county, was almost okay. Then he would turn into a screaming maniac; his face red, his neck veins protruding, kicking trash cans and throwing anything he could get his hands on. I tried to stay away from him.

He wanted me to buy his house in north city. I looked at it. It was like YMCA camp with bunks, commodes, and tables with benches.

He had so many children that he couldn't keep track of them. He and his family went to a police picnic at a park in the city. After the fun and games, they loaded up and went home. After a while they realized they had forgotten one of the kids at the park. They returned and retrieved him.

He was schmoozing me with his cop charm when he pitched me on buying his house, smiling and cracking jokes. He could have been a good salesman instead of a broke cop. I had heard that all of north St. Louis was going to be black. I declined. The charm stopped immediately. He turned back into cop supervisor.

Bob Scheetz was for all accounts a good man. He would never cheat on his wife and he was honest. He would preach to us at roll call about the perils waiting for us on the street: women, booze, graft. He felt we, as a group, were his children. He sincerely did not want any of us to go astray.

But he was frazzled and confounded with a type "A" personality. All things, family and police, had to be just right or he would become frustrated and lose it.

He was basically a low profile guy. Most of the other platoon commanders were always schmoozing for new "aces" or entertaining their old "aces." "Aces" got people promoted.

Business people, politicians, people with means and power rule in the game of politics. The more friends an up and coming commander had, the better his chances of being promoted.

James Hackett, who was a lieutenant, like Bob Scheetz, was always in competition with him for promotions. He was the exact opposite of Scheetz. He was a champion schmoozer. He lived for his career and his friends, who just happened to be powerful businessmen in the community. He was a high profile guy.

But Jim Hackett didn't have the shtick that Bob Scheetz carried. Hackett wasn't humble. He had no humility, and he didn't have nine kids.

When promotion time rolled around, Bob Scheetz would visit his friends from St. Louis University, classmates who had gained prominence, doctors, lawyers, accountants, judges.

They remembered him as the nice guy who had to leave college because he had so many kids. He was the poor guy who had to join the police department to survive.

Bob gave the persona of a beaten down man. He looked and acted the part. He would wear his commander uniform when he visited their offices.

It was the equivalent of a homeless veteran wearing his war medals on his drab green field jacket. How could a friend or a casual observer not respect the man and pity his circumstances?

He had been a star basketball player for St. Louis University. He got married, became a cop, and continued having kids.

He had a part time job as security/delivery man for area jewelers. Many jewelers purchased diamonds, gold and other precious stones from burglars. They needed a reputable person to convey the stolen jewelry to the Paul Brown or Arcade Building in downtown St. Louis for resale.

Der Fuehrer, who fashioned himself as "beyond repute" and actually was, worked most of his days off picking up and delivering contraband. He could be seen at area malls, going into and leaving jewelry stores, carrying a black satchel with that maniacal look on his face.

I saw him one bright summer day. My wife and I were in a mall, and I almost bumped into him as he strode out of a store. I mechanically said, "Hi, Lieutenant."

He reared up at me. "Don't call me lieutenant. I'm picking up and delivering jewelry. I don't want anyone to know what I'm doing." He felt like he was James Bond on a secret, undercover assignment. The crooked jewelers were laughing up their sleeves at him as he walked out of their store.

He, like all St. Louis cops, lived off of entitlements. Most of his friends were people who could help him in an emergency: plumbers, mechanics, used car dealers, shoe salesman, clothing salesman, grocery store owners, small businessmen who could and would help him and his family survive. He later became Chief of Police.

The small folks, the ones who had helped him during his salad years, never forgot him or what they had done for him. They had friends who were cops, and now Chief Scheetz was in a position to help them.

When a St. Louis cop is asked what he wants from the police department, his answer is usually, "a promotion."
Chief Bob was being bombarded with requests from old friends who wanted him to do something for their friends. And he also had the St. Louis University Alumni "aces" who wanted payback.

His temper became worse. His aides, lieutenants in his office, ran the police department. It was all he could do to keep his friends at bay.

It is why chiefs of police in this city have so many specialized units. It's the second choice of most cops. They get to wear jeans and "T"'s, drive a city car and wander around the city at will. The cops without aces stay in the districts, fighting drunks, getting shot, and answering radio assignments.

I could tell that Lieutenant Bob Scheetz was as serious as a heart attack as we travelled north on Page Avenue. I was asking myself, "What does Der Fuehrer" want from me?"

Finally he broke the silence, "What did you do with Paul Kramer's money and his jewelry?" Der Fuehrer asked.

At first I was surprised at the question. But I quickly gained my composure. This was a good job for me, but it wasn't good enough to be accused of being a thief. "I didn't have his money or his jewelry," I responded. .

"He had money on him," Der Fuehrer continued, "ten-thousand dollars in cash. He had another ten-thousand dollars-worth of jewelry. His family didn't get it when they took possession of his property at the morgue. That means you took it."

"He gave me his gun and badge," I replied. "I packaged it and turned it into the property room. He gave his cash and jewelry to the female who rode to the hospital with us. I think she was his niece."

He pulled the car into the Eighth District station. We got out and I followed him inside. Captain Jim Reddick was the commander of the eighth. He was an old prize fighter, and he had a fierce reputation. He would reach across his desk and wallop folks who disrespected him or gave him reason. It was old time law enforcement. I'd heard he had knocked some cops out, ones who he didn't see eye to eye with.

I didn't know what to expect from this encounter. He shook my hand and showed me a letter Paul Kramer's sister had written to him asking him to get her brother's cash and jewelry from the thieving cop who had stolen it from his family. That thieving cop was supposedly me. I wasn't taking this accusation lightly.

I was waiting for things to get physical. The old Captain didn't know my background. I had been in fights with guys bigger than him. I was a street kid. All of my life I had been played lightly. It worked out for me.

"He gave it all to his niece," I said with a smile. "It was never in my possession."

"I'll check this out," he replied. I shook his giant hand and we were out of his office. Lieutenant Scheetz later told me that the niece admitted to her family that she had Paul Kramer's money and jewelry. It made me realize that a cop could and would be accused of anything, and that he was presumed guilty until proven innocent.

Chief Scheetz's wife died. He remarried, a younger gal, and he retired. They made plans to move to Naples, Florida. It's what the cops in the trenches dreamed of.

The good guy cop with the state representative brother came into the station one day shortly after we rode together and resigned. The supervisors tried to talk him out of resigning but he would not listen to them. He handed in his badge and gun and walked out.

I found out later that his wife was seeing another man while he was risking his life on the city streets. He followed them, and when they came to a stop light he calmly walked up to the vehicle and shot the guy through the window six times with his department revolver.

Remarkably the guy lived. He was treated at city hospital, and after he was released he left town. Allegedly, there were Mafia members in the cop's family, and they advised the victim to relocate, quickly. The cop was never arrested, not even questioned about the incident.

Shortly after the good guy cop quit, Lieutenant Scheetz ran in to a burning building and rescued several ghetto dwellers from certain death.

The good guy cop, and ex-fireman had advised me not to do it if the opportunity arose. Apparently nobody advised Lieutenant Scheetz of the long lasting effects of smoke under pressure. He was sickly for months after the incident, coughing up black soot and he was forced to have tests on his kidneys. He was awarded for his heroism.

In the 1970's Eugene Camp, the chief of police, was in charge of the entire police department. The Chief of Detectives was John Doherty whose responsibility was the department's investigators.

These guys didn't like one another. Both had been big time politicians in competition for the Holy Grail (chief's job), and Gene Camp won the contest. As I said previously, the job paid $35,000 a year. Either of them would have killed to get it. To the cop on the streets, they were demi-gods, wealthy and powerful.

To the slick businessmen and politicians in and out of the city, the cops jockeying for the chief job were jokes. John Doherty was aligned with wealthy and powerful Syrian power brokers in south city, as well as state senators and representatives. But he also had Auggie Busch on his side, the most powerful man in the region. He had a country club membership, played golf with millionaires, and told them cop stories at the nineteenth hole.

Obviously, the Busch family was at the top of the royalty totem pole in the St. Louis region. For a mere cop, even a high ranking cop to be personal friends with one of them was mind boggling.

I doubt any cops kids were playmates with Auggie Busch's kids. Money associates with money, except with John Doherty and the Busch family. The Busch/Doherty friendship was one of power, a quid pro quo example of the "good old boy" system.

When the Busch kid killed the Lay's potato chip kid in the Busch mansion in St. Louis County, before the county police were called, the Busch family called John Doherty. He was on the scene when the county cops arrived.

John Doherty had a house in south city but he never went there. He lived in St. Charles County, near a lake. When he ran out of beer the Bush clan would deliver it to him via helicopter. He was on the payroll of Eugene Slay, wealthy business tycoon and close friends of national mafia members. Doherty was his security consultant.

The smart money was riding on Doherty to become the next chief of police. It was a done deal until Gene Camp befriended a surgeon at City Hospital number one, Doctor James F. Cooper.

Dr. Cooper's brother in law was Warren Hearnes, the governor of the state of Missouri. Gene Camp rose from Captain to chief in two years leaving Doherty standing at the altar.

Dr. Cooper became the department surgeon and the head of the police department medical division. The medical division was a big deal. It had offices attached to St. Louis University Hospital. There was a full medical staff just for the health and welfare of city cops, and sometimes their families. There were several other surgeons working part time at the medical division, and full time nurses and physical therapists.

There were cadets assigned there. They were police department employees who wished to be police officers but were too young. Most of them were right out of high school, and had a relative or political friend who helped them get hired. They were required to attend college while working for the department.

They were mostly gofers for whom they were working. It was like a mini-police department within the real police department. They even had rank for some if they wanted it. It showed the cadet the structure of rank, and it showed how they could obtain a higher position within the department when they became real cops.

The department was slowly making cops out of the youngsters, slowly leading them toward the thought process of being a St. Louis cop; obey without question and inform without remorse.

Doc Cooper always got the cream of the crop to work in his medical division. Most were athletes in high school still lifting and training and impressing Doc with their youth and enthusiasm.

Doc was in charge, and it didn't take anyone long to figure out that he was the guy who could help them into a groovy investigative job when they became cops.

Steroids were new and legal at that time. Doc made them available to whomever wanted them. Cops overdo most things including weight training. The cadets copied them. Cops, old and young, and cadets were using anabolic steroids to become super humans and super cops. It had to be okay, Doc Cooper said it was.

Eventually these overstuffed cops, who looked like side show freaks, began experiencing side effects of the anabolic steroids. Some died at young ages. Some committed suicide. The fed eventually ruled anabolic steroids illegal. But some of the young cadets were hooked on the massive muscular look. Many later became cops. Some quit and pursued other interests. But the damage had been done. The youngsters were hooked on the thought of being super human.

On March 9, 1971, the ROTC building at 4200 Forest Park Boulevard was bombed. The building was in my assigned area. I had worked the afternoon watch and had answered an alarm sounding at the building earlier in the evening.

In those days, when a burglar alarm call came out, two officers were sent to the scene. The outside of the building is checked for any signs of a forced entry, and the officers ask the dispatcher if an alarm man was en-route.

The company who had installed the alarm had a team of alarm specialists with keys to the front doors who go from business to business checking on buildings and resetting alarms that are accidentally set off. The alarm man did not show up at the scene of the ROTC building. My partner and I checked out the perimeter of the building and went back in service.

My partner on that night was Patrolman Charles . We were from the same eastside berg, were about the same age and background (he was an ex-Marine also), and had become St. Louis cops at about the same time. We didn't know one another prior to becoming partners in the Ninth District.

Patrolman Charles was an ambitious guy. He wanted to be a detective, but he didn't have the political clout or the time on as a patrolman to be appointed to a detective bureau.

But those little facts didn't alter his plans. He was a glory hound, stopping and searching cars between radio calls, stopping pedestrians and searching them for contraband or weapons, and arresting almost anyone who violated any crime that warranted an arrest. He was a by-the-book-cop.

As the months rolled by and Patrolman Charles hadn't been discovered by some cop demigod and placed in a bureau, he became a sour guy. He had always gotten what he wanted. He was an only child, a good athlete, and a good student. Guys like him get their pick of most things in this world.

Patrolman Charles and I were in the Marine Corps about the same time, but we were actually in different Marine Corps. I finished boot camp, was sent to Camp Pendleton, and trained as a machine gunner. I trekked a super heavy gun around Camp Pendleton, training for combat.

I went to Okinawa and continued to train for combat, living in the jungle, sleeping in the rain, and eating C-rations. The training never stopped. I was a grunt for four years.

Patrolman Charles became a military cop right out of boot camp. He was sent to Honolulu, became an investigator for the Corps and arrested fellow Marines for indiscretions to the Military Code of Criminal Justice. He was a "spook."

He was a special guy for most of his life, but not in the St. Louis Police Department. Not unless you have an "ace."

Patrolman Charles did some deep thinking about his dilemma. He was an excellent softball player. He joined the softball league which was formed and coached by the detective sergeant of the Ninth District detective bureau. Cops who wish to be leaders don't just lead within their individual units. They can't stop leading. They form softball leagues and lead off-duty.

Before long he became Detective Charles, a detached detective in the ninth bureau. He was a thinker and he thought and planned about how he was going to get the notoriety due him.

Square mile hospital was having a tough time with car theft. There were dozens of cars a week stolen off of the street at the hospital. They were broad daylight thefts. People would come to visit friends or relatives in the hospital, come outside, and their car would be gone.

Detective Charles initiated a plan. He and another district detective on loan to the bureau got permission from square mile hospital for access to their roof. One of the cops would get on the roof with binoculars and scan the area for car theft. They would take turns, one on the roof: one day, the other on the roof the next day.

If they observed a car slowly making its rounds near the visitor parking, the guy on the roof would alert the guy on the ground, and he would watch the guy until he made his move to steal a car.

They would catch them in the act, busting the steering columns or using keys which were made on the spot with key machines.

The plan proved lucrative for Patrolman Charles. He was referred to as "Roof Top," and he received the notoriety that he was in need of. He was now a special guy again.

There was an article in one of the major newspapers touting the car theft busting tactics of "Roof Top," and he was now known throughout the city. Car theft was one of the biggest crimes in the city. It kept some potential visitors from entering the city limits. The word in St. Louis County was "If you love your car, don't drive it to the city."

"Roof Top" now had upward mobility. He was assigned to the prestigious Intelligence Unit. It was the Chief's private unit. Only his friends went there.

But at that time there wasn't much going on in intelligence. Dope was now the recognized problem of society in the country and especially in St. Louis. He campaigned for and was eventually assigned to the Federal Drug Enforcement Administration Task Force.

It was the pinnacle of law enforcement for a city cop. Neat cars to drive, undercover assignments, pay like a federal agent, and the main reason: the cop was completely away from the city police department.

The cops were treated like feds, carried fed credentials, and worked through the United States Attorney's office to prosecute their cases.

"Roof Top" was intelligent enough to see that this federal "gig" was his door to fame; he only had to find a way to widely open the door and keep it open.

He knew of a family of criminals, headed by a middle aged Italian fellow named Joseph Olivastro. Joseph wasn't a Mafia character, he was just a hustler and a journeyman criminal. He did what he could, illegally, to make a decent living.

He had two sons, Anthony (Tony) and Joseph Jr. (Jo Jo) who reaped the benefits of having a crook for a dad. When the sons were adolescents, Joseph Sr. purchased a modest home in the Ladue School District in an affluent, ritzy suburb of St. Louis. Joseph Sr. was a thinker. He wanted his sons to go to school, be friends with, and to associate with rich kids.

This elaborate plan worked. Tony and Jo Jo graduated from Ladue High School and were friends with rich and powerful young adults.

Joseph Sr. wasn't any different than the other parents of Ladue kids. Money was the goal of both social groups. Greed brought Joseph's kids to Ladue. It brought the doctors, lawyers and business folks there also.

Anthony and Jo Jo Olivastro concocted a scheme to travel to Florida, purchase marijuana and cocaine, and to transport the drugs back to St. Louis and sell it in taverns and night spots.

It wasn't a new idea. It had been going on in St. Louis for decades. It's where "weed" came from. The jet setters in St. Louis desired …..."weed." It was the drug of choice with folks who could afford to purchase it.

"Roof Top" infiltrated the Olivastro crime family. He gained their trust and they even thought of him as their friend. It wasn't an easy thing to do. It started with informants.

" Roof Top" was a strong personality when he desired something. One of his main attributes was that he didn't look like a cop, and he was a good actor. He eventually passed himself off as a drug dealer looking to gain new footing in the Ladue area.

Anthony and Jo Jo Olivastro desired the financial help of several of their Ladue childhood friends. The selling point of the business venture was the markup of marijuana and cocaine. It was a sure fire way to get richer quicker. A couple of Ladue's up and comers jumped on the plan. They had the cash, the Olivastro's had the moxie, and the operation was a success for a while, until "Roof Top" came on the scene.

"Roof Top" made several undercover buys and had plans for the group and he to purchase a shipment of drugs that he was going to bring into the St. Louis area, via private aircraft. He got close to the family and their rich friends which meant they got close to him.

During one meeting they invited a close friend, (Jimmy Cohen), who was a criminal, had been to prison, was a noted tough guy, and boasted that he could spot an undercover cop in an instant.

"Roof Top" was afraid DEA surveillance would be spotted. He requested that surveillance not be used. "It's either surveillance..... or a "wire," his DEA supervisor advised him. "Roof Top" figured he might be searched for a wire so he declined the wire and chose surveillance.

DEA surveillance has always been a weak tactic. The agents conducting the surveillance are in essence working for someone else's drug deal. They aren't totally focused on some other agent's glory, especially a detached cop's glory.

During the meeting Jimmy Cohen showed up and advised the Olivastros that he had spotted surveillance, probably DEA, around the house they were meeting at. Cohen then did a cursory search of "Roof Top".

He came up with a "throw down gun" in "Roof Top's" boot, no wire or anything incriminating. "Roof Top" had bogus identification in his wallet. Cohen examined it. He advised the Olivastro's not to deal with "Roof Top" and that he was probably a DEA agent.

"Roof Top" left and told the Olivastros he would be in touch with them for the "big" deal. Greed overcomes common sense. The Olivastro group and the Ladue rich kids wanting to be richer than their crooked businessman dads continued to wait for "Roof Top's" big deal.

"Roof Top" had been keeping the United States Attorney's office apprised of his progress in penetrating the Olivastro crime family. The Assistant United States Attorney in charge of the case was totally focused on "Roof Top's" case. These guys are graded buy the U.S. Department of Justice on the quality of the cases they prosecute.

Criminals are divided into groups of importance called G-deps. An important criminal successfully prosecuted is a feather in the hat of the prosecutor, which means he will get a pay raise and gain the respect of his peers.

The cops who are risking their lives jumping through hoops, ruining their marriages, drinking too much, and hardly ever getting any sleep are largely forgotten by the federal government and the Assistant United States Attorney after successful prosecution.

But before and during the investigation and during the prosecution and trial, the Assistant United States Attorney is the cop's best friend. They schmooze the cop investigator, counsel him, even offer to play "father confessor" to him.

"Roof Top" confessed some of his undercover cop sins to the Assistant United States Attorney. To "Roof Top," the case was premier in his thought process. Nothing else mattered, not his marriage or his health or his self being. The case prevailed. It meant notoriety, fame, and success.

The Assistant United States Attorney didn't see it that way. He rebuffed "Roof Top" in his office. "Roof Top" walked out in a daze. He thought he and the AUSA were brothers in arms against the enemy.

He went back to the DEA offices in fashionable Clayton. The Special Agent in Charge called him into his office and advised him he was being sent back to the police department, immediately.

The case went on but the Olivastros and their rich Ladue friends were offered a deal to plead guilty to a lesser charge without going to a trial. They took it.

All of them did a little federal prison time. The case would have probably been thrown out if their lawyers had demanded a trial. Anthony and Jo Jo did the most time since they came from a criminal family and enticed the other greedy participants with the promise of quick cash. Who could resist such an offer?

There was a wealthy kid who came to the attention of law enforcement mainly due to "Roof Top's "stellar investigative techniques.

Mark Molasky inherited his wealth. His dad was in the media distribution business and had amassed millions. He worshipped Mark, and gave most of his fortune to him.

Mark Molasky was a strange looking fellow, but he had boat loads of cash and he was a young man. He always had a dynamite looking gal at his side, living with him, or accompanying him to local events where he could be seen by the "regular people" of the region. Money can't buy love, but it can buy beauty.

Mark owned a mansion in Ladue, near Ladue Road and I-64. The young and rich criminals befriended by "Roof Top" would go to Mark's home for poker parties. After getting Mark stoned on cocaine and weed, they would systematically cheat him out of his fortune.

Mark came from artistic and cultured parents. They gave him artwork and items of intrinsic value to display in his home. When the group of rich criminals left Mark's home with most of his cash, they would also steal his artwork or anything else they could get their hands on.

When he would wake up the next morning from a cocaine/poker binge and notice the missing artifacts, he would ask the wealthy young crooks about the evening. They would tell him that he lost the art work in the poker game.

Mark Molasky was a scofflaw. He felt above any law, state or federal and did his own thing. His reputation among cops and agents was growing, but he was basically left untouched due to his financial status.

Whenever a federal agent or a cop investigator went to his mansion to interview him, he would not speak to them. He referred them to his attorneys. Mark was always on the cusp of something illegal, and it was always something stupid, like a woman saying he forced her into a relationship, or a gambling debt he was trying to collect, or drug usage. He was super rich but a low-life.

Business people in the region did not want to do business with him because he was so unpredictable. But as with all criminals, rich and poor, they always lead themselves into the path of lady justice.

Mark and his gorgeous new wife got involved in a sex crime. The new wife left him and agreed to assist the state in his prosecution.

He sold his mansion and moved into a condominium in Ladue. "Roof Top" and I, who were now partners in the Intelligence Unit, his first assignment after returning to the police department from DEA, decided to interview Mark Molasky. It was part of our job description. There is always some bit of criminal information gathered during an interview.

Riding with "Roof Top" in the ninth was an unusual experience. He was eager to prove himself in those ancient days. I understood his plight although I didn't approve of it. Trying to be better than your fellow man wasn't my forte. It was boring to me and small.

He had planned his ascent in the police department the way big business executives plan their successes. They climb to the top of the food chain because they are convinced they are number one and the other cops are below them in stature.

Having him as a partner two times in one lifetime was even more unusual. He was now an angry man. In his mind he had failed. His long term plans had disintegrated, but he didn't blame himself. He was unable to rationalize the experience.

In the Marine Corps every Marine is a basic rifleman. No matter what you become or where you are assigned, you are a rifleman in the eyes of the Corps. It is the same mindset in the police department. Each cop is a basic street cop. Cops are demoted and transferred daily for almost nothing. If they do something real stupid and the royalty can't protect them, they are fired, sometimes sent to prison.

I gave "Roof Top" my philosophy on the police department and law enforcement in general, but he wasn't buying it. He would drive the detective car while I sat in despair wondering what this madman was going to do next. He would bang on the dash, the door panel, the steering wheel with his fists as he had fits of rage, cursing and expounding. He would stomp his feet on the floorboard and kick the underneath part of the dash as he cursed the Assistant United States Attorney who betrayed him. The cigar in his teeth would spit fire on the windshield as he raged.

In the Intelligence Unit, partners usually accompany each other on any assignment or any time they leave the detective car. We were deemed "undercover cops" and we were always there for each other. It was an unwritten law. If a partner got into a jam alone, the supervisor would ask his partner, "Where were you? You are supposed to stay with your partner no matter what."

The rage didn't diminish with "Roof Top." He wanted revenge for what he perceived to be an attack against his loyalty and his reputation. He constantly drove around the United States Court House, as if he was gaining his courage to go in and confront the Assistant United States Attorney who had betrayed him.

On a bright fall day he parked in front of the courthouse. "Let's go inside for a while," he said.

His jaw was set and he had the look of a madman. "I'm not going in there "Roof Top," I replied. He lit a fresh cigar and climbed out of the car. He was gone for an hour, came back and slid inside. He had had a confrontation with the Assistant United States Attorney, he eventually told me. I didn't ask for any gory details and he didn't tell me what had transpired, but he seemed more readily acceptable to what cards life had dealt him.

Our mission was to interview Mark Molasky. Being clumsy and uninformed, we drove to Mark Molasky's mansion, parked in the front, trekked to the door, and rang the bell. We were prepared to barge in and demand to speak to Mark Molasky. It's what city cop detectives did at the time.

A man in his sixties came to the door. We thought maybe he was a servant so we identified ourselves and told him our intentions. He advised us that he had purchased the mansion and land from Mark through an attorney and that he was going to tear the mansion down and build luxury condominiums.

Always searching for information, we asked him if he knew Mark. He said he knew of him and that he would not deal with him personally. Business transactions were handled through an attorney. He told us where Mark had moved.

"Roof Top" and I headed for the Molasky condominium parked and rang the bell. A servant came to the door, we did our shtick and Mark came to the door. We told him we wanted to interview him. He motioned for us to come in. I was shocked. It was "Key Stone Kop" time.

He paused and studied us. We began by asking stupid questions. We weren't prepared so "Roof Top" started talking about the poker games and cocaine and weed.

It was awkward and unprofessional. Mark held his hand up as if he was asking us to stop. We waited for him to speak.

He said, "Aren't you here to tell me about my wife? She left two hours ago and told me she was going to commit suicide. I thought you were here to inform me of my wife's death." The interview was over. "Roof Top" and I walked out. Eventually state indictments came out. Mark Molasky and his wife went to prison.

Mark Molasky's wealth could not save him from child sex violations. He spent several years in the Missouri State Penitentiary and eventually died there.

The other Ladue kids got out of prison and resumed their lives of privilege. I still see their photos in the Post society pages attending concerts and lavish dinners for charity. Their arrest was just a little bump in the road to success.   If you are rich and you wish to be richer you have to sometimes take chances. It's what America is about, taking chances to gain more wealth.

"Roof Top" never did recover from his ordeal at DEA. He had never been rebuffed in his life. He had always been a winner. His attitude was bad when he came back to the police department. It fueled his anger and ruined his career. He was friends with Chief Eugene Camp. He went to the chief and asked him to transfer him back into the narcotics division. Chief Camp was an intelligent man. He knew "Roof Top" was damaged goods, but he probably observed a glimmer of redemption in him.

He transferred "Roof Top" to the Bureau of Investigation. He was now working for Colonel John Doherty. Detectives who work for Doherty are clean shaven and wear a suit or sport coat with a tie. "Roof Top" sported a beard. Dressing up for him was a clean black "T" and an old pair of jeans.

Colonel Doherty advised "Roof Top" of the dress code. "Roof Top" rebelled. He advised Doherty that he was sent to the Bureau of Investigation to go in to narcotics, and that he needed his beard for undercover work.

"Roof Top" disrespected Colonel Doherty. It was considered sacrilegious to disobey or be rude to the Chief of Detectives. Disrespecting a demigod was another capital offense in the police department.

Colonel Doherty had friends and relatives working for him who never forgot "Roof Top's" disrespect of their idol. The disrespectful incident would come back to haunt "Roof Top" in the near future.

"Roof Top" loved horses. He owned several and rode frequently. He took a farrier course in Springfield, Illinois, and learned how to make and fit horse shoes. He eventually quit the cop job to become a farrier.

But that didn't last. The thrill of narcotics investigation called him. He became a Jefferson County, Missouri, deputy sheriff. He was good at anything meticulous. He wrote up a grant request to start a small county-wide narcotics unit.

The federal grant was approved, and he was in charge of the unit. It was a big success. He had a good bunch of guys working for him and he was reaping the accolades of the ruling class in Jefferson

County.

I was eventually sent to the DEA Task Force. I was again being assisted by "Roof Top". We were semi-partners again. Whenever he needed "buy" money, he would come to DEA for the cash.

It's the way the federal law enforcement agencies get their stats up. If the case is successful, DEA takes the case federal, and a bunch of federal agents get the credit for the arrests and seizures. Since he and I were old friends, I usually accompanied the federal cash.

"Roof Top" was calmer than I remembered him, but he was still a by-the-book cop. The job came first with him, nothing else mattered. He was now divorced; the little country drug unit was his wife.

"Roof Top" had a drug deal he needed financial assistance with. He came to DEA and explained it to the bosses. He wanted to make a big buy of meth at a trailer court out in the boonies. He needed approximately $8,000.

I was given the cash and ordered to meet "Roof Top" at his undercover office. I signed the cash over to him, and we took off for the lakeside trailer court in the middle of nowhere.

"Roof Top's" undercover agent went inside the trailer and after approximately ten minutes, came out with the dope. The scenario is to then go back inside the trailer and seize the government funds.

It was raining and cold. We stood outside debriefing the guy who made the buy, a Jefferson County deputy sheriff working undercover.

There was a high ranking Jefferson County deputy accompanying us (Ed Kemp). He was actually in charge of the scene. We forced open the trailer door and stormed in with our guns drawn. We arrested the dope dealer. The search for the government funds was to no avail.

The trailer was packed with junk, like a hoarder lived there. The high ranking deputy took the handcuffed dope dealer out into the rain, "Roof Top" and I followed.

It was pouring and the dope dealer was soaked. "Where did you hide the money?" the senior deputy asked.

"I'm not telling you anything," the dope dealer replied. The deputy hit him with a cattle prod. It sparked in the rain and the dope dealer came off the ground and landed on his knees. "I'll show you where it is," he finally said.

We recovered the $8,000. It was remarkable how whenever "Roof Top" and I worked together there was some sort of controversy.

Nothing was ever smooth. But that is the dope game. It's all about money. The dope dealer doesn't want the dope. He wants the money it brings.

The federal government doesn't want the dope; they want the proceeds of the sale. Big dope dealers are super wealthy. The government wants large seizures. You have to take off small dealers to get to the bigger dealers.

"Roof Top's" Jefferson County gig sadly came to an end. A high ranking relative of Colonel John Doherty retired from the St. Louis Police Department and took a job with the Jefferson County Sheriff's Office. Vengeance was his.   Doherty's relative was close friends with the sheriff. Fate plays a big role in law enforcement. Country cops and city cops believe anything they hear. "Roof Top" paid for his disrespect of Colonel Doherty.

He was sent back to uniform and again he was crushed. In his mind he was too valuable to ply the county roads in a marked car. He was an undercover guy. He quit in protest.

"Roof Top" got a job with DEA as an analyst. He sits in an office all day typing reports for the federal government. They "birddog" for information on dope dealers. One of their investigative tools is access to IRS records concerning the incomes of friends and associates, past and present, enemies, past and future; and people they are just curious about.

It is profiling via the government computer. The trick is to find someone who is living beyond their means. In the minds of the federal bureaucrats, this is prima facie evidence that this person is a dope dealer. They have federal meetings to discuss the findings. The analyst is praised for his covert computer investigation. They plan how they are going to seize the alleged drug czar's assets, cars, boats, house, bank accounts.

Most of the time there is a reason for prosperity in the United States of America. We are all supposed to be rich. It is what the country was founded upon. I went to visit "Roof Top" in his office several years ago.

He was sitting in a little cubbyhole, toiling over a computer, making himself satisfied that he was a clerk for the government. We talked about his past. He had done the impossible; he had infiltrated a rich kid dope ring, and they all went to prison. He received no accolades for this improbable task.

He was commander of a country drug unit, had organized it and made it successful. He had the respect of the guys who worked for him. I felt strange seeing him working as a clerk.

He sensed I was taken aback by his meager federal existence. He told me some of the DEA agents were going to take him on a dope "deal" with them. Most of the agents I had dealt with at DEA couldn't infiltrate a drug ring. They have informants and guys like "Roof Top" to do their dirty work

They couldn't make undercover dope buys. They left that task to confidential informants with a badge, DEA agents description of cops with information on drug dealers. I left "Roof Top's" office with an empty feeling in my gut. I haven't seen him since.

On the evening of the bombing of the ROTC building on Forest Park Boulevard, in the "bloody" Ninth District, "Roof Top" and I, after handling the first alarm sounding, were lucky and got off on time. At 11:15 p.m. another alarm sounding occurred at the ROTC building. This time several officers and a supervisor responded. They were met by an alarm man who had keys to the building. The officers and the alarm official entered the building and were checking it for any sign of a burglary when a large bomb went off inside of the building.

The officers were knocked to the floor, some thrown several yards, some suffered concussions and hearing loss. They were conveyed to the hospital. The fire department was contacted. As firefighters entered the building to investigate and extinguish any possible fires, a second bomb went off inside of the ROTC building. Several firefighters were injured and conveyed to area hospitals.

It seemed that the bombs were timed to go off so that first responders would be injured or killed. On March 10, 1971, the Globe Democrat Newspaper received an anonymous letter allegedly from the bombers.

In the letter they referred to the bombing as a "deed" and a "concrete action against the "amerikan" government, the number one enemy of all people." The typewritten message was addressed to "Dear sisters and brothers. The bombing occurred on International Women's Day."

I had a chance to read the investigative report. The burglary was quite sophisticated. Spikes were nailed into a utility pole at the rear of the building. The burglar/bombers climbed on their spikes until they reached the regular climbing spikes installed by the telephone company. They stepped onto the roof of the building and entered the building through an elevator housing after sawing through a wooden grillwork.

The cop brains charged with solving this deed stated they were looking for a political activist who was also a professional burglar. They admitted they did not know of any such suspect.

In the rubble of the ROTC bombing, investigators found some electrical wiring, flashlight batteries, and a timing device. As of this date, no arrests have been made.

The bombers were apparently on the roof when "Roof Top" and I were checking the perimeter of the building. Or they were inside setting the timers on the bombs. A cop never knows what's behind a closed door.

In the day to day police business cops were being shot like battlefield warriors. Doc Cooper's considerable clout within the department, getting cops promoted and transferred to neat detective jobs continued and grew. And he was a great surgeon. He was a combat surgeon in Viet Nam. Gunshot trauma was his specialty, a good man to have on the St. Louis Police Department staff.

Most cops wished to be friends with Doc Cooper. A cop approached Doc with the idea of forming an intramural football team. They already had a name for the home team: "St. Louis Razorbacks."

Doc hit the field running. He along with some cronies organized a game with the Kansas City, Missouri, police football team. There was friction between the two teams. Both were controlled by the state, through statute, which meant the state of Missouri controlled their pay and benefits.

With Warren Hearnes as the governor and the brother-in- law of Doc Cooper, Kansas City cops felt they were being short changed. For once, St. Louis wasn't the bastard child of the state. Sadly that didn't last long.

The football game was a big deal. It was played at a high school stadium in Kansas City. Doc Cooper was on the sidelines, treating injured players, cheering and rabblerousing, pacing like Joe Paterno.

He shouted his displeasure at questionable calls. A fight broke out between some K.C. cops and some of St. Louis' finest on the field.

Doc was right there on the field observing as the fight was broken up.

Doc was born and raised in the boot heel, but he loved St. Louis, and he loved St. Louis cops. The Razorbacks won the game. Afterward, on the way back to St. Louis, he took a contingent of his closest cop friends for a personally guided tour of the Capital Building and the governor's mansion in Jefferson City. The working poor cops were mesmerized by the event and bragged about it for years.

It was time for St. Louis to shine again. The cops had Doc Cooper, Governor Hearnes, and the state democratic party behind them. And they had federal cash supplying the department and the city with funds to modernize the ragtag political police department.

The ghetto dwellers had socialized housing and federal cash behind them. The cops had an old fashioned and poor police department. The cops and the poor folks were riders on the same horse. The existence of both groups depended on who was going to get the most cash from the fed and the state.

In actuality, without the poor ignorant blacks, the police department could have been cut in half. Most of the beat cop's shift was catering to, transporting, counseling, preaching to, arresting, going to court and/or educating poor black folks.

They were riders on the same horse, but they were facing each other and fighting over who was going to be the jockey. The poor blacks won the battle. They got billions for replacement housing. The cops got millions.

The goal of many of the cops in those days was to get a bachelor's degree and go into federal law enforcement. From all appearances, the St. Louis Police Department was never going to be a real job, not something a guy or gal could support their family on. Pay would always be minimal because the state controlled our pay raises.

The driving force within the police department was prestige. If you had a prestigious assignment, like Burglary—Robbery, Homicide, or Intelligence, then you had prestige. Everyone else didn't. Chief Gene Camp decided who was going to get these plum assignments.

Doc Cooper helped his friends. The district cops, doing almost all of the work, coming face to face with danger on every call, working the worst hours, were the lowest cops on the pecking order totem pole. And they still are.

The cops who sat in an office with their nickel plated magnums in shoulder holsters, their personal coffee cup, secretaries to do their typing, personal department cars to ride to free lunches in and to take home, and a rolodex of political friends, had prestige.

Most district cops longed for a prestigious position. There were only so many available so Chief Camp would invent new investigative units and then place them under the bureau of investigation, Colonel John Doherty's bureau.

One such unit was the Strategic Operations Deployment Division, SODD for short. Sergeant Glen Lodl was a supervisor in SODD. He was a flashy guy, a television cop series kind of a guy. He dressed the part: casual, jeans tight fitting, T-shirt, large nickel plated magnum in a shoulder holster, leather bomber jacket. He acted the part, almost professionally, sultry and serious; all cop, all job, no gray area. Glen Lodl was a get-the-job done at any cost kind of guy.

Glen Lodl idolized Gene Camp. At the beginning of most months he would take an envelope to Camp's office late at night and place it on his desk chair.

Glen Lodl came from a police family. Glen's dad, Bill Lodl was a city cop. As in many cop families there had been marital problems with Bill and Velma Lodl. Velma had moved out of their South County home and moved in with her son, Glen in the city. Glen was in the police academy at the time.

Divorce was imminent; Bill and Velma were bickering about the disposition of the house in South County. Bill had told a neighbor that if Velma took the house he would turn on the gas and do away with both of them.

Coworkers stated that Bill Lodl left work at the old twelfth district station in a good mood, smiling and joking. He drove to the 3400 block of Locust where his wife worked. He observed her walking on Theresa Avenue toward Olive with a coworker. Bill stopped his car and asked Velma to get in with him so they could talk. Velma refused and kept walking. Bill stopped the car, got out and took his wife's arm. He tried to force her into his car. She begged him to stop and told him he was hurting her. He released her and she kept walking.

Velma took a short cut through an alley in an effort to lose Bill. She was headed for the bus stop at Grand and Olive and was in a parking lot when Bill, who had parked his car and gotten out, accosted her again, grabbing her arm, trying to force her to come with him.

Bill pulled his off-duty revolver with his left hand and held onto Velma with his right. Velma pulled away screaming hysterically.

Bill shot Velma five times with the snub nosed gun and then shot himself one time in the chest. Both were pronounced dead at City Hospital number one.

I had heard the story. All of the old cops talked about it and all of the other tales of horror concerning murder and city cops. It became obvious to me that if you are a friend, relative, or associate of a St. Louis cop you should be cautious of what you do or say. They are not to be trod upon.

Bill and Velma's son, Glen was an ambitious cop. He started a security company (L&R Security) and was successful at running it. Lt. Colonel William Brown hated Glen Lodl. Maybe he felt Glen shouldn't have been a cop because of his traumatic youthful domestic experience. Colonel Brown dogged Glen Lodl, accusing him of using the police department as a tool to gain business for his security company.

Glen was transferred to a district but still had prestige. He drove Caddys with mobile telephones in them, and he conducted security business while on duty. Colonel Brown was trying to force him to take an early pension. The police department was the only family Glen ever knew. Leaving it would be like leaving home and never being able to return. The department was his mother and his father; the cops he associated with were his brothers and sisters.

Glen married a woman younger than he. She was small and cute and energetic. Glen signed the security company over to her. He was now free to continue his life as a police supervisor in the department.

In the police business there is usually a domestic issue in our personal lives that needs to be dealt with. The job is the other woman, the mistress who demands all of our time, on or off duty. She makes us distant at times, sad, or giddy. She controls our emotions. Wives hate her, and they grow disillusioned with us, the cop. It happened with Glen and his cute wife.

I answered a call for an alarm sounding at Glen's security company, ironically on Locust a couple of blocks east of where his mother worked. Glen had committed suicide a couple of months prior to me getting this call. The brass in the police department didn't see this as an unusual occurrence. It was business as usual; Go to the funeral, give condolences to the family, and go back to the office and drink coffee.

Glen's cute widow met me at the security company. It was a false alarm. I asked her about Glen and his obvious problems. She told me she knew he was going to kill himself. Friends advised her that his plan was to kill her first then kill himself. She went into hiding until Glen did the deed. She either closed or sold the security company.

Gene Camp hated dealing with the state legislators over pay increases because they always made him promote someone he didn't wish to promote. It was quid pro quo in its finest form: "You want a pay raise for your cops, we want this list of cops promoted." The department went many years without pay raises because of this mentality.

Doc Cooper always advised his cop friends to look elsewhere for a career. Most of his close friends graduated from area colleges and left. Many of his friends become successful people: The Honorable Clifford J. Proud, Federal Magistrate for the Southern District of Illinois. John Vollmar; College professor, Art Dwyer; radio personality and owner/originator of the Soulard Blues Band are just a few of Cooper's friends who made good.

He and Gene Camp were idolized by about half the department. The other half idolized John Doherty. Cops were always looking for someone to look up to. Camp had a business degree, Doc Cooper, and the chief's job.

John Doherty had aces, contacts and a huge reputation. But he didn't have direct access to the governor and that is what it takes to become the chief of police in the City of St. Louis.

The state controlled the police department in those ancient days, a holdover from the Civil War. The state didn't want the Union leaning city to use their police force as a militia against the confederacy. The state took control of the department and the governor appointed four civilians from the city to be police commissioners. The fifth member is the mayor. The governor advises the board president whom he desires to be the chief of police. The president advises the board members. Eugene Camp was a shoe in.

There are idols within bureaucracies. It is what makes the system work. The less fortunate idolize their supervisors and the bosses expect complete loyalty from them. Cops are so down trodden that if a supervisor is just nice to them they fall all over themselves. They instantly admire a cop supervisor who praises them from time to time, and they will do whatever he asks them to do. He will defend their name and them if need be.

The supervisors are always testing your loyalty and the underling knows this fact. You act as a pet, a trained dog who will fetch on command. If you hesitate or refuse to show undying loyalty then you are discarded for someone who will. It instills fear in the subordinate. He feels power by being one of the chosen ones, he does what he is told.

One of the stories about John Doherty was that he killed a gangster with his bare hands. He had told the gangster, Isadore Londe to get out of town, and that if he ever saw him again, he was going to kill him.

Apparently Londe was seen by Doherty leaving the old twelfth district station. Doherty confronted him on the steps of the station house and beat him, killing him.

As I examined this story, I figured that almost any cop who knew how to fight with his hands and feet could probably beat almost any suspect when they are in or around a police station. The suspect might get a punch or two in, but he can't win because an army of cops will come to the aid of the cop.

I also wondered how any cop, anywhere in the City of St. Louis could get away with such a beating. To kill someone with just your hands is difficult to do. I found out it was myth. Just another story to beef up someone's hero resume

The city police flew under the radar for decades. No one in outstate Missouri cared anything about what went on in St. Louis. The folks in neighboring Illinois couldn't care less what happened just across the river from them. City politicians did what they wanted and were happy with their independence so long as they could get federal cash for their poor blacks to dole out as they wished.

In the early 1950's, specifically 1953, a couple of Kansas City bar flies, Bonnie Heady and Carl Hall, conjured up a plan to kidnap the son of a wealthy Kansas City Cadillac dealer.

Bonnie Heady went to the Notre Dame de Scion Catholic School in Kansas City, told the nun in charge that she was to pick up Bobby Greenlease because his mother, her sister, Virginia Greenlease, had suffered a heart attack and was wanting to see her son. The nun turned the six year old over to her. Bobby freely took her hand and they walked out together. She transported the boy and herself via taxi to a parking lot in downtown Kansas City where Carl Hall was patiently waiting in a Plymouth station wagon.

The boy was chatty and happy to be with them as they drove into the Kansas farmland. Carl brought the Plymouth to a stop in a field. Bonnie climbed out and took a walk with their boxer dog. Carl clumsily, brutally, murdered the boy in the seat of the Plymouth. They buried the boy in Bonnie Heady's back yard in St. Joseph, Missouri then sent a ransom note to Robert Greenlease Sr. They demanded $600,000 in twenty's and tens for the safe return of Bobby Greenlease Jr. They got it and headed to St. Louis.

They barhopped in St. Louis. Carl purchased a steel footlocker and a large suitcase then transferred the ransom money into it. They befriended cabbies and pimps, prostitutes and bartenders. A prostitute saw the footlocker full of cash.

The owner of Ace Cab Company, Joe Costello, an underworld associate, got word of them, their cash and their drunkenness. Joe Costello called a cop friend, Lieutenant Louis Shoulders, a shake-down cop, murderer, and ner de well. Their plan was to steal the cash from Carl Hall and Bonnie Heady. They figured it was the Greenlease ransom money, but it didn't really matter to them.

Lou Shoulders advised his substitute driver, Officer Elmer Dolan, that they were going to meet Joe Costello, crook and cab company owner. Elmer, no doubt worshipped Lou Shoulders. He was his supervisor. He respected and trusted him and his judgment.

Hall and Heady were staying at a hotel at 5613 Pershing Avenue. Dolan and Shoulders barged into the room and arrested Hall while Costello waited around the corner. They seized the footlocker, drove Hall to a district station, and booked him in. They later found out the cash in the footlocker was for certain the ransom money, and they turned it in, but it was shy by $300,000.

The case and the missing money made national news. J.Edgar Hoover was incensed about the missing cash. Shoulders and Dolan were sent to prison. The missing $300,000 was never found.

Seventeen years later when I became a St. Louis police officer, people were still talking about the missing money. When Elmer Dolan was released from prison, John Doherty was a hotshot, high-ranking detective in the Bureau of Investigation. He had subordinates who idolized him.

He wanted that missing money. He and his trusted men put Elmer Dolan under surveillance thinking he would lead them to the cash. They were like school children with a treasure map, but the part of the map describing where the treasure was buried was missing.

The problem was these were children with badges and guns, homicidal children, unconscionable and above the law in the city where nobody cared what happens with the police.

Doherty and his men eventually rousted Elmer Dolan from a bar in south city and conveyed him to police headquarters. John Doherty beat him with his fists trying to find out where the ransom money was hidden.

Elmer Dolan didn't know. He eventually died a broke and broken man. John Doherty came to his wake. Elmer Dolan's wife asked him to leave.

It was typical of a cop commander in the day. Their opinion of themselves was so high they couldn't figure why someone would hate them for handcuffing and beating their loved one. "What's the big deal? I was doing it for the city."

Elmer's son became a St. Louis cop, resigned after several years, and went to work for the federal government. Lou Shoulders son became a union organizer. His car was blown up with him in it at an outstate lake in the mid 1980's. The kidnapping, the missing ransom money, and the crooked cops brought worldwide attention to the St. Louis Metropolitan Police Department.

The unwritten creed of the police department was to take care of your friends and the relatives of your friends. This enormous task rested on the shoulders of the chief of police. Before any decisions were made on transfers, promotions or discipline, the chief had to figure who was friends with whom. He had staff who kept the crony books straight, and they would advise him on current and past friendships.

One such friend…. based on a family member being courteous to Gene Camp while acting as a servant at a country club, was Sergeant Andrew (Mickey) Davis. The sergeant had been hired, promoted, and given good positions within the department, but he felt the need to look elsewhere for employment.

He quit but didn't stay gone for long. When you are favored in the police department, it isn't easy feeling comfortable someplace where you actually have to show progress in your field of endeavor.

Mickey was rehired as a police officer. Gene Camp then reinstated him as a sergeant and placed him in the Bureau of Investigation, (narcotics division.) He had prestige.

On October 22, 1970, a sixteen year old girl went to the Ninth District station and advised officers that she had been brought to St. Louis by a man and woman for the purpose of prostitution. She said she had been injected with some kind of a drug by the man and woman, and that she had smoked some type of dope with them. She said the man and woman were from Detroit and they were staying at the George Washington Hotel at 600 N. Kingshighway. She added that they had a large amount of narcotics with them.

The girl was turned over to juvenile authorities, and since there were narcotics involved, the narcotics unit was contacted. This was the beginning of a three part stage play that was so bizarre it could not have been scripted.

Two squads of narcotics detectives (four detectives) went to the hotel to interview the couple the girl had named. The name she had given them wasn't their real name. They were registered at the hotel under the names Wesley Copeland and his wife Goldie.

The narcotics cops went to the room, knocked on the door, and then kicked it in. The man in the room pulled a 45 automatic on them and the woman with him brandished a rifle. The narcotics cops backed out of the room and called for backup.

Narcotics Division was under the command of Colonel John Doherty, so the Burglary—Robbery Division, Strategic Operations Deployment Division, and any detective who wished to get involved rushed to the George Washington Hotel.

My old Irish sarge, Sergeant John McGuire, contacted me on the radio and told me to call him at the station. I knew what he was going to tell me: "Stay away from the George Washington Hotel." He knew I was curious and that I ventured out of my assigned area frequently. I went to a couple of call boxes, but none of them were operable so I did what most cops do, I went to a bar.

I called the station on a bar phone and asked for him. He got on the phone and said ,"Stay away from the George Washington Hotel."

I asked, "Why?"

"It's prime for disaster, and I don't want you there." I felt crushed that I was missing out on a major hostage situation, but I stayed away for a while.

I kept circling the vicinity, getting closer and closer, until I was on the perimeter. There was a Mobile Reserve officer blocking the street at Euclid and Delmar so I stopped and talked to him while the event began to build.

The Mobile Reserve Division, which is a uniform city-wide patrol division, cordoned off the entire block. The area was sealed. A canvass of the area revealed the Copelands' automobile, a newer model Cadillac. Bureau detectives communicated with the couple by telephone.

Captain Harry Lee, Commander of the Ninth District ordered all police personnel out of the hotel until they could initiate a plan to arrest the couple.

Sergeant Mickey Davis disobeyed Captain Harry Lee's order, went to the room, and knocked on the door. He figured since he was black, and the couple from Detroit were black, he would be able to communicate with them and defuse the situation. His plan went awry. They held him hostage for six hours, at gunpoint.

I listened to the Mobile Reserve officer's radio as I sat in my cop car and envisioned what I was missing I was a rooky cop; this was real police work. I yearned to be a part of it but I knew it wasn't going to happen for me, this time.

The interview of a possible narcotics violator had turned into a hostage situation with a mini-cop-demigod being held hostage. Mickey Davis was personal friends with the chief of police. He was a special guy. It was time to break out the heavy hitters.

John Doherty, Chief of the Bureau of Investigation and his henchman, Sergeant Glen Lodl, head of the Strategic Operations & Deployment Division (SODD) responded to the scene. Also in the fray was Lieutenant Fred Grimes, another killer cop from the old days of law enforcement. They were scrambling to get Sergeant Mickey Davis back.

I listened to the closed circuit Mobile Reserve radio. The cop royalty demigods were talking over each other, barking orders and getting their voices onto the tape recording, for every word uttered on a St. Louis police department radio is taped.

The tapes would be studied and transposed. Police commissioner would have a copy of the incident. The commanders would be under scrutiny.

Colonel Doherty and Lieutenant Fred Grimes worked out a plan. They told the Copelands they were going to allow them to leave St. Louis without charges if they released Sergeant Mickey Davis. They told them they would bring their Caddy up to the front of the hotel. The keys were obtained and a uniformed officer was sent to get the Copeland's car.

The black couple didn't realize that disrespecting John Doherty or his band of henchmen was, at the least, a beating offense. Taking a St. Louis cop hostage, and then being set free for the offense is considered a capital crime in this city.

The Copelands agreed; Mickey Davis was freed. They walked out of the hotel together. It was retribution time. Doherty briefed his hit crew, and they set themselves up to watch the Caddy. The Caddy was brought up to the hotel entrance, but there was a glitch in the plan. Somebody in the command field didn't like the idea. The plans were put on hold. When the Copelands were out of the hotel waiting for their car, they were arrested.

Before, or during these plan changes, someone ordered Patrolman Steven Georgeff assigned to the Mobile Reserve Division, to drive the suspects Caddy to headquarters. He eagerly jumped in the Caddy and took off toward downtown St. Louis, probably happy to be away from the mayhem, indecisiveness, and blundering of the command rank.

The cop demigods didn't call the hit crew off. The plan stayed in effect. Patrolman Georgeff made it as far as Boyle and West Pine. An undercover police car driven by Sergeant Glen Lodl pulled alongside the Copeland's Caddy. It was dark and the shooter, Detective Rich Kuklajon, Glen Lodl's sidekick and attack dog, fired a shot from his .357-magnum into Patrolman Georgeff's body.

The caddy crashed into a parked car. But there was more than one shot. Someone else inside the undercover cop car fired into Patrolman Georgeff. He was shot two times, once with the .357 magnum and once with another caliber weapon.

Patrolman Gerogeff was severely wounded, shot several times in his side and shoulder. He was in critical condition but survived. Doc Cooper saved his life.

Rich Kuklajon stated he accidentally shot his magnum. He was supposedly pointing it at the driver thinking it was Wesley Copeland trying to get Copeland to stop the car and surrender himself when the weapon discharged. Kuklajon stated his weapon went off one time.

But Georgeff was shot twice. Someone was riding in the back seat of the undercover cop car. Maybe Colonel John Doherty. Maybe that's why he didn't call off the hit crew. He was with them and didn't know the plans had changed.

It must have been someone of stature, a member of the cop royalty club, someone who wanted to even the score for Detroit scum coming to St. Louis and causing a big mess for our city cops to clean up.

Disrespecting the city and its band of blue warriors the way Copeland did is at the least a torture first offense, then a death sentence. Wesley Copeland was sitting in a warm police car being interviewed when Patrolman Georgeff was shot. He was eventually released, returned to Detroit and was shot and killed by his uncle over a money dispute.

Congressman Bill Clay wrote a letter to the Board of Police Commissioners demanding a full inquiry. He wanted a grand jury investigation or a House of Representatives probe into the incident. He called the incident a "breakdown in law and order."

Doc Cooper reiterated that Georgeff was shot twice with two different weapons. Another opinion was needed so a different doctor examined Georgeff and stated he was shot one time with one weapon. It was a battle of the two leading factions.

When the dust cleared, Detective Kuklajon was ordered to receive reinstruction in the use of firearms because of his carelessness in discharging his gun and wounding Patrolman Georgeff. City cops weren't allowed to carry magnums. It was unlawful for Kuklajon to carry one.

Sergeant Glen Lodl received a three day suspension for failure to supervise Rich Kuklajon. The third person in the car was never identified if there was a third person. Maybe Glen Lodl leaned over and fired into Steve Georgeff at the same time Rich Kuklajon fired.

Steve Georgeff was eventually given a disability retirement. His life was changed in an instant. I had contact with a relative of Steve's. He told me Steve didn't live a good life after the shooting and that he died a young man.

Rich Kuklajon's explanation to his peers? "It was a mistake." Detective Kuklajon had prestige; He was one of Colonel John Doherty's henchman. The system was backing him 100 percent. Patrolman Georgeff didn't have the backing of the dictatorship.

As all of this material was not made available to the rank and file cops, they had to read about the incident in the newspapers. I pondered long and hard on it. I compared Rich Kuklajon and Glen Lodl. I didn't know them personally. I would see them in the district stations.

They were flashy detectives: well dressed, shiny big magnums in shoulder holsters. The district cops looked up to them. They were free from the radio.

But Rich Kuklajon and Glen Lodl were not the same kind of guys. Rich would kill to stay in the limelight. He was a showman plying his trade and doing what he was told. He was a member of an elite undercover group of guys and he enjoyed it.

Glen Lodl was 180 degrees from Rich. Glen was a congenital killer. If he wouldn't have been a cop he would have been a hired killer for organized criminals. It was what he desired.

Rich Kuklajon eventually resigned to sell real estate. He also died a young man.

'JEWISH LIGHTNING'

Story two:

Even though the federal government was instrumental in providing assistance for the majority of the citizens of the City of St. Louis in one form or another, the government wasn't thought of as socialistic.

The police department was completely socialistic. The medical division, operated by Dr. Cooper with a full staff: nurses, doctors and assistants and secretaries was just one example. He surgically removed a Marine Corps tattoo for me, free of charge. Cops would go to his house unannounced, eat food from his refrigerator, guzzle his expensive collection of fine wines, swim in his pool. Doc just laughed it off. He was one of the boys and that was important to him.

Whatever a cop wanted or needed, there was someone in the community who would give it to him free of charge or at a discount. Food, cars, services, clothing. There was always a "police discount" involved. It easily and quickly became a "way of life" for city cops. We, as a group, felt entitled to these perks, and if they weren't forthcoming, the cops advised other cops of the merchant who denied them of their entitlement. It was barter, donate, discount, or be placed on the blacklist.

The city of St. Louis as a geographic entity was used as a lab rat for the federal government. The city was unique in a way that we were on our own in the scheme of politics. We were not part of a county, and not completely recognized by the state in which we were housed. Politically, it was the state of Missouri and then St. Louis.

Added to these political realities, were big-time racial problems from more than half of the residents being poor and black. The fed spent billions building the Gateway Arch, and the Poplar Street Bridge, connecting Illinois with downtown St. Louis by a modern bridge, but they didn't finish the Arch project.

The Arch grounds were cut off from the rest of the city by Interstate 70. It was difficult to access the Arch grounds or the riverfront, the only natural attribute the city had. It was fun to look at the Arch grounds and the riverfront, but they were not available to pedestrians who wished to casually walk and enjoy it.

The Poplar Street Bridge, commonly referred to as "the tunnel project," incorporated trade and labor unions from both sides of the river. Organized crime in Chicago saw this as an opportunity for growth. The crooked labor and trade unions in that city flooded the little and corrupt town of East St. Louis, Illinois, with union thugs.

Buster Wortman was the organized crime boss on the eastside. There were ghost employees; workers who never showed up on the work site and still got paid big money, including overtime cash. Buster Wortman decided who was going to get hired, and who wouldn't have to show up for work and still get paid.

The Chicago thugs eventually infiltrated the St. Louis, Missouri, trade and labor unions. They took them over through intimidation: beatings and murder. All of the trades were bossed by a new organized crime king pin in Chicago, Joey Aiuppa, a throw back of the old Al Capone gang.

It was as if the federal government was watching this experiment through a fish bowl: politicians in white coats with food and electrical wands, feeding and shocking to see where the St. Louis lab rat would run for food or shelter.

What most humans and lab rats desire most is peace. There was nowhere to go in the region for that commodity. No matter what your occupation or job description, the citizens of this berg were scrambling.

The slick businessmen in the city were making big money through the trickle-down effect of socialistic government subsidies. Most city business owners knew that the only real dollar was the tax-free dollar, and most money generated over the counter was cash. Credit cards weren't popular yet.

The mayor during the building of the Poplar Street Bridge and the Arch grounds was A.J. Cervantes. Life Magazine did an expose on organized crime and corruption in St. Louis. There was a large photo of A.J.Cervantes tending bar while mayor for an organized crime party. He was rubbing elbows with the Mafia, Chicago Mafia who penetrated the sleepy and small/big city of St. Louis and took control of the trade and labor unions.

The fed was huge, but you could randomly stop a person on the street, white or black neighborhoods and ask them if they knew what the IRS was or what it meant to them, and get a response of, "Who?" Government was huge and nobody knew it, not in the city of St. Louis, anyway. The government to most St. Louis residents meant a monthly check, nothing else.

The rumor among the movers and shakers of the city was that the mid-part of the city was someday going to be the garden spot of the state of Missouri. Businessmen with money were snapping up any kind of real estate they could find in the mid-part of St. Louis, including the Central West End.

They bought warehouses, old factories, vacant lots, tenements, old hotels, any real estate that became available. One whole stretch of Olive Boulevard was purchased, renovated, and turned into restaurants, night clubs, and antique shops. There were unique, antique gas lights lining the streets so they named it Gaslight Square.

It was an instant hit and gained worldwide acclaim as the place to be seen in the Midwest. Big name entertainers performed there: Barbra Streisand and the like. The restaurants were four-star, and you could dine street side and watch the parade of beautiful people walking by dressed in their finest. St. Louis was on the map because of Gas Light Square. It thrived for years.

But there is always a glitch in neighborhoods in St. Louis. As the poor blacks grew dissatisfied with public high rise housing, they started the move westward toward Gaslight Square and the Central West End.

The single family homes in the neighborhood were brick which made them attractive to the federal government. Citizens on welfare were given rental subsidies for brick homes. After a couple of years, the neighborhoods surrounding Gaslight Square and most of the middle part of the city were inhabited by poor blacks.

There was always a parking problem at Gaslight Square. You had to park on the street most of the time, then walk several blocks to get to the restaurants and clubs.

People walking on the street through the black neighborhoods were robbed. In some instances young women were brutally raped on tenement porches and in barren front yards hidden by overgrown shrubs while their date or husband stood by with a gun to his head, witnessing the dastardly deed. At the least, cars were vandalized, stolen, burned for no reason except that the people going to Gaslight Square were white with money to spend and cars to park in the neighborhoods, and in front of their homes.

But patrons kept coming. Many would take taxi cabs so they would not have to park in the black neighborhoods. The R&B bands were the draw. St. Louis has always been keen on Rhythm & Blues bands. R&B lovers could hop from bar to bar and listen to big name performers from Texas, Detroit, Chicago and St. Louis. The street was still packed with the "beautiful people".

Beer and booze weren't enough of the downers for many of the party goers. Many sought out "weed" to help them party through the night. "Weed" was at the Square, but you had to know someone who was "in the know" to obtain it.

The doormen or bouncers at the nightclubs were "in the know" for anything or anyone at Gaslight Square. If you were a doorman or a bouncer, you had many friends and contacts for almost anything.

The Whiskey A-Go-Go, 4212 Olive, was one of the most popular clubs on the Square. It had good entertainment and gorgeous Go-Go dancers in gilded cages above the bar gyrating to the loud R&B.

The main doorman/bouncer at the Whiskey A-Go-Go was Ray Lawrence. He grew up on the eastside. He was a big tough guy who had been fighting all of his life. But he could be a schmoozer if he wished to be.

People liked him. All sorts of people, crooks, cops, customers just wanting to enjoy an evening out with their wives, people who didn't care about anyone's past. People who lived for the moment. That is what nightclubs are for. A place to forget about the past and escape into the present.

As in all nightclubs, there are a certain amount of ner' de wells who are regular customers. Ray Lawrence knew these customers and he would treat them with respect as long as they didn't start trouble at the club. His job was to keep the peace. Usually all he had to do was to approach a troubled individual, and any trouble within the confines of the club would cease.

On October 22, 1967, near closing time there was a large argument inside the Whiskey A-Go- Go. Ray Lawrence was outside on the sidewalk laughing and talking to the bar-hopping night club set. It was part of his job: know the patrons.

The owner sent a waiter to inform Ray there was trouble inside the club and they needed him, quickly.

Ray rushed in, 220 pounds of muscle, tattooed and bulging.

He ordered the group of young guys to leave the club. One of them, Thomas Callanan, twenty six-year old son of Lawrence Callanan, head of the Pipefitters Local 562, pulled a thirty eight caliber pistol and shot Ray Lawrence in the left shoulder.

Ray spun with the impact of the bullet which went through his body and into the wall behind him. He started wailing on Callanan with rights and lefts. Callanan ran from Ray and exited the bar via a back door.

The police were called. Ray Lawrence was rushed to City Hospital, admitted and treated. Ray Lawrence made a statement that Thomas Callanan shot him.

Witnesses corroborated his statement. An arrest order was put out for Callanan. The following day: business at the club resumed as normal. Under usual circumstances that would have been the end of the story.

Ray Lawrence checked himself out of City Hospital and vanished. Five days later Thomas Callanan turned himself into then Major John Doherty, Assistant Chief of Detectives, at his office at police headquarters, accompanied by his attorney, Richard L. Daly. Callanan declined to make a statement.

Shortly thereafter victim, Ray Lawrence, appeared at police headquarters. He had changed his statement. He advised that Thomas Callanan was not the man who shot him October 22 at the Whiskey A-Go-Go. He stated that he and Thomas Callanan were the best of friends. Witnesses also recanted their statements, saying that Callanan was not the man who shot Ray Lawrence on that fateful night. The charges were dropped against Thomas Callanan.

But this little shooting in Gaslight Square made big headlines. The end had always been near for the entertainment oasis in the middle of the ghetto.

Much of the region was aware that local 562 was a gangster union, controlled by the Chicago Mafia, the "Outfit," ruled by Joey Aiuppa. The square was on its way down. The middle-aged "square" customers of the nightclubs didn't want to be caught in the crossfire of spoiled gangster sons whose lawlessness went unpunished.

State Liquor Control Supervisor Harry Wiggins filed three charges against Whiskey A-Go-Go. One of the charges was that the owners knowingly allowed a convicted felon (Ray Lawrence) to work at this establishment in violation of state law. Whiskey A-Go-Go lost its liquor license temporarily, bur eventually reopened. But the crowds that once thronged to the nightspot were dwindling.

Ray Lawrence and I grew up in the same eastside berg. He came back to town with a new Mustang convertible, a new wardrobe, and was flush with cash. He was the victorious kid who went to the big city, broke, hung out at Gaslight, and came home with folding cash.

I asked him how he did it. He advised me that after Tommy Callanan shot him and after he was admitted to City Hospital, Lawrence Callanan, Local 562 leader, Tommy's dad came to the hospital.

Lawrence Callanan convinced Ray Lawrence to check himself out of City Hospital and to come with him. Ray complied. Ray said Lawrence Callanan took him to a hospital at Lake of the Ozarks and checked him in as an outpatient.

He was given access to a suite at Lodge of the Four Seasons and was asked what kind of a car he would like to have. He said, "Mustang convertible." He was taken to a dealership and picked out his Mustang.

He was given a credit card and told to buy himself a new wardrobe of clothing. Ray spent largely. As his condition improved, Ray was given thousands of dollars in cash and advised to go to police headquarters and to tell the detectives that Tommy Callanan was not the person who shot him at the Whiskey A-Go-Go.

Ray complied and came hone a hero. He told the story in bars in the little eastside berg. Ray hardly ever had to buy a drink. He was bigger than life and resembled a cartoon character. Eastside folks flocked to him.

Ray eventually married a girl who had ultra-religious parents. They were leery of Ray but eventually accepted him. He and his wife had a child. Ray became an ordained minister.

Tommy Callanan had his legs blown off in a car bombing. It was a broad daylight bombing in Spanish Lake. When his Lincoln was blown up, it rolled into a school playground where students were playing soccer. He had a twenty five caliber automatic in his pocket when police loaded him onto the stretcher to go to the hospital. He survived the bombing, and also survived a second bombing. He eventually died a young man.

On April 30, 1969, in an alley between Delmar and 4100 block of Washington (rear of Gaslight Square where patrons parked their cars),

Patrolmen Gerald Walters and Donald Nilhaus received a radio assignment for a "barking dog."

It was 2:00 A.M. and the Gaslight patrons were long gone for the night. But there were other folks lurking in the darkness. When the "squares" go home, the ghouls come out.

At Sarah & Olive, just one short block from Gaslight Square, there were houses of prostitution lining both sides of the street. A 1920's era hotel was on the south east corner, and one block south, there was another depression era hotel at the corner of Sarah and Westminster.

Heroin, which was the readily available drug for the city dwellers, was for sale on the street and in any of the hotels, day or night. There was always street activity.

Patrolmen Walters and Nilhaus had been on the police department for about five years. In a district like the ninth, a cop learns quickly to be reactive instead of proactive. All a cop has to do is to answer the radio and wait for the event of the night to happen.

They were driving through the alley looking for the person who called about a barking dog when they saw a shadow alongside the alley.

Patrolman Nilhaus was driving. He shouted to the shadow, "Did you call about the barking dog?"

Paul T. Cortez, twenty five years old, mumbled something, then pointed an automatic pistol at them, and started firing into the police car.

Walters said he didn't know what was going on since he was in the passenger seat. He stated he remembered Nilhaus asking the guy if he had called the police, then he saw Nilhaus' hair stand up on his head, like he had been struck by lightning.

He said Nilhaus tried to climb over him to get to the passenger side door, and then Walters said he heard the shots from the automatic pistol. The first shot struck him in the ankle as he and Nilhaus rolled out of the police car and onto the alley pavement.

Cortez shot five times with the automatic. Walters stated he knew his ankle was broken when he tried to stand up to shoot back at Cortez.

Walters and Nilhaus began firing back at Cortez, striking him in the head and neck. When the shooting stopped, Walters was shot in the left ankle and right leg and Nilhaus was shot in the left leg.

They called for help on the police radio, advising they had been shot. Scores of city cops responded. The shooter was already dead, but several responding cops shot into his body.

The cops knew Cortez was dead. They weren't trying to kill him again. They were killing the audacity of someone who would shoot a cop. Cops and criminals shoot each other. Nothing will ever change that fact.

Cortez was taken to the morgue. Walters and Nilhaus were taken to the hospital. Walters was eventually given a disability retirement. Nilhaus stayed on the police department. He did thirty years and retired.

Nilhaus was a body builder, and it was rumored throughout the police department that he used anabolic steroids. He changed his first name, legally, to "Rocky." He was a power lifter and carried photos of himself power lifting enormous amounts of weight, veins and muscles bulging, red-faced and straining.

Patrolman Nilhaus was retired for a short time when he decided to have knee surgery to repair a tendon. It was supposed to be a minor event. He died when a blood clot travelled to his brain.

The customers stopped going to the mid-city oasis of food, entertainment, booze, and beauty. The trendy restaurants and night clubs closed up, leaving the abandoned place with barren streets.

As in all entertainment areas that fall on hard times, a lower class of entertainment takes hold. I came to the area as a cop in 1970. I had gone there as a guy just home from the Marine Corps in 1966. I was mesmerized, but I didn't frequent the Square, just visited once in a while. It was expensive; I was a factory worker.

Just four short years later, I was a cop assigned to the district where Gaslight Square was located. The Square was really on the skids by then, and as usual, the business folks who were trying to hang on would storm into Captain Harry Lee's office and complain that they were barraged with criminals, and that they never saw a cop.

I was assigned as a beat man on the Square. Harry Lee called me into his office and told me to go into the businesses on Olive and Boyle and get the name of the bar tender. I would advise the bartender I was walking a beat and that if he needed anything I would be available.

There were probably only six or seven businesses left. Two were gay bars, two were black soul type bars, and there were a couple of hippy bars. All of the customers and employees hated cops, authority, uniforms, and structure. But I did it, just to please Harry Lee and to keep my cop job. I didn't wish to go back to the daily grind of the factory.

When I wandered into the gay bars, the patrons would hoop and scream obscenities at me, call me a girl, and try to block my way to the bar to get the bartender's name. Guys would be dancing and necking with other guys, dressed in weird garb, and all with long stringy hippie hair. No one ever tried to touch me. I had drawn a line in my brain that if anybody ever tried to lay a hand on me I was going to attack them.

I had a different reaction in the hippy bars. I was greeted with stares of hatred. Even the bartenders were hateful and insolent. Some of the patrons would stare at me and then spit on the floor.

In the black bars, the bartenders were usually friendly, but the patrons were hateful, even asking me, "Why you in here, white boy pig cop?"

There was a small independent radio station at the corner of Boyle and Olive. The employees were amateur's playing whatever they wanted, joking on air, allegedly smoking dope; long hair and beads type of guys and gals.

City narcotics raided the place one cold night while I was walking the beat. They paraded all of the workers out into the cold and then into the paddy wagon. They were all Grateful Dead lookalikes. I asked one of the hippy-looking detectives how much dope they had recovered. He showed me a bag of marijuana that would fit into the palm of my hand.

I nodded and walked away. I knew district cops who carried that much dope on them at all times for personal use. Cops were smoking dope in police cars between calls. Most cars had coolers of beer in them. It was toward the end of the Viet Nam war. The guys who came back from that war, on the most part, didn't give a damn about anything or any rule.

They had seen their friends killed or maimed, and they had seen the federal bureaucracy in action. The war was lost and they didn't trust anything bureaucratic.

A lot of the cops had long "hippie type" hair. They would buy wigs, stuff their hair up and under the wig, and come to roll call. They looked stupid, but that didn't deter them. To most cops this was an eight-hour gig and there were sixteen more hours in the day for them to wear their long hair and hippie clothing, just to fit in and to get girls.

Comparing today's cop with the cops in the 1970's, in this futuristic era of police work; computers, cameras, microphones, stun guns instead of night sticks, pepper spray and criminal psychology, little has changed with the cops or the crooks. The people haven't changed. The street is still the same.

Cops are still one on one with the bad guy. Poor folks still demand and receive ninety percent of the street cop's attention, cop's pay is inadequate and the non-working poor folks are still winning the war against the establishment.

Instead of wigs to hide their long stylish hair, the young cops wear portable sleeves to hide their tattoos.

As the Square dwindled away into oblivion, hippie type communes moved in to take up the empty footage of abandoned businesses. Ten or fifteen men and women, all staying in the same structure, all dependent on each other for survival.

They would combine all of their cash, food, booze, and clothing and try to live a free and peaceful existence. Most were from out of town. Many came here to go to college, dropped out, and didn't wish to go back home to Nebraska or Kansas so they were taken in by the communes.

Heroin was prevalent, but the Narcotics Division didn't score any large seizures. It was as if they didn't care about where the heroin came from or who was bringing it into the region. The detectives were satisfied with making small arrests, mostly unwarranted, and thrown out by the circuit attorney.

Detectives Mel Wilmoth, Skip Ruediger and Glen Vaughn, in narcotics, got a tip there was some dope in a commune in the west end of the city. They went to the site, an apartment house slum near Washington University.

They had no search warrant. They planned to use the same tactic the narcotics team used in the George Washington Hotel fiasco. They entered the apartment building, searched for the apartment, and listened at the door. They were satisfied they had the correct apartment, but instead of knocking on the door and forcing their way in, they decided to use a subterfuge to make the occupants open the door and come out into the hallway.

The cops had been drinking beer, and the group had beer cans with them that they had just emptied. Some cop had the idea to start kicking the beer cans up and down the hallway. That would make noise so that the occupants would be curious, open the door, and maybe venture into the hallway.

The detectives kicked the beer cans, the apartment door opened just enough for the detectives to look inside. It was their chance: they forced their way into the apartment with their guns drawn, an illegal entry for law enforcement.

A hippy college student drop-out who was concerned about the neighborhood sat on a couch with a twenty two caliber survival rifle.

The guy in the apartment with the gun was like most of the commune dwellers in St. Louis. Nobody really knew who he was. It didn't matter to the drop outs living in the commune. The gunman said he was from San Francisco and that made him more acceptable.

Even hippie commune dwellers who had grown up in St. Louis had an inferiority complex about being from St. Louis. San Francisco was where the action was: free love and dope.

The stranger from San Francisco had asked a friend to loan him a gun for protection because he had gotten beat up by a motorcycle gang, and he was in fear of his life. His buddy loaned him the $15.00 single shot twenty two caliber pilot survival rifle.

He had it on his lap when Mel Wilmoth and the other detectives rushed into the apartment. He fired one shot, striking Detective Mel Wilmoth in the abdomen. He fell and uttered, "My God, I've been shot. Get me a cruiser."

The San Francisco stranger was also shot and killed. The other occupants of the apartment were arrested. Detective Wilmoth was rushed to Deaconess Hospital.

He was operated on several times. Citizens and cops gave scores of pints of blood for his transfusions as he lost blood. He subsequently died of the single twenty two caliber gunshot to the abdomen.

The San Francisco stranger was identified by his personal identification as Bernard Weiss Jr. from a Chicago, Illinois, suburb. But as the investigation went on, the investigators found that Bernard Weiss from the Chicago area was still alive and attending college in another state.

The shooter had a tattoo on his forearm that read "Dirty Denny." An occupant of the apartment "commune" told investigators that the shooter said he was from San Francisco. They narrowed their search and contacted that city, mentioned the tattoo "Dirty Denny," and were told the shooters name was Dennis McMahan.

Homicide located Denny's mother. She said she had not seen her son in years. He was apparently a brilliant boy, a choir boy who had grown up in a broken home in Los Altos, California.

For some reason Denny had changed. He would leave and not come home for days. He was sent to a private boarding school for troubled youngsters. On a field trip he left the group bus to use the restroom and never returned. Denny's mother donated Denny's life insurance to the Wilmoth family.

There was a big shake up in the Narcotics Division. Most detectives got transferred back to uniform (they lost their prestige), and some of them resigned. Glen Vaughn came to the ninth and I was his occasional partner.

Most of a cop's shift involves trading stories with his partner. Glen told me the Mel Wilmoth story. He also told me that Detective Wilmoth executed an unarmed burglar in a service station on the south side.

Wilmoth wanted to impress Colonel John Doherty, Chief of Detectives with his dedication. Apparently it worked. John Doherty had him transferred in to narcotics shortly before he was killed by Dirty Denny.

The funeral was a chaotic but sad affair. Family members screamed his name and sobbed. Police officers were shaken and somber. His wife took the family and moved to Florida. A family member committed suicide with Mel's gun in Florida. New cops gained prestige with transfers to narcotics.

Patrolman Gregory Chase came back to the department from the army and a stint in Viet Nam. He had been in the ninth before he got drafted, did his time, and came back. I was to be his partner, Lieutenant Bob Scheetz informed me.

On the day before I was to begin my partnership with Greg, he jumped a stolen car and was pursuing it. We were standing in the rear of the Ninth District station awaiting our scout cars to pull up so we could change shifts. There were about ten of us in the back and about ten cops in the front of the station all waiting for their cars to arrive.

It was late in the afternoon, about 3:00 P.M., and Greg was on the radio calling out the streets he was on while he was pursuing the stolen car. "East on Lindell," he called out, west on Olive Suddenly the car was coming toward the Ninth District station. "He's going west on Lucas, heading past the station," Greg shouted.

The car headed down Lucas right by the ten or so cops waiting for their cars on this bright summer day. As the stolen car got in front of the station and the cops, all of them pulled their weapons and fired at it as it sped by, nonchalantly, as if it was scripted. In those days, it was the right thing to do.

Greg was right behind it; the stolen car crashed on Lucas, Greg chased the driver on foot and arrested him. It was a big deal in the annals of police history, namely because the owner of the stolen car was a big-time physician and a golfing buddy of Colonel John Doherty.

Greg and I were partners for a brief time. On a bright Sunday morning Greg and I were riding together in the north part of the district. The desk sergeant had read off at roll call that there was a house in our area where, reportedly, heroin junkies were frequenting.

Greg Chase would not miss a chance to make an arrest. He loved locking people up. He headed toward the house. We parked in front and walked toward the front porch. There were approximately six ghetto scofflaws sitting on the porch. I didn't know what was going on; I just followed Greg's lead.

He pulled his revolver and told them to get their hands up. We searched them. They were all armed with pistols, some of them exotic automatics, German and Japanese. All of them were heroin addicts and were having signs of withdrawal.

We called for a paddy wagon and an assist. Patrolman Donnell Whitfield showed up along with some other officers.

Donnell seemed to be upset that Greg and I had entered the house and were searching it without a warrant. "It's a search incident to an arrest," Greg said. "The front door was standing open." Donnell and Greg glared at each other. "You're just upset because your ace, Jet Banks, owns this house," Greg said. Donnell sped away in a huff.

"Who is Jet Banks?" I asked.

"He's a state representative, a politician with clout, a businessman. He's rumored to be a heroin trafficker," Greg replied.

We conveyed the now unarmed heroin addicts to the district station. We checked the serial number on the guns in our newly purchased computers (courtesy of the federal government) and found that one of the German guns, and the Japanese Gun had been stolen in a home burglary in upstate New York.

A large black man stormed into the station wearing a security guard's uniform. He demanded to talk to Harry Lee. It was Sunday; Harry Lee wasn't working. He demanded to speak to the watch commander. There was a sergeant who was acting as a watch commander.

Jet Banks was out of control and getting angrier as he screamed at the sergeant. The sergeant calmly told him to leave the station or he would be arrested. Jet stormed out. It was my first encounter with State Representative J.B. Jet Banks.

Clarence Harmon was a district detective. He was smooth, personable, and smart. He attended college like the rest of us dreamers of the future. But for Clarence the dreams were a reality. He was older than the rest of us, maybe by ten years, and he already had several years of college under his belt before he came to the police department.

Chief Eugene Camp was always looking for talent, and he was particularly interested in talented and educated black cops. Clarence was introduced to Chief Camp and a friendship ensued. Clarence had access to him and eventually was transferred to the Intelligence Unit: Camps personal investigative unit.

Chief Camp hated Jet Banks. Jet put pressure on Chief Camp to give cushy investigative jobs and promotions to his friends. The chief had no choice; the state legislature controlled all pay raises and funding of the St. Louis Metropolitan Police Department. There were times when the chief told Jet to forget the pay raises. We all suffered for that lack of leadership.

If you were a friend of Chief Camp, then you had to be an enemy of state representative, soon to be State Senator, J.B. Jet Banks. Camp thought Jet would just fade away, and he wouldn't have to deal with him. Or that he would be killed, or arrested, disgraced, and that his political career would end.

It didn't happen. Jet just got more powerful as the years clicked by. He was a state representative from 1969-1976, and a state senator from1977-1992. He was even the majority floor leader for most of the 1980's. Jet had the police department sewed up.

I was in the Intelligence Unit with Clarence Harmon. He was my direct supervisor. He hated Jet as much as Eugene Camp. Rumors swirled about Jet and his dope dealing, trafficking, financing. But they were just rumors. No agency ever had anything substantial on him.

There was never an arrest. He was accused of having political rivals killed, of arson, having people beaten. None of it ever substantiated. Clarence hounded him with every piece of information available to him. Jet laughed at him.

Some black politicians: Alderwoman Mary Ross, and Jet Banks, brought comedian/activist Dick Gregory into the city to protest the closing of Homer G. Phillips Hospital.

There were always white city politicians trying to close the all black hospital. It was mostly a welfare hospital for blacks, free and a drain on the economy of the city. It was socialism at its finest.

A new mayor ran on the promise not to close Homer G. Phillips. He was on television and looked directly into the black faces of St. Louis and declared that he would not close Homer G. Phillips.

But Vince Schoemehl was a true politician. He was in office for several months before he reneged. He made a big push to close it. The black masses and black politicians were incensed. They had trusted whitey one time too often. They wanted vengeance.

Clarence and I worked the protests. They were peaceful but tense. Finally, Mary Ross and Dick Gregory, in demonstration, laid down at the middle of the intersection of twelfth and Clark, police headquarters.

"Let's arrest them," Clarence said. We had to carry them into police headquarters. We took them into the fourth District Detective Bureau and subsequently booked them for some insignificant crime, maybe peace disturbance.

Dick Gregory knew Sergeant Clarence Harmon. They spoke to each other like opposing generals on a battlefield. Clarence was scolded for being a black man helping the white establishment. Mary Ross agreed with Dick Gregory.

I was just there witnessing this personal assault on Clarence. I was like a fly on the wall. I did what white cops do: arrest black folks. With Dick Gregory, Alderwoman Mary Ross, and Sergeant Clarence Harmon, the incident was personal.

Clarence eventually became the Chief of Police for the City of St. Louis. He succeeded Robert Scheetz. Eugene Camp had been gone for years, but Chief Clarence still hated Jet Banks.

Clarence would have been the best chief the department ever had, or ever would have. But there is always a fly in the ointment in the cop game. Politics screwed Clarence Harmon. The majority of the Honorable Board of Police Commissioners, appointed by the governor, were loyal to Jet Banks. At least one was related to him. It was no secret in the black community that Jet and Clarence were natural enemies.

Any power that was given to Chief Clarence Harmon by state statute or city charter regarding the operation of the St. Louis Metropolitan Police Department, ie, promotions, transfers, or pay raises was all subject to the police board's approval.

The board garroted and put short pants on Chief Clarence Harmon. It was sad to watch. He retired after three years as chief. When a cop and a politician go head to head, the politician is always the winner.

Clarence then went full bore into politics. He ran for Mayor of the City of St. Louis, was elected, and served one term. As mayor, he sat on the police board as the ex-officio member, right alongside the Jet Banks' crusaders who sabotaged his position as chief. Clarence is retired and living in St. Louis. Jet Banks died while vacationing in Las Vegas.

Gregory Chase was all cop, and proficient, and I learned a lot from him. He had favor with John Doherty due to the arrest of the guy who stole his golfing buddies, (the doctor's car). Greg was eventually transferred to the vice division.

He would act as a decoy wherever there was prostitution. He was in the now defunct Gaslight Square area, sitting in an undercover car acting like he was wanting to buy dope or hire a prostitute. It is what undercover cops do.

A street creature jumped into Greg's undercover car and put a gun to his head, demanding Greg's money. But he made a fatal mistake. Greg was a cocked gun waiting to go off, and he hated the street creatures more than anything else in the world.

Greg smiled at the guy, then grabbed the gun and pushed it away from him at the same time while he grabbed his own Colt thirty eight revolver. Greg said that he probably could have continued to fight with the guy over control of the gun, and maybe didn't have to kill him, but he reasoned, "The guy was going to kill me. It was the law of the street, kill or be killed."

Years later, at the same location, an undercover cop, Detective

Gregory Erson, acting as a decoy for prostitution, did not fare as well. He was shot while seated in his undercover cop car. He died at the scene.

Greg Chase did twenty years on the department, retired and went to work for the state as a liquor control officer. He was an interesting guy to work with, and I learned his version of the creed of law enforcement from him: "Tell them what they want to hear."

The problem with the creed is that cops use it daily, almost on every call for service. Cops eventually live by the creed, and subsequently the creed enters into most factions of their lives. It follows them home and they begin using it on their wives and children. They feel that whatever someone tells them is the result of the creed, so they believe no one outside of the cop job, not their closest friends or relatives.

The creed is one of the reasons cops are distrusted and untrusting. Loved ones and associates recognize the creed, but don't know what it is. It's why cops are divorced so often and why their children hate them. The creed quickly becomes the cop curse.

There were cops joining the police department in droves. The word had gotten out that the fed was paying for cops to attend college. There was a possibility to beat the system if the cop was slick enough. Several cops would enroll in the junior college and never show up for a class.

Many instructors were intimidated by the crazed city cops. They went along with the program. They would allow the cop to take a final test, and if he passed it then he would pass the course.

At the junior college in the city the black cops would befriend campus security cops and persuade them to enter the instructor's office at night with a master key and copy semester tests and the answers.

The cop would study the test for a couple of hours, take the test, and pass it with a B. In the city cop business you have to make your own success.

Patrolman Billy Robinson was a police academy classmate of mine. He wasn't like most of us Viet Nam veterans with a bad attitude. He was a college kid. It's all he had ever done in his life. He had grown up in the city, was half white, and spoiled.

While in the academy, Doc Cooper came to our class and gave us a lecture about bullet wounds, the city hospitals, and his medical division. He asked the class if they had any questions.

Billy Robinson told Doc Cooper that he had been a pre-med student in college. He received no comment from the Doc. The rest of the class moaned. Billy had a tough time passing the weekly academy tests. It was doubtful he was in that particular curriculum.

Billy was sent to the Ninth District with several of us. We all "snapped in" fairly well at the ninth. Billy was in love with his department issued thirty eight caliber revolver. He kept it with him at all times. He was a conscientious cop.

We were on the same watch and we rode together frequently. In the early 1970's, on the afternoon watch on New Year's Eve, we received an assignment for a disturbance in a slum home.

It was way below zero with snow on the ground. We trudged our way to the house, and we could hear gunfire or fireworks coming from inside. The door quickly opened; a woman ushered us in.

"He's upstairs," she began. "He's drunk and he keeps throwing firecrackers down the stairs. He's my husband and he's scaring the kids and me, and I want him out of here."

Sensations and images flash through a cops mind during disturbance calls. Weapons, for one. Most homes in America have at least one weapon. Most have dozens and they are strategically placed around the house in case someone invades their castle. The cops don't know where they are. The drunk maniac does.

Another problem is either going upstairs to arrest someone or going downstairs to arrest someone. The cop is at risk during these encounters. He can't see what is going on above him or below him.

One of us asked the wife if there were any weapons upstairs with her husband. "He has a BB gun," she replied, straight faced.

We went to the foot of the stairs. Billy called up to the closed door at the top of the stairs for the guy to come out and walk down the stairs to talk with us.

The door opened and a string of firecrackers was tossed at us, exploding around our heads. A gun barrel came out the door and was pointed at us. It didn't look like a BB gun to me. It was big and wide, like a shotgun.

The firecrackers made us angry. The gun pointed at us made us even angrier. We rushed up the stairs, Billy in the lead. He was the first one to begin the assault.

We charged into the room. The guy was still pointing the gun at us so we jumped him, disarmed him, and subdued him. The gun was a .410 shotgun with deer slugs in the chamber. It would have killed Billy if the guy had fired it.

Billy was a brave cop. He just didn't get any peer respect. Cops need respect from their peers. Cops spend more time with other cops than they spend with their families. For that reason, Billy covertly searched for a way out of the cop job.

He invited me to his grandmother's home in the West End. It was a grand old home with a big porch. It was where he grew up, apparently raised by his white grandmother. He didn't identify with the black cops, and I was about the only white cop he would be friendly with.

Race was a dilemma with Billy. Most of the time he would act like a white guy, but occasionally, in the report room where most of the cops hung out between assignments, he would make a feeble attempt to act black.

It always came out clumsily. It was as if a spoiled white guy, one who grew up in affluence was trying to be black. The black guys and the white guys shunned him.

The other black cops in the district were disrespectful to Billy. We all had lockers in the basement of the district where we could hang clean clothing and a new uniform. Billy wore expensive clothing and he would have a couple of shirts and slacks hanging in his locker.

Some of the black cops somehow gained access to his locker combination. If one of their shirts was soiled they would get into Billy's locker and grab one of his expensive shirts.

Billy mentioned it to me. He was upset that his clothing was disappearing. He observed a fellow black cop wearing one of his shirts and he questioned him about it. The cop wearing his shirt called Billy a "pussy" and asked him what he wanted to do about it.

I knew Billy Robinson was a man and not a pussy. But the distinction between the two Afro-American men was blaringly obvious. One light, one dark. Black men are certain they are more manly than white men. It's basically a myth. I've seen white guys beat black guys on a one on one fight. Problem is that if a white guy is fighting a black guy, other black guys will assist their compatriot. Whites won't.

I figured Billy Robinson had been bullied for his entire life by real black guys since he grew up in a black neighborhood. Maybe it's why he became a cop. But he wasn't a kid anymore, and he wasn't living in a black neighborhood. He was at work, trying to survive like the rest of us.

It was difficult for Billy to accept that he was an outcast from his black cohorts. The pressure mounted within him. I could see it. He would date black girls and then white girls, and he always brought them to the station to show them off.

He purchased a new car, a white Pontiac Trans Am with a big blue eagle emblazoned on the hood. It was a fast and neat car. He rented an apartment in fashionable North County and occasionally he and I would ride to work together. He always had his department thirty eight near him while he drove the fancy and fast car.

Billy was in St. Louis County, driving his car and became involved in a road rage incident. A white guy gave him the finger and Billy became enraged. He motioned for the guy to pull over They both did, climbed out, and got nose to nose. Billy told the guy he was a city cop. The guy told Billy he wasn't in the city now. Pushing turned to shoving.

Billy had no idea who he was messing with. The guy was a Golden Gloves boxing champ and he lived for the fight. He punched Billy's face and chest with several well aimed punches.

Billy was dazed and backed off. Instinctively Billy drew his department issued thirty eight revolver. The gun was his only friend, except for me.

The boxer backed off after seeing the pistol; he turned as if he was going to run. Billy shot one time. The bullet entered the boxer's buttocks and lodged in his bladder.

The fighting stopped. The county cops and an ambulance arrived on the scene (St. Louis County had ambulances). Billy told his story while the boxer was being sped away to a hospital.

As far as the St. Louis Metropolitan Police Department was concerned Billy's actions were justified. The St. Louis County cops had no problem with the shooting.

But the boxer lost time at work. The surgeries were expensive for his family. He suffered severe hardship. He sued Billy in civil court.

Billy had no money. All he had was his beloved Trans Am hot rod. The boxer took it. Billy was now driving a junker like the rest of us.

Billy quit the cop job. He tried to be a salesman, but that didn't work for him. He went back to college but failed. He was gone for several years, and he was re-hired by the department. He came back to the Ninth District.

He wasn't there long. He quit again. By this time he had married a gal with a good job. They purchased a condo in the Central West End. They had a child and Billy was a stay at home dad. I would see him occasionally walking his dog and his kid. He seemed relaxed and happy. He died in his early fifties.

The locker fiasco with Billy and his black cop associates concerned me. Apparently anyone with desire could gain entry to any locker in the building.

Lieutenant Bob Scheetz knew there was a problem with marijuana in the police department. He did not want his men to dabble in drugs. The cops didn't realize it, but whenever they confiscated weed from a person on the street, and didn't arrest the subject, in many instances the person who lost his stash would telephone the station and ask to speak to a supervisor.

Anonymously they would advise the supervisor that patrolman so and so took their dope without arresting him or her. "The cop took it for his personal usage," they would say. Weed was difficult to get in St. Louis. Heroin and cocaine was readily available. The public desired "weed."

Lieutenant Scheetz would check the records to see if any marijuana was turned in to the department lab. Then he would go to the cop's locker in the basement with an extra key and see if it was there.

He would call the officer into his office and confront him with the "weed" taken from his locker. The cop would never have a viable excuse. Some said, "I got it for my girlfriend" or some such other weak excuse.

The lieutenant would give the cop the opportunity to resign, or he would be arrested and brought up on charges. There were a few guys on my watch who rapidly quit the department. They were black guys, not friendly with Billy Robinson.

I emptied my locker and told the person in charge of them that I no longer desired a locker. Anyone could gain access to it or place anything inside of it.

Eventually the department instituted a drug screening program. Many cops quit after being told to report to the hospital for a drug screening. It was the end of an era.

Donnell Whitfield and I rode together for a twenty-one day stretch on the night watch. He grew up in the Ninth District. He knew the people there, and they knew him. He wasn't someone to cross. He was quick with his hands and feet and he would knock a ghetto scofflaw out in a second. Unlike most of the old cops, he didn't need a lead-loaded sap or a squad of fat cops to assist him. For some reason he referred to me as "Junebug."

On a domestic disturbance in the early morning hours, Donnell and I received a radio assignment to an apartment house at the corner of Taylor and Olive. A lady came to the door with a bloused eye, torn clothing, crying, and distraught. The people living there didn't have a telephone. A neighbor had called.

I got the impression that Donnell knew the lady with the swollen eye, but I didn't ask. "Where is he?" Donnell asked. She motioned toward the back of the apartment. Before we could go back there a large young man appeared in the living room where we were standing.

"Did he do this you?" he asked. The lady nodded in the affirmative. The man tried to back away. Donnell caught him with a left, knocking him down. He got up and Donnell got him with a couple of rights and lefts rendering him unconscious, lying beside the couch. "If he ever does this to you again, you call me. Understand?" The lady nodded and we left. "That's street justice, Junebug," he said to me.

Donnell Whitfield rose to the rank of Captain. He took an early retirement due to an incident that I never understood. I often wondered if he was "setup" due to his close association to Senator Jet Banks.

Rossino's Restaurant was in the basement of an apartment building at Sarah and West Pine. The owner was friends to cops. He believed in the cop philosophy: feed cops cheaply and they will hang out in your establishment. If cops are there, maybe bad guys won't be. The food was good, the waitresses pretty, and even the booze was discounted for Ninth District cops. A kid I went through the police academy with, Patrolman Jerry, was lucky like me, and got assigned to the Ninth District right out of the police academy.

Jerry hung out at Rossino's. Like Billy Robinson, he wasn't like the rest of the Viet Nam veterans and bad attitude guys in the class. He was studious and serious. And he was also young, just barely twenty-one, the age required to go to the academy.

Jerry was also enthralled by the cop gun the police department gave us. I could see it in his eyes when they passed the new steel blue thirty eight revolvers out to us, still in their boxes, covered with brown paper and protective oil. It was mesmerizing to many of the recruits. They had probably been bullied in their youth and dreamed of having an equalizer like the thirty eight. Even the smell of the weapon was enticing.

To the military veterans it was no big deal, just something that will rust if you don't clean it often. It was big, difficult to conceal, and if it was used as a striking tool, instead of a killing tool, could be damaged to the extent it would not fire. If we desired a smaller weapon, to carry off duty, we would have to purchase it ourselves.

Jerry was stationed at the bar at Rossino's, off-duty, drinking after hours, when for some unknown reason he pulled out his department revolver and shot the bartender in the head.

The owner, who was a big thinker and slick, realized that this incident could be harmful to his business, and his liquor license. He came up with the idea to move the body out to the sidewalk so that it would be on city property instead of his.

While a waiter and Patrolman Jerry were carting the shot bartender out to the sidewalk, the slick businessman dialed the Ninth District station and advised the desk officer that a person had been shot outside the restaurant. He also called Captain Harry Lee at his residence (most businessmen selling booze had Harry Lee's home number) and advised him of the incident.

Patrolman Jerry was almost cop royalty. He had prestige within the department even though he had only been an employee for a year. His sister was one of Chief Eugene Camp's girlfriends. Harry Lee dialed Gene Camp's residence and advised him of the incident. They devised a plan.

The cavalry arrived, led by an old white haired sergeant who had seen almost everything in his life. Upon arriving at the scene, the old sarge was advised by the radio dispatcher to call the captain at home. He did and was advised of the prestige Patrolman Jerry carried.

The sarge had seen hundreds of cover- ups. He asked Patrolman Jerry what happened. Jerry told him the truth. He took the lad to the side and counseled him. Jerry agreed that when he was showing the bartender the gun, it for some reason went off in his hand and struck the bartender in the head. All of this happened on the sidewalk of the north east corner of Boyle and West Pine.

The bartender was whisked off to City Hospital number one in the back of a paddy wagon. Jerry was whisked away to the Ninth District station. The bar area was cleaned, the restaurant was closed, the bartender lived to tend another day.

Harry Lee and the white haired sarge were in good standing with the chief, and all parties involved were satisfied with the outcome.

But there was a glitch in the plan. The chief, Harry Lee, the white haired sarge, and the slick businessman didn't take into account that Jerry had prestige along with another attribute; He had a conscious.

When it came time for Jerry to write his rendition of what happened at Rossino's Restaurant, Jerry told the truth. He also mentioned the cover-up. He was ordered to change his report. He refused.

Jerry showed up for work the next day like nothing had happened. The cops in the district station had heard about the shooting, and the cover-up.

Harry Lee called Jerry into his office. Several of us watched at the door as he stood tall before the Captain's desk. He had done the unthinkable; the chief had stuck his neck out for him, along with Harry Lee and the old sarge, and Jerry had sold them down the river. "Why?" Harry Lee screamed at him. "If you are that damn dumb then you don't belong in this job."

Jerry stared like a Hindu priest teasing a king cobra. He had no defense. "I'm going to put you on a foot beat on Franklin Avenue, across the street from Pruitt Igoe, and I hope one of those Maryland farmers kills your ass. Get out of my office."

Jerry walked out with his head down. I watched him and wondered if he would ever survive this event. He would be ostracized by his peers within the police department. No matter where his sister's boyfriend sent him, he would be rejected. He walked a beat on Franklin Avenue for a week or so, then resigned. The young cops were observing the police life unfold before them.

Another one of Chief Camp's friends arrived in the district. He was treated with kid gloves, just like all of the chief's cronies. They always got the best assigned areas with places to eat and interesting views.

The officer was young and eager. He wanted to show the chief that he was worthy of being a detective. It was always that way and to the casual observer it was embarrassing.

He almost always worked the Central West End which is predominantly white. He became involved in an altercation with a white kid from West County. The kid mouthed off to him, which is how street encounters begin. They usually end with the instigator going to the hospital for head stitches.

But this young cop didn't carry a wooden night stick. He carried a steel six cell flashlight. He clobbered the mouthy white kid over the head with it and killed him.

The killing was deemed justifiable. The influential cop faded away, never to be heard from again.

The old supervisors were dropping like flies from terminal disease. A district sarge, Sergeant Dutch Brinkman, was shooting pool in a downtown bar with a guy he didn't know. He and the guy got into an argument; Dutch pulled his forty five automatic and pointed it at the guy. The gun was taken away from Dutch and used to kill him.

My old Irish sarge, John McGuire, spoke to me about the incident. "Number one," he began, "Dutch was in a bar where he wasn't known, gambling with strangers over a pool game. Number two, Dutch was carrying a weapon that is not authorized by the Board of Police Commissioners. Number three, Dutch flourished the unauthorized weapon thinking he was going to impress the guy he was gambling with. The law enforcement code is to never un-holster your weapon unless you are going to clean it or kill someone with it. Get the picture?"

"Yes, Sarge," I muttered.

As is almost always the case in life, cops, like most folks can't stop doing their jobs after their shift is over. Fireman, doctors, mechanics, when we leave our jobs after a shift, we still have our professional hats on. It's why the cop job has such good vacations. It usually takes a week to relax and mentally remove the cop hat.

Some folks are born to be cops. They have an uncanny ability to see crime or criminals far beyond what the ordinary cop can see. C.C. Smith was one of these cops. He was a legend in the Ninth District. I was fortunate to work with him on occasion. The problem was that when you got into a police car with him and headed to your assigned area, you never made it. You would have an arrest and be back at the station in minutes.

He would say, "There goes a stolen car." Or, "There's dope in the trunk of that car." Or, "That guy's armed, is a felon, and is wanted."

C.C. Smith should have gone far in his chosen field. He was a natural. But downtown bureaucrats weren't impressed with good police work from black cops without political affiliation. C.C. Smith knew he wasn't impressing anyone, except the cops he worked with. That was enough for him.

But he couldn't change hats when his shift ended. He had gotten a tip that a felon wanted for robbery was hiding at an apartment in Pruit Igoe. He went to the apartment, off duty, knocked on the door and announced himself.

The wanted guy came to the door, opened it, and shot C.C. Smith to death. His demise was taken lightly by the department. It was kind of like he had just gone on a long vacation. People forgot him almost immediately. The natural without political friends was dispensable.

There had been a police radio missing for months. It was an expensive item, and the city would have to write it off if it wasn't located. The radios were referred to as "miniature radios," but they were far from miniature, and they were portable. Anyone wishing to investigate or continue doing police work after his shift wanted one.

C.C. Smith was doing police work off-duty. He was alone. He was out of his district. It was as if he was trying to get killed. But his death wasn't in the line of duty. There was no glory attached to it. The missing radio was found on his body. In the thirty five years I was a city cop, I had never met another natural like C.C. Smith.

In contrast to C.C. Smith was Fred Grimes. Fred was a killer and a tough guy. He was the most intense guy I had ever seen. A lot of cops act their way through this business. A gun and a badge allows them to act tough.

There are cops who had never been in a fight in their lives who, with political friends or relatives, made rank and were awarded with office jobs for the rest of their careers.

They would sit behind their desks, bellies bulging, jowls shaking, and threatening to kick the entrenched beat cop's asses in the districts for some act a cop had or had not done to their liking.

They go through their entire working lives thinking they are tough guys. They eat free, drive company cars, play golf on duty, answer to no one and live the life of a dignitary.

Fred Grimes was not one of those guys. If Fred Grimes ever told you he was going to kick your ass, it would be wise for you to take a vacation or call in sick.

Fred was a killer, a black man with police work on his agenda, and he had political friends to back him up. He went up and down the ranks. He would make rank and then get it taken away from him. It did not deter him. He was a killing, beating force to be reckoned with, in the black criminal community.

In the 1950's the department introduced a new weapon to fight street crime, the "whippet shotgun." The whippet was a sixteen-gauge short barreled, short-stock weapon with a lanyard, or strap going through the stock.

The weapon was made for detectives. The strap would fit around the detective's shoulder and the weapon could be easily concealed under a jacket or coat. It was pump action and could be fired rapidly. The detective just had to grab the weapon, turn it toward the criminal and start firing and pumping. Fred Grimes killed three-guys with it during the first week he had one.

Fred was on his way down by the time I got to the Ninth District. In fact, he was in the Fourth, Pruit Igoe's District. I had heard about him and I had met him. He was always intense, like a ticking time bomb ready to go off.

He drove the police vehicles aggressively with his intense look, jaw jutting out, teeth clenched. He was always on a mission.

Whenever I arrested someone I always had a chance to talk to them after the initial arrest. There is plenty of time between the arrest, booking and transport to the downtown holdover.

St. Louis was big on the "who do you know game"? The arrested subject would initiate the game. For the ghetto folks, crime was a game. They knew most of the aggressive cops. It was all part of the game. Names would fly around, some I would know, some I didn't. The name Fred Grimes always came up. When it did, I would ask the guy, "Did he ever kick your ass?"

"Hell yeah," they would proudly reply. I could never figure out if they were bragging or complaining, or if they were just relieved that Fred beat them up instead of killing them. Fred died a young man, shortly after the George Washington Hotel incident.

The young cops continued to go to college. It seemed to be the only way out of the police life. We carried too many classes per semester, read and studied in police cars during the night watch, worked straight night watches so we could attend classes during the day. Professors were threatened if a poor grade was rendered. The socialism of the police department was being used in college.

There was one real smart guy on our watch, Mike Williams. I had always felt that the instructors in the classes I took were actually not speaking to me. Most of what they said went over my head. In reality, they were speaking to guys like Mike Williams.

Great students have the ability to decipher what the instructor is saying, make copious notes, and regurgitate the information at test time. Mike Williams was that guy.

He went to St. Louis University. I attended the University of Missouri, St. Louis. Mike helped his friends. Had I gone to St. Louis University and taken classes with Mike Williams, I would have become a good student. Mike was an ex-Marine, like me, but he was highly decorated and a war hero.

Another cop on our watch was Amiel Cueto. He was from the eastside, like me, but he was a motivated fellow and ambitious. He was a cop so he could take advantage of the veterans on the job training program, and to get some experience in law enforcement, like most of us.

But unlike most of us, Amiel Cueto had power across the Mississippi River in St.Clair County, Illinois. His best friend, soon to be Congressman Jerry Costello, son of a former Sheriff of St. Clair County, packed influence in the eastside region, and clout in the federal system.

Amiel Cueto was aware of the future he could have if he could just get through the curriculum at St. Louis University. He was an average student in a place where average students fail. He became good friends with Mike Williams. Mike tutored him through to his bachelor's degree.

But Mike Williams wasn't finished with the challenge of academia. He decided to go to law school. By then, Mike Williams and Amiel Cueto were the best of friends. Mike took the law school admissions test and was quickly accepted into St. Louis University's law school. He prepped Amiel for the test, and Amiel passed it due to a minority deferment. Somewhere in his family tree was a Spaniard, considered a minority by the school.

Mike went to class and took notes, precise and excellent, then tutored Amiel and another cop, Sergeant Dan Cregan. Mike helped

Amiel, Dan, and several city cops complete the curriculum at St. Louis University Law School. They all graduated. Mike took the Bar Exam and scored highly. It was now Amiel's turn. Mike tutored Amiel and he passed the Bar.

Amiel quit the St. Louis Police Department, returned to St.Clair County, Illinois, and eventually went into the law business. But something was missing with Amiel. He had power, influence, and a law degree, but he didn't have the brain of Mike Williams at his disposal.

Mike had taken a job with a Jones Act lawyer in downtown St. Louis doing Rail Road and Barge Lines litigation. He wasn't making any money, per se, but he was out of the police department and he was using his mind instead of wrestling black activists in the Ninth District.

Amiel asked Mike to join his law firm in Belleville. Mike accepted. For approximately thirty years they worked together in the crooked, good old boy environment of southern Illinois, making loads of money.

But there was a problem. Amiel was making most of the money. Amiel kept promising Mike Williams a big payday that never came. Mike was patient and rational, and he was making a good living, but he was the brains of the firm, guiding the haphazard Amiel Cueto out of trouble at every turn. Mike figured he deserved more.

Power eventually corrupted Amiel Cueto. He was a feared litigator in the courtroom, (even the judges feared him,) and a force to be reckoned with outside of the courtroom. He was certain there was nothing, short of murder, he couldn't do in St. Clair County, Illinois. As is usually the case, Amiel's power led to federal criminal charges against him which led to incarceration.

In the late 1980's, Amiel Cueto met gangster, Thomas Venezia. Tommy Venezia was a pimp, murderer, dope dealer and big time gambler who started his crime career in St. Louis, then eventually moved his empire to St. Clair County.

He and Amiel became good friends, and Amiel was his lawyer. Amiel's ability to twist the law in St. Clair County got Tommy Venezia off of the hook on a concealed weapon charge that could have gone to federal court for a Felon in Possession of a Firearm. Venezia admired Amiel for that experience. Amiel admired Tommy Venezia for being an outlaw and being successful at it. It led to a friendship that proved fatal to Amiel Cueto. He was mesmerized by Venezia.

Venezia enticed Amiel to go into the gambling machine business with him. I was in a federal law enforcement agency at that time, and I heard about the relationship between them. I was shocked.

I had worked with Amiel Cueto, and I had investigated Tommy Venezia. Amiel hated organized criminals. Right out of the Police Academy Amiel was chosen to work undercover in downtown St. Louis and to frequent the organized crime-owned "B" girl bars, acting like a John looking for a prostitute.

When confronted by the criminal bar owners (pimps), Amiel would attack them with his fists. He despised them and what they stood for. He was an eastside kid brought up around low-life Chicago style mobsters. Amiel had "heart" and he had character. He would never back down from a ghetto scofflaw or an abusive supervisor. But Amiel had apparently changed.

Mike Williams counseled Amiel. He told him Tommy Venezia was a pimp and a murderer. He begged Amiel to back off his friendship with Venezia.

Amiel became angry. He pointed his finger at Mike and said, "Tommy Venezia has more character and more integrity than any lawyer I ever knew." It's why they call them pimps. They pimp people into doing things they would normally never do. Pimps remove heart--- they destroy character. It's how they make a living.

The partnership between Venezia and Amiel Cueto was apparently successful. Both were indicted federally. Venezia testified against Amiel Cueto. It was what the U.S. Attorney's office wanted.

Amiel took the stand in his own defense. It was a huge mistake on his behalf. He was surly, arrogant, and unprofessional. He acted like a gangster, an eastside martyr who couldn't be convicted because he had the judge and prosecution in his pocket. It backfired on him.

During a recess in the trial Mike Williams attempted to counsel Amiel. "What are you doing, Aim? You are acting like a damn gangster on the stand. You are slumped over, legs crossed and laid back and surly. The jury doesn't like defendants who act like that. They are going to convict you if you don't straighten up. Remember how they taught us to testify when we were in the police academy? Sit up straight, answer the questions and don't act like an asshole."

Aniel's response was, "I'm acting the way those people expect me to act. This is the eastside. They respect me for what I am, not for what the government said I did."

Mike Williams walked away from Amiel shaking his head in disbelief. Mike knew the end was near for the power broker, Amiel Cueto. It would also be the end of Mike's tenure with the law firm. After Amiel went to jail Mike purchased a building on West Main in Belleville, Illinois, and opened his own law firm. One of Amiel's brothers became a circuit judge and the other one stayed at the original law firm.

Amiel had the power brokers in St. Clair County: a United States congressman, millions of dollars in the bank and Mike Williams big brain backing him, but he could not counter Tommy Venezia's testimony against him

Somehow, Amiel Cueto forgot the valuable lesson we are taught from our youth: "There is no honor among thieves."

Amiel Cueto was sentenced to seven years in federal prison and lost his law license. After six years, he got out of prison, a broken man.

Mike Williams and Amiel Cueto became bitter enemies. He wrote letters to Mike trying to restart their friendship. Mike told him that if Amiel ever got within striking distance of him, he would attack him.

I examined the contrast between Amiel Cueto and Mike Williams. Mike was a Viet Nam veteran, Marine Corps Recon, a decorated war hero.

Amiel Cueto was drafted for a two-year hitch in the Army. As soon as he graduated from boot camp he was stationed in Washington D.C. as an M.P. Amiel told me Congressman Mel Price helped him get the safe and prestigious duty assignment. The clout came through St. Clair County Sheriff Costello. Cops in police cars tell their life story, and anyone else's story who is not in the car with them.

The good old boy system is alive and well in America. Amiel Cueto lived off it and thrived. He always had someone helping him.

Both he and Mike Williams were Ninth District cops: both lawyers who came up the hard way, working their way through college and law school.

The difference in them was that Mike Williams truly desired to help his friends. He got satisfaction in helping people.

Amiel's only friends were a congressman in St. Clair County, Illinois, and his brothers. Everyone else was an adversary, except for the scumbag Tommy Venezia.

But when dealing with wealthy scumbags there is always an innocent party who becomes a victim. The victim this time was Jennifer Anderson, twenty-one, Tommy Venezia's live-in companion.

Both of them were found dead, shot to death in Venezia's home in Belleville, Illinois. Jennifer was apparently a victim of circumstance. She was a pretty girl, a 2002 graduate of Belleville East High School, a bar worker, and an employee of a topless club in Sauget.

Her obvious fatal mistake was taking up with Tommy Venezia, but wayward girls, on their own, are only interested in surviving. It is a hard scrabble life on the eastside. Working the bar scene, topless bars especially, leads to an association with the dregs of the earth.

Tommy was no doubt interested in her beauty and her youth. Jennifer was seeking security and money, something she had probably never experienced. For whatever the reason, the two took up residence together in Belleville, Illinois, after Venezia completed his prison sentence. He and Cueto were released at about the same time.

The Belleville, Illinois, Police conducted a stellar crime scene investigation. Venezia's body, a gunshot wound to his right temple, was found in a recliner in a bedroom with a thirty eight caliber revolver on his abdomen.

Anderson's body was found on the kitchen floor with a bullet wound from the same revolver in the back of her neck. It was estimated that Anderson was shot a few hours before Venezia shot himself. The Belleville Police deemed it a murder suicide.

St. Clair County, Illinois. Coroner Rick Stone conducted a coroner's inquest on the deaths. At the hearing Rick Stone approached the Anderson family to offer his condolences.   Michael Anderson, Jennifer's father, stated to coroner Rick Stone: "I believe they were murdered. Everyone wants to believe this was a murder-suicide. I don't trust the investigators. I don't trust you. I was at the crime scene."

Stone slowly moved away from Anderson and said, "Be real careful before I lock you up." The verdict came back murder-suicide.

When Michael Anderson was asked who he thought killed his daughter and Tommy Venezia, family members quickly cautioned him against responding.

Tommy Venezia met his demise in July of 2002. Amiel died in June of 2012. The government estimated they had incurred over forty-eight-million dollars in their illegal gambling machine enterprise.

Back to the old Ninth District-----The cops attending college were edgy. Two cops got into a fist fight in the roll call room over the affections of a young girl residing in the district. One of them wore a wig. His wig got knocked off, and his long stringy hair was let down over his collar.

The lieutenant came to the roll call, after the fight and observed his mullet. He was forced to get a haircut and to stop wearing the stupid wig.

A cop with domestic problems walked around the station saying, "I want to kill somebody." His wife came into the station house, and they had a battle at the front desk while the rank and file stood and watched. She left in a huff. He went to the downstairs restroom, crying.

He returned with his hand on his revolver, still chanting, "I want to kill somebody". As luck would have it, he got his chance. A scofflaw ghetto resident came to the rear area of the station and challenged the cop. They fought and the guy went for the cop's gun. The cop pulled his weapon and wasted him.

The Viet Nam war veteran cops were beginning to graduate from college. It was a race to the federal law enforcement offices to obtain applications.

Most of them started with the FBI, then worked their way down to the Treasury jobs: Secret Service, Customs, ATF. Some went to DEA, but that was not their first choice.

As usual in the crook and cop profession, there was a glitch. The fed wasn't hiring just any cop with a degree. They only wanted the best of the litter. The fed thinned the herd by giving a pre-employment test.

Most cops are not good with tests, especially government tests. They are designed to identify character and intellectual flaws in the applicant's consciousness and sub-consciousness. Most of the degreed cops weren't being hired.

If a guy could pass the Treasury math test he would be hired without a degree; that fact had not changed. The young cops felt they had been had. The old timers laughed at the young cops. Their delight in the young cop's failure only added insult to injury.

As a group of educated cops, we were trapped. We were still answering radio calls to the ghetto, playing servant to the ghetto scofflaws, taking them to the hospital, tending to their needs, and being hated for our toil, while the test takers of the world were bagging the big federal law enforcement jobs.

But most of the young Viet Nam vet cops realized that they possessed something that the politicians, the slick businessmen, the ghetto scofflaws, and the career criminals didn't have: immunity.

We could speed, drive drunk, beat people with our fists, club them with night sticks, or steel flashlights, and even shoot them, and get away with it. It's what kept us going in the job.

And we also had discretion. When we slipped into our police car for an eight-hour shift, we decided who went to jail, who went to the hospital, who went to the morgue.

A cop does whatever he desires to do, in most cases. He just has to be able to explain his actions. If his explanation is plausible, then it's okay. Who else has that kind of power?

One of the cops, Patrolman Paul, called the CIA and demanded an interview. He told them he was a Viet Nam vet, a college graduate and a big city cop and that if he didn't get an interview, it was a violation of his civil rights.

The CIA guy told him that he would interview him, but he didn't want him to come to any CIA office, that instead he would meet him at a hotel and interview him covertly, in the lobby. They agreed on the Holiday Inn Hotel at 301 S. Grand.

The cop showed up with his resume, dressed in his best J.C.Penny off-the-rack suit and waited for the CIA agent to approach him.

They made eye contact and with a nod they walked toward some overstuffed lobby chairs near the south wall. The CIA guy turned the chairs so that their backs would be facing each other; they sat, the backs of their heads almost touching.

The interview began: Their personal conversation began. The cop tried to turn around and speak to the agents head but the agent told him not to try and face him, just to speak at the wall and that he would hear him, and that this was a CIA clandestine meeting. The CIA guy told him to hand the resume over his right shoulder. The cop complied.

There was silence while the resume was studied. They spoke of the cop's job, his military experience, his wife and family, his college experience. Finally, the CIA guy asked the crucial question: What do you want to do for the Central Intelligence Agency and the United States of America?"

"I want to kill people," the educated cop replied. It seemed that it was the proper answer for the cop. It's what most Viet Nam vet City of St. Louis cops wanted to do. But being a hired killer/cop wasn't enough to be hired by the CIA.

All it took was a good aptitude for test taking. He didn't get hired. He didn't even get an application. Eventually, he was hired by the Naval Criminal Investigative Service (NCIS) and moved out of the area.

My old Irish sarge, John McGuire, died. A young sergeant was sent to replace him. His name was George Clobes, a cadet in his youth, but not one of Doc Cooper's friends. But he was close friends with Chief Eugene Camp.

Unlike Sergeant McGuire, George Clobes was brash and unfriendly. He believed in the old way of doing supervisory police work. He had learned his lessons well from the old guard at headquarters. Abuse your underlings, and then after the beating, praise them. It worked for some of the guys. He had a following. Some cops would do anything for him. I wasn't one of them.

Sergeant Clobes believed in entitlements. If a cop without rank or prestige had a pretty wife, George felt he was entitled to the wife. It only made sense in his brain. I have rank and I'm George Clobes. This guy has no prestige and thinks he's better than me because he has a nice looking spouse, so I will take his wife away from him. This was proper thinking in the social confines of the St. Louis Metropolitan Police Department.

George exercised these entitlements, and he was proficient at it. He broke up several marriages (not his own), and he was proud of his escapades. The cop wives didn't have to violate their vow of marriage and enter into the darkness of infidelity. He gave them the opportunity and some took it.

George was proficient at other things: he carried a large lead-loaded sap in his belt, tucked in between his belly and his waistband. He was quick and good with the sap. It was his trademark. He even carried it when he was off duty. In a bar fight, he could grab it and strike with it before anyone knew they were being struck. Most thought it was a fist. The guy had talent.

One of the victims of George's police wives venture, Patrolman Barry Lalumandier, came across George in a south side bar. Barry always had a beautiful wife. His first wife succumbed to George's charm. While Barry was working the night watch, George was romancing Barry's wife. The marriage ended. George had another notch on his revolver grips, and the whole department got a chuckle out of it.

For a guy like George Clobes, it was good publicity. He was revered by the other commanders. It was considered "good police work" to show the non-prestigious cops that they were nothing but radio slaves. Who do they think they are having pretty wives?

Barry had had too much to drink. He wasn't a fighter; he was a lover. He mentioned to George (who by then had already been promoted to Lieutenant) that George had broken up his marriage, taken up with his wife while he was on night watch duty, and that he was rotten to the core for doing so.

George struck Barry several times in the face with his magic, lead-loaded sap. Barry went down and didn't get up. George strutted around like he had just won the world bar fighting championship. Barry still didn't come around; somebody called an ambulance.

Barry was rushed to square mile hospital and eventually regained consciousness. His facial bones were crushed. He had a severe brain concussion. He was sent to the operating room. His present wife, Peggy, who was in actuality prettier than any of the other police wives, arrived at the hospital accompanied by Barry's best friend, Detective Tom Rangel. After several surgeries he was sent home to recuperate.

Barry subsequently sued George Clobes for the attack and the injury. George had to take out a loan on his house to pay Barry. But George faced no disciplinary action from the police department.

The unofficial opinion of the administration of the police department was that the women George Clobes pursued didn't have to go with him into a sinful, adulterous relationship. He didn't force them. It was the woman's fault, and it was Barry's fault for allowing it to happen, and for approaching George about the incident.

Barry recovered from the George Clobes' beating. His new wife, Peggy, left him for a fireman. He divorced her and lost most of what he ever had, including a gorgeous spouse. Even his best friends forsook him. He did thirty five years on the police department, retired, and took a job as court security with the St. Louis County Courts.

George Clobes was close to having thirty plus years on when he died. He was playing golf with some of his cop buddies when he suffered some sort of seizure. He died on the golf course. His golf buddies gave him CPR until an ambulance came and carted his body away. Apparently he was dead when he hit the ground.

For some reason George had a following. His friends started a George Clobes Memorial College Scholarship fund. They solicited cash from businessmen, cops, lawyers, anybody they could put the arm on. I often wondered if any of Barry Lalumandier's kids went to college with money from the fund.

On December 3rd, 1972, I was working the night watch, in the Gaslight Square area. The street creatures were out: prostitutes, pimps, dope dealers, and customers. The pimps patrolled the streets giving the appearance they were protecting their girls, but in reality they were counting the johns who paid the street girls for sex. The pimps were businessmen; the bottom line was the dollar.

The street cops, like me, stopped the pimps periodically, pulled them out of their Caddy's and Lincolns, searched them and their cars looking for guns, then threatened them. We all hated them for putting girls on the street.

They seldom had any contraband. Most were tough guys who could handle any situation without a gun. If a john was rough with a girl, and a gun was involved, the pimp would smooth the situation over, then get even with the john at a later date. The johns always came back. Sometimes they came back and were killed in an apparent street robbery. It was retaliation.

The street dealers hardly ever had any dope on their person. It was usually hidden near them, or they would make the initial contact with the buyer then meet at a different location. It quickly became an exercise in futility.

I received a radio call for a fire at 4254 Maryland Avenue, just blocks from Gaslight Square, and one block north of Lindell Boulevard. The call was routine for cops. The fire department does all of the work; the cops usually just block off the streets with their scout cars.

I slowly arrived on the scene. A couple of fireman were dragging a body out of the two-story house. The fire was all but knocked down by the time I arrived. Neighbors were in the street. Some came over to the front yard and viewed the burned up human remains of the home owner.

I was used to big spectacular fires. The mid-section of the city, now blighted by crime and poverty, was being burned to the ground.

There was a big fire at least once a week. Warehouses, apartment buildings, old hotels that were now abandoned tenements, all were heavily insured; real estate investments that could not fail due to the popularity of Gaslight Square, were mysteriously catching fire. Gaslight Square had become a failure. It had been the cornerstone of the economy in midtown St. Louis. Investors wanted out.

Some of the fires were obvious arson but some went unclassified. The people setting these buildings on fire were becoming sophisticated. The arson investigators from the police department, and the fire investigators from the fire department called these fires, "Jewish lightning."

A fire captain came to my scout car and asked me if I had gotten the radio assignment. I said, "Yeah," reluctantly.

"You will have to convey the body to the morgue and write a report. This is arson with a fatality. The victim was at the base of the stairway. We ran over her body as we ran inside the house to fight the fire. We didn't see her until after the fire was knocked down. The neighbors say her name is Opal Stillman, white female about sixty."

A neighbor came over to me, "I heard a loud explosion, and I could hear her screaming for help; I couldn't get to her in time. The fire was horrendous." I got his name and jotted down what he told me.

I called for a paddy wagon; it arrived and we, the paddy wagon driver, Patrolman Bob Scott, and I placed the burned cadaver onto a stretcher and slid it into the paddy wagon. We headed for the morgue.

The victim was a female. Her upper body was burned to where she didn't look human. Her body had burst open from the flames. I had never viewed such a gruesome sight, not even in the Marine Corps. She smelled of gasoline. I filled out the morgue forms and transferred the burned corpse onto a steel table, tied a tag to her right big toe, and left the morgue. My job was complete, I thought.

A week went by and I was summoned to coroner's court. In the City of St. Louis, in those ancient days, the coroner was an elected official who investigated suspicious deaths and made determinations on the treatments and the remains of the dead. If a physician didn't, or wouldn't sign a death certificate, then there was a coroner's inquest. In a city of poor folks, like St. Louis, the district cop went to coroner's court often.

I was subpoenaed to coroner's court, showed up, and was sworn in. I took the stand and answered the questions pertaining to my radio assignment and what I found when I arrived. I was excused but I decided to stick around and see what the initial investigation had revealed.

An arson investigator, Detective Thomas O'Connor, was sworn after me and took the stand. I had met him before and I knew his demeanor. He was all cop: intense and honest, like a television investigator. He would dig for the truth in a case until he got to a relevant conclusion.

Detective O'Connor testified that the investigation at the scene revealed a strong presence of gasoline throughout the house, and it appeared that the victim, Mrs. Stillman may have been in an upstairs bedroom, possibly retrieving something of value while the fire was being set on the stairway, blocking her escape. She apparently made it to the base of the stairway and was burned alive.

The coroner asked, "Did your investigation reveal that there was another person involved in the arson and the death of Mrs. Stillman?"

"Yes," Detective O'Connor replied.

"And what other facts did your investigation reveal, Detective O'Connor?"

"That Mrs. Stillman left her entire estate to an automobile firm officer at Yates Oldsmobile. She had apparently purchased Oldsmobiles from this person for the past eighteen-years. The legacy includes a 155 acre farm in Southeast Missouri, the Maryland Avenue home, life insurance, and $5900 in jewelry. The beneficiary, when questioned, told me that he advised Mrs. Stillman in business matters, in addition to selling her cars. He was the executor of her estate."

"Anything more to add, Detective O'Connor?"

"Yes, we located a new Oldsmobile parked on Lindell Boulevard that had been lent to Mrs. Stillman by the automobile officer pending the arrival of her new car."

I walked out of the court thinking deeply about the death of Opal Stillman. It appeared that while she was in the upstairs bedroom, an accomplice started the fire on the stairwell landing, trapping her and killing her. By the evidence presented at the hearing, the finger of accusation was pointed at the automobile officer at Yates Oldsmobile.

Life went on for me; college, wife, crazy job, and dreams of a future. About a month later I met up with Detective Tom O'Connor at headquarters. I asked him about the case of Opal Stillman.

"The car dealer, executor of her estate, had an appointment for a polygraph examination here at headquarters," Detective O'Connor replied. "He didn't show up. I called him and asked if we could re-schedule the appointment. He said, "No.""

"You think he was the accomplice who killed her?"

"No doubt in my mind," he replied. "And another thing. The guy's friends with almost all of the high ranking cops in the Ninth District, and many more in headquarters. He loans them cars to take on vaca-tions. The whole case has been shoved under the table. Go to the rec-ord room and try to get a copy of the report. You won't get it. It spells out the conspiracy between this guy and his salesman against that old lady. Nothing will ever come of it. A loaner car is a big deal; bigger than murder."

"You mean there was someone else?" I asked.

"Yeah, one of his salesman was in on it with him. We went to the farm down in Southeast Missouri. There were plastic bottles of gaso-line stored down there in a barn. We asked the old man, the victim's husband, what they were used for. He said, "They told me it was Jew-ish lightning." The old man had dementia. He probably won't live much longer. The car dealer got the entire estate of Opal Stillman."

The years clicked by; I got transferred to the Intelligence Unit. I saw Tom O'Connor in the hallway on the fourth floor. He was vocal and upset. He had been passed over for a promotion to sergeant. Shortly thereafter he quit the St. Louis Metropolitan Police Depart-ment for an investigative job with the Illinois Division of Criminal Investigation. I saw him periodically over in East St. Louis, Illinois. We checked on gangsters living on the eastside. He was still an intense guy, stopping cars by himself in and around the gangster hangouts.

Years had passed and I was about to leave the Intelligence Unit. I had read in the St. Louis Post Dispatch that the officer in the car deal-ership (Yates Oldsmobile) was in trouble with and being prosecuted by the Internal Revenue Service. He was now the owner of the dealer-ship, and it was no longer called Yates Oldsmobile.

He had refused to cooperate with the government, and it appeared he was going to court to fight them. The world had changed. Almost all citizens, even street people knew who and what the IRS was, by then.

I pondered the Opal Stillman murder case. I could still picture her burned cadaver in my mind, and the smell of the gasoline and the burned flesh. I thought about what Tom O'Connor had told me about the police report and the investigative report. I wondered if I could retrieve it.

I went to the record room, wrote her name on a report request, the date and time of the incident, and handed it to the clerk. She checked the files and told me there was no such report. Tom O'Connor was correct in his assumption.

I wandered over to the morgue and asked for the report. It took about ten-minutes and I had it. I wasn't certain what I was going to do with it, but I took it over to my little cubby hole office and read it.

The report was expertly written, informative, and raised suspicions about the car dealer and his salesman. I had worked with IRS agents in the past. It was part of my job as an Intelligence Unit detective to work with feds. Actually, the IRS special agents I had worked with were good guys, just like most cops. We all had one thing in common--- get the bad guys. They did it by finding out where the cash went. I wondered if the IRS knew about the windfall the car dealer received when Opal Stillman left this earth.

I telephoned the IRS office and received the name of the agent who was working the case. He called me back. I asked him to come over to the office and that I had something for him to read. He did. He read the report, thanked me and left with it.

Shortly thereafter, the car dealer pled guilty to the tax evasion charge the IRS had on him. I wondered if I had granted retribution to Opal Stillman with my investigative actions.

I remembered the car dealers grown children coming in to the Ninth District station, brash and upset over parking tickets given to them. They would walk right into the watch commander's office and challenge the lieutenant on duty.

In my mind, this offense was worse than the Black Liberators coming by and shooting up the station. This was a face to face threat by some cheap suit wearing young men with chips on their shoulders.

They would sneer at the watch commanders, and toss the parking tags onto their desks. The watch commanders would not look at them. They would take the tickets and keep their heads down. I made a move to extract one of them from the office. I was told not to take action. The brash young men walked away laughing.

A car to take on vacation is a powerful tool for a crook to possess. It makes murder feasible. I played it out in my mind----Opal Stillman probably went to the car dealer, a person she trusted, and requested his help in burning her home for the insurance money. She had larceny in her heart-------no good could come from it.

The car dealer no doubt knew he was the executor of her estate, and was set to get most of her estate upon her death. When Opal went upstairs to fetch something the car dealer doused the stairway with gasoline and ignited it as he ran from the house. It was almost the perfect crime. It was the perfect murder.

'BLACK LIBERATION ARMY'

Story three:

The Black Liberation Army, not to be confused with the St. Louis street gang, the Black Liberators, was a spinoff of the Black Panther Party, a national group of black terrorists set on killing police officers, judges, and any established white order of law enforcement.

The Black Panther Party was originally started by Huey Newton and Bobby Seale in Oakland, California. They recruited other activists to patrol the black ghettoes in California to protect the residents there from police brutality.

I had seen black militants in the Marine Corps while stationed in California. The California blacks I was stationed with, lived with in Marine Corps barracks, and went into the jungle with, were different than the blacks I had grown up with and gone to school with on the eastside.

They were dissatisfied but so were American Indians, American Hispanics and guys who came from the swamps of Louisiana or the hills of West Virginia. Nobody was happy in the Marine Corps so I didn't dwell on their plight.

It was the colonization of the black race that struck me as odd. Not only in St. Louis with Pruit Igoe and the other poor housing projects that cops spend most of their on-duty time in but also in the black neighborhoods. It seemed to me that wherever there were large numbers of blacks, they were colonized. I didn't experience this colonization until I became a St. Louis cop in 1970.

The Black Panther Party was gaining power within the state of California. These guys, Huey Newton, Bobby Seale, Stokely Carmichel were big talkers, smart and articulate, and they could convince almost any crowd that revolution was the only answer to black equality. One of the things they preached was that the police were the military arm of the government and should be destroyed.

During their insightful speeches, they would casually say with a smile, "Have you killed any white people today?"

J.Edgar Hoover said the Black Panther Party was one of the most serious threats to the security of America. He formed within the Federal Bureau of Investigation Cointelpro, an acronym for Counter Intelligence Program.

Basically, through false letters written by the FBI to Huey Newton, Bobby Seale, Stokely Carmichael and other top officers within the Black Panther Party movement, the FBI caused distrust, confusion, and the eventual down fall of the party. The stragglers left from the party formed the Black Liberation Army.

On October 22, 1970, the BLA placed a bomb in a church in San Francisco during a funeral of a police officer killed in the line of duty.

On May 21, 1971 members of the BLA participated in a shooting of two New York City police officers.

On August 29, 1971, three BLA members walked into a police station in San Francisco and murdered a desk sergeant.

On January 27, 1972, the BLA assassinated two officers in New York City.

On February 2, 1972, at approximately 9:45 p.m., Patrol Officers Richard Archambault, aka "Frenchy" and Larry Tinnell, aka "Craz" were patrolling in car 9 Charles-8.

It was a depressing part of the City of St. Louis. The business section of the area was north Grand Boulevard with the focal point being a doughnut shop at Grand and Cass. It's where the weary cops hung out between calls for service. It was one of the few white owned establishments in the area. I had been assigned to the area many times. When I came in to work and observed the work sheet and found out my area for the evening was 9 Charles-8, I became instantly depressed.

There was nowhere to eat, nothing to look at but slum dwellings, nothing to do but watch the world go by at Grand and Cass.

For some unknown reason, Grand and Cass was the crossroad for criminals anytime, day or night. If a cop sat at the intersection of Grand and Cass and watched the cars going north and south, he would come up with a fugitive, or at least an occupied stolen car.

I had done it many times. Boredom would set in at about the same time, three hours into your shift, and like an animal going to the watering hole, or migratory bird flying south for the winter, the 9 Charles-8 cop would glance at his watch and say to himself, "I think I'll go set up at Grand and Cass and look for an interesting car to stop." It was almost always fruitful.

It seemed like when I was assigned to the area, I was a one man car. In fact, I almost always rode one- man; I kind of preferred it. I was always intent on doing my own thing. It was the biggest perk of being a cop. You are on your own, alone in a cop car.

I was no stranger to Grand and Cass. I was involved in a fender bender car crash on the way to work at the Ninth District. I was a little late for roll call and wasn't paying attention to the cars coming and going. A car pulled out of a parking spot south bound on Grand, and nailed me.

I went into a business and called the station. My car was junk before the accident. It was all I could afford at the time. I had only been a cop for about a year.

The accident happened across the street from the Black Muslim Mosque, and as one would imagine in that area, it was a Black Muslim who hit me.

Several police cars came to the scene. I was one of "them," a good-guy cop against the Muslims, in the minds of the responding cops. They put the Muslim guy in cuffs and conveyed him to the station.

There were several older cops at the station. They hung out there smoking cigars and swapping war stories. Nobody really cared in those days. There were always enough cops on the street. There were cops bumping into each other.

The Muslim guy was led into the report room, still cuffed, and placed at a table in a chair. The older station house cops wandered in. They had heard about the accident via the station gossip trail which went from one end of the station house to the other instantaneously.

It was like a stage play but without a script. The mission of the play-with-out- a script on this fine winter evening was to force the Muslim to pay for the damage to my piece of junk car. I sat back and observed.

I figured the Muslim thought he was going to be beaten at any moment, but he held his own. In those days, most of the Black Muslims were converts from the prison system. I was almost certain this guy knew the system well enough to know that if he wasn't beaten, he would probably be walking out of the station house, with at the most, a traffic ticket which he would beat in city court.

The old cops badgered the Muslim, asking him about money and how he planned to right this wrong by giving me a couple of hundred dollars for the damage to my car. The play was amusing for a while but soon grew old and tiring. I knew this guy didn't have any cash.

If he did have money to pay me, I was reluctant to take his money. I had friends in the car business who would fix my junker for almost nothing. It was an accident. Who cared? But the play continued on.

Eventually, a big-wig from the mosque showed up at the station. He asked for his buddy and was escorted to the report room. This guy was big and impressive looking. He wore an expensive suit, was in shape and healthy looking. Much more impressive than the old station house cops who lived on cigars, fast food and booze.

I figured this was scene three of the play and it would soon be over. The old cops then badgered the new guy, blowing cigar smoke in his face and threatening him and his mosque. They were intimidated by him. The threat of violence was building; I could see it.

Eventually the word got to the watch commander. He came in and ordered the old cops out of the room. He removed the cuffs from Muslim number one, and he and Muslim number two walked out of the station house.

In 1975 I graduated from the University of Missouri. I felt like I was going to be moving on soon: federal law enforcement maybe, or something better than being a St. Louis cop.

I hadn't walked up to the stage to get my degree diploma, yet, but I had finished the curriculum and was in a holding pattern wondering what I was going to do with myself.

I was working the afternoon watch, winter time, and I had a female reserve officer with me. It was dark by 5:00 p.m. and the reserve officer was frightened, I could sense it. Her name was Ouida Baynham. She was a secretary by trade, but she wanted to be a St. Louis cop. I didn't really know her. That's the way it usually worked when we had reserve officers. They would just show up at roll call and the watch commander would place them with a one man car as a back-up.

Sergeant John was our supervisor. He was an unhappy fellow, and he drank too much. He didn't drink on duty, but he drank heavily after work. He would come to work in a bad mood daily. He wasn't a nice guy to work for because of his mood swings.

Most of the time he stayed in the station and did his homework. He, too, was a college student, but unlike most of the other cops who went to college so they could leave the department, he studied to gain rank in the department. He was friends with Chief Camp. In order to get Chief Camp to back you in a promotion you either had to be educated or politically connected. It helped even more if you were both. Sergeant John knew this fact. He ran for and was elected as a trustee to the pension system. The state legislature and state legislators were immensely interested in our pension fund.

Any increase or decrease in our benefits came from the state legislature. Sergeant John, like so many officers of rank before him, was elected as a pension trustee. He was now a cop state legislators were interested in. Our fund had hundreds of millions of dollars in it, and it still does.

State legislators still have immense interest in the fund. So do lawyers, fund managers and cops. Politicians, cops and lawyers monitor and manage the fund. With that combination, what could possibly go wrong?

Sergeant John was subsequently transferred to the Vice Division. He had a squad of men assigned to him, and they harassed and arrested the prostitutes and pimps in the ninth. After their crusades, he and his crew would sit in his detective car in the parking lot at the rear of the Ninth District Station, drink, beer and smoke cigarettes. He was eventually promoted to lieutenant and then to captain. He died without getting any of his pension.

Cops are observant creatures. It's what we do most, observe, adjust our lives to suit the moment, and try to achieve a specific goal. For some cops promotion is the goal, and they will resort to anything to achieve it. Lie, cheat, steal, or desecrate.

Such was the case with Police Officers Anthony Daniele and Walter Klein. They were voted in to the pension fund as trustees. Anthony was the chairman of the fund. As I previously stated, prominent people were familiar with and interested in the fund. Trustees of the pension fund come into contact with these folks on a daily basis.

If a prominent person in the community can steer pension business to a friend or business associate, it can mean cash, probably under the table cash, to all parties involved. Hundreds of millions of dollars of invested pension fund cash can boost the revenue of the investment firm doing the investing.

Donald Anton, a prominent attorney in the St. Louis region some-how came in to contact with Patrolman Anthony Daniele and Patrol-man Walter Klein. To Anthony Daniele, this contact quite possibly meant a sure fire promotion to sergeant for him. To Walter Klein, it probably meant cash.

There is a member of the Honorable Board of Police Commis-sioners who sits on the pension board as well as the trustees and a member of the mayor's staff. Donald Anton was apparently wired in with one or more of these folks. Anthony Daniele was star struck.

Daniele and Klein tabled and voted to move some of the fund to a brokerage house where somehow Donald Anton was connected.

The fund was churned which is the illegal buying and selling of stocks which increases the commissions of the participants. Daniele and Klein allegedly received kickbacks from the fund from the churn-ing. They both went to federal prison.

But before going to prison, Anthony Daniele went to a police commissioner's office in downtown St. Louis and took him hostage. He held the commissioner at gunpoint for hours. The reason for the hostage-taking apparently stemmed from the inability of the police commissioner to grant Daniele's promotion to sergeant, which is what lawyer Anton promised him.

Danielle had allowed one or more influential professionals, law-yers, investment counselors, businessmen and politicians to fleece the pension fund. He was an observant cop but his plan backfired on him.

Reserve officers were armed, carried night sticks, and handcuffs and wore the same uniform cops wore. But they weren't cops.

Reserve Officer Ouida and I received a radio assignment to a two family flat at Grand and Cass for an accidental injury. The flat was on the second floor. We trudged up a long staircase to a landing.

There was a lady standing at the landing talking to us as we climbed. I was in front and I made it to the landing and a young black guy rushed me at a full run from a hallway running perpendicular to the stairway. I didn't know it, but he had just stabbed his brother with a butcher knife.

He and I tumbled and rolled down the long stairway and landed at the foot in the entry hallway. Both of us were dazed by the fall down the steps. He was scrambling for my cop thirty eight revolver. I could feel him thrashing at the holster. It's what bad guys do when fighting cops.

We began rolling around on the floor, fighting and wrestling, grappling for control. We both got on our feet and began fist fighting. We were exchanging punches in the little semi-dark vestibule, and finally Ouida came down to the foot of the stairs with her night stick in her hand.

Ouida was a good gal, but not St. Louis cop material. I was hitting the guy with everything I had with my fists but not really hurting him. He was landing on me, counter punching me.

The guy was young, probably sixteen, and I didn't want to shoot him, but I was considering it. His mother was standing at the top of the stairs watching the fight. I grabbed Ouida's night stick and clubbed the guy in the center his forehead. It knocked him out cold.

We didn't have radios. The guy's mother had to call the radio dispatcher and inform her of the fight and injuries to both of us. Our supervisor didn't even respond to the scene.

I was laid up for about three weeks. When I graduated from U.M.S.L.I could hardly make it up to the stage to receive my diploma.

Ouida became a St. Louis cop. She was critically beaten on a peace disturbance call by a guy. The pension system gave her a disability pension but she didn't last long. She died shortly after retiring.

Sergeant John made lieutenant shortly after my fall down the stairs at Grand and Cass. When he went to vice, a new supervisor was transferred in, Sergeant Neal.

There was a night and day difference between Sergeant Neal and John. Neal was a funny guy and he wanted the best for his troops. He had come from the Burglary Robbery Division, a Colonel John Doherty unit.

Neal would tell us stories of being in a downtown bureau. We all wanted to gravitate there someday. I listened intently to the stories he told me.

There was camaraderie in a specialized unit. The group detectives always worked together; most worked the same hours and didn't have to attend college on their days off. They had already arrived at their destination within the police department.

Neal always had a flashy girlfriend. The guys in Burglary Robbery were no doubt jealous of him. He had an apartment in fashionable West County, but he wanted to be one of the guys. It was important in the cop/specialized unit game.

He invited his work buddies to his apartment for a quiet card game and some light libation. One of the cops got drunk and subsequently fired his thirty eight detective special into the floor of the apartment. Neal lived on the second floor.

Neal hustled the cops out of the apartment and went to bed. The next day there was a knock on his door. It was the gentleman downstairs in the apartment below his. He asked Neal about the shot that was fired. Neal played dumb.

The neighbor held the bullet in his hand for Neal to peruse. Then he stepped off several feet in the middle of the room and knelt down. He found the hole in the floor where the bullet ripped through the floor and into his apartment.

Neal knew he was had. He told the neighbor he was a city cop and that his rowdy buddies from the department came over and drank too much. One of them played with his gun and it discharged accidentally. The guy accepted Neal's story and asked him to make sure it didn't happen again. They exchanged telephone numbers and became neighborly.

Neal was getting married to one of his flashy girlfriends. His cop buddies wanted to have a few casual drinks with him on the evening before the wedding to celebrate the ending of his bachelorhood. It's a big deal amongst men, losing your freedom to a flashy gal.

Neal cautioned his friends. "No shenanigans, right? I don't want to walk down the aisle with a black eye or worse."

"No," they assured him, "just a few drinks among friends."

Neal welcomed them into his apartment with open arms. They were his fellow warriors, men he trusted with his life. As the apartment door was closed, one of the cops jumped on Neal and got him in a headlock. Another one handcuffed him behind his back.

While he was being held down on the floor, they undid his belt, unzipped his trousers and then stripped his trousers and underwear off of him.

One of them displayed a can of black paint and showed it to Neal before he sprayed Neal's penis and scrotum with a liberal coat of enamel.

They got up and walked out of the apartment leaving Neal to fend for himself. The only person he knew in the building was the downstairs tenant who had been leery of Neal and his maniac friends ever since the bullet came whizzing by him as he watched television.

Neal got to the telephone and with his hands cuffed behind his back and managed to dial the downstairs neighbor. The neighbor reluctantly came to his aid. But time was of the essence. Neal was desperate to get the paint off before it completely dried.

Neal opened the door for the neighbor and showed him where his handcuff key was. The guy took the handcuffs off, shook his head, and walked out. Neal worked most of the night trying to remove the paint. Not all of it came off.

Neal was personal friends with Kenny Rothman. It was an easy friendship; they were both the same religion, and Kenny liked cops. He desired to help cops and he had influence.

Kenny Rothman was a state senator for a long time and he eventually became Lieutenant Governor. He was a Democrat and he was associated with Democratic city politicians.

Kenny Rothman waited for the Governor, Kit Bond, to leave town. By law when the governor was out of state, the lieutenant governor assumed the duties of the governor.

In the fall of 1982, Kit Bond was out of state. The Cardinals were playing the World Series, and the whole city was abuzz. It was packed with baseball fanatics.

I was a detective in the Intelligence Unit. Part of our responsibility was to provide protection for politicians and dignitaries. I was told to go to Ken Rothman's home in Ladue, pick he and his wife up in an unmarked police car, and take them to the World Series.

I figured I would convey them and then wait in the police car for the game to end. Kenny Rothman didn't want that. He wanted me to accompany them for the evening so I did. He told me to refer to him as Kenny. Our first stop was at the Busch private room. We had fresh shrimp, prime rib and all of the beer we could consume.

From there we went to the Busch's private box seats, right behind home plate. The beer kept on coming. It was a great night for a cop. I drove them back to Ladue like we were old friends.

The president of the Honorable Board of Police Commissioners was Theodore McNeil. He was the first black police board president and he was a visionary. He wasn't quite like Dr. Martin Luther King, but he envisioned a cohesive population of blacks and whites living in peace in the City of St. Louis.

Cops could live outside of the city at the time. Hardly any cops lived within the city limits. St. Louis County was a place to get away from the city crime and congestion.

He made it mandatory for newly hired cops to move into the city. His rule stuck for nearly three decades and it placed a hardship on cops with children. There were few city schools where city cop's kids could feel comfortable.

The cops had to work constantly in order to pay for private schools. That meant no vacations, no new cars, and no frivolous purchases. For a city cop during those years, if their wives didn't have good paying jobs, it was like living in communist China.

Kenny Rothman was a political ally of Theodore McNeil. Their association was good for Sergeant Neal. But even as a supervisor, Neal wanted to make arrests. He was on the street most of his shift looking for bad guys.

St. Louis boxing legend Leon Spinks had just defeated Muhammed Ali. He was now the Heavy Weight Champion of the World. Most cops in the City of St. Louis were familiar with Leon Spinks. He was a semi-police character with an appetite for heroin.

Leon came back to his hometown and frequented the black nightclubs and restaurants, signing autographs, shaking hands, and getting the respect he always had desired.

Sergeant Neal was on the street, working the night watch when he observed Leon at a White Castle hamburger fast food restaurant.

Leon was standing in the parking lot shaking hands and talking to his fans. He was a celebrity no matter what his past had been. Sergeant Neal pulled the police car into the lot, climbed out, and approached Leon.

They had a short conversation: Neal did a cursory search of Leon, including his wide brimmed hat. Inside the hat was a "button" of heroin. Neal arrested the "champ," handcuffed him and placed him in his police car.

Neal was a happy cop. He was going to get notoriety. Kenny Rothman and his political friends would see him on television. He booked Leon and placed him in a cell at the Ninth District.

Leon had been in jail before, and he wasn't the only heavy weight champion of the world who had been in the Ninth District holdover for possession of heroin.

Sonny Liston was a St. Louis native, a Ninth District police character, and a jail bird due to his heroin addiction. The old detectives in the ninth watched for Sonny Liston.

He stood out in a crowd of street people buying and selling dope at Sarah and Olive, and he had been warned by the district detectives to stay away from that neighborhood. He did not heed their warning.

Sonny was arrested numerous times for possession of heroin, and when he was arrested, he resisted arrest. The Ninth District detectives were just like most cops in those ancient days. They drank too much, smoked cigarettes, were not in physical condition, and had soft bellies.

But when Sonny Liston was in their district buying and using heroin, these normal doughnut-eating cops would turn into super athletes. Sonny was beaten up several times by the Ninth District cops.

Sonny was an ex-con and he hated cops. When he was under the influence of heroin and was approached by a cop, he became belligerent. Belligerence always led to a beating no matter who the recipient was.

Maybe that's why Sergeant Neal wanted to arrest him. Maybe he thought Leon would resist arrest like Sonny Liston. But Leon didn't resist. He took his plight like a champion.

The newspapers got word of Leon's arrest. It went viral. Sergeant Neal was basking in his own glory. But there was a fly in the ointment. The mayor and some of the city fathers didn't appreciate the fact that a city police sergeant arrested one of the city's returning heroes.

Neal was chastised by the chief for not using restraint. He stayed in the office a little more often but was still a good supervisor to work for.

He was promoted to lieutenant, took an early retirement from the city, and became the chief of police of a county municipality. It seemed like the good supervisors never stayed with the city.

I eventually was transferred to the Intelligence Unit. My partner was Detective Tom Rangel. Our boss, Captain George (Bud) Nintemann was on us daily about arrests and stats. He never let up. He threatened to transfer us if we didn't make a felony arrest daily.

We were looking for a Cadillac which had been stolen by two rapists. They beat and raped an old lady and took her Caddy. One of them apparently told the old gal that they would drop her Caddy at Grand and Cass. It was fitting. Grand and Cass was the crossroads of hell.

We sat up there, right at the intersection, and lo and behold there was the Caddy driven by the two rapists stopping at the light, south bound.

I was driving and we were in a "funny car," a non-descript civilian style vehicle. I drove toward the Caddy and blocked the southbound lane with the funny car.

Tom Rangel and I got out and pointed our little snub pistols at the windshield. The guys inside of the Caddy pointed their bigger automatic pistols at us.

Tom and I shot at the bad guys thinking our bullets would penetrate the windshield. They didn't. We were required to use police issued ammunition. It was low velocity, soft nosed, and worthless. The ammo would not kill anyone unless you hit a soft vulnerable area, like a temple or liver or sometimes a gut shot. If it hit bone it would not penetrate.

The driver of the Caddy placed it in reverse and tore off, north on Grand, backwards. He swung it around with us running after it, shooting at it. One of our bullets blew out the rear window. They were eventually caught and went to prison.

But this story isn't about me, or Tom Rangel or Ouida Baynham or Sergeant Neal. It's about Frenchy (Richard Archambault) and Craz (Larry Tinnell). Two of the Ninth District's best.

There is a saying in the cop business that all cops learn quickly: "You're the cops. You can do anything you want to do so long as you can write yourself out it."

I knew I could depend on myself. I knew I could write well enough to cover myself. Thus, I didn't mind being alone in a cop car for eight hours or more. But the cop in a one man car wasn't always alone. He would get two man assignments and another car would assist him. Or he would get a call to go to the station for a prisoner run. Both assignments were bled to the max when 9 Charles-8 was your assigned area.

Another problem was the speed of the vehicles on Grand going north and south. The cop cars didn't have radar. I was a cop for thirty-five years and I have never even held a radar gun in my hand.

But if you were set up at the intersection watching for that one car that hits you in the eye as suspicious, you had to act fast because it would be gone in seconds. You would have to drive like a madman, weaving in and out of traffic, honking your horn, and motioning for people to get out of the way.

A siren or red roof lights would spook the driver, and you would never see the car again. Sirens and roof lights were only used when you pulled the car over, if you found it.

It is a game of chance for cops. Cops call it "jumping on cars." Like any game of chance, there is always a down side. At the least, you will probably have to fight the prospective criminal after you get the car stopped. In 9 Charles-8's neighborhood the chances of the guy being wanted are great. A gun or drugs would probably be in the vehicle, but you would have to get the driver outside of it to search him and the car.

And if you don't have to fight the driver, you may have to fight with one or all of the passengers, depending on the severity of the crime they are about to commit or have already committed. And the cop, always in the back of his mind, has the question, "What if they come out shooting?"

All of these possibilities race through a cops mind whenever they jump on a car in a ghetto somewhere in the world. It's no different in England, Tokyo, Moscow, or St. Louis. Crooks are the same everywhere, so are the cops.

In the cop business it always amazed me how the supervisors determined who was going to partner up with whom. It took some soul searching to make these two-man teams.

They didn't wish to have two laid back cops together, and they didn't want to have two aggressive cops in the same car.

Frenchy was a laid back likable guy. He was always smirking or smiling. He was a lover, not a fighter, but he would go along with almost any program. He could be aggressive if that is what the circumstances called for. He was a great cop respected by his peers and his supervisors.

Craz, as his moniker revealed, was an aggressive cop. He longed for and pursued notoriety. There wasn't much glory riding around in circles in 9-C-8's blighted area. Craz wanted to be a detective. They got the glory. Uniformed guys got the shaft.

These were political times in the St. Louis Police Department. A promotion to sergeant would cost the ambitious cop $3500. The cash went to a state representative via a trusted associate. The hook was, "You'll make it up in one year after you are promoted."

Most of the cops were promoted in this fashion. When they were promoted, they usually went to a district to do their years awaiting retirement. Guys like Craz didn't wish to participate in the promotional merry-go-round. Most of the supervisors in the Ninth District were promoted politically.

The political supervisors sat in their offices and judged the cops on the street. That was their job: judging, signing tickets and reports, and going home on time. Aggressive cops like Craz were a thorn in their side. It meant controversy, arrests, injuries, hospital details, and misconduct allegations. Craz rocked the boat.

Craz knew the system. It didn't take long to figure things out. He strived to be a super human cop. He desired awards, arrests, and recognition. He received an award from the State of Missouri for an arrest he initiated, alone on a dark night.

Had he been a prestigious cop, a detective or a cop with an important relative or friend, he would have been given a luncheon, an award ceremony, and the award would have been presented to him from the Chief of Police. Craz's award was mailed to him. No award ceremony for this worker of the police department.

Frenchy went along with the program with a smile and a chuckle. Neither of them cared about anything but police work. Craz was as great a cop as Frenchy but intense to the point of being crazy.

It was an hour before relief. Having known both Craz and Frenchy, I suspected that Frenchy was looking forward to getting off on time and drinking beer with his cop buddies.

I would suspect that Craz was stressed because he didn't have an arrest for the night. Craz was driving, Frenchy was no doubt scrunched down in the passenger seat smoking and waiting for the final hour to go by.

A car zoomed past them heading north on Grand, a black and green Oldsmobile four door with a cardboard license plate with Michigan stenciled on it. It was a perfect car stop.

Craz jumped on the car and activated the roof lights. The car pulled to the curb. It was occupied by four black guys. Craz walked up to the driver's door and asked the driver for his driver's license. Hardly anybody had a driver's license in 9 C-8's area. Craz probably thought he would get a summons arrest for the driver and at least one warrant or wanted case from the other three passengers in the vehicle. Cops didn't get paid overtime in those days. It was all for glory.

Frenchy took a stance at the rear of the Oldsmobile near the right passenger door standing on the sidewalk. The driver didn't give Craz his driver's license. The rear window of the Oldsmobile came down at about the same time the passenger was reaching inside of his jacket to presumably give Craz his driver's license. Instead he and the other passengers started shooting at Craz and Frenchy.

The interior of the Oldsmobile lit up like a Christmas tree from muzzle flash as the occupants fired at the officers. The first shot was fired from the right rear seat of the Oldsmobile. It hit Frenchy in the belly button and lifted him several feet into the air. He slammed down on the sidewalk, and Craz and Frenchy pulled their revolvers and returned fire.

Craz was quick-footed as well as being quick-witted. Several bullets whizzed by him making holes in his cop jacket. He fired into the car six times and observed the driver of the Oldmobile slump due to a shot in the back of his head from Craz's thirty eight. Craz was out of ammunition and was in the process of reloading as he ran toward the rear of the Oldsmobile.

Frenchy wasn't as lucky. He was shot four times, in both legs and the abdomen. He fired five times with his revolver as he lay on the sidewalk.

Lowly patrolmen didn't have personal radios. Those were reserved for supervisors and detectives. The fire power that came from inside the Oldsmobile was overwhelming, especially when you are firing back with thirty eight caliber revolvers.

Twelve gauge shotguns were issued to each police vehicle, but they were locked in a carrier located in the trunks of the police cars.

It appeared that Frenchy and Craz were on their own with the four armed madmen who later turned out to be members of the Black Liberation Army fleeing Black Muslims in Detroit and heading to the deep south for safety as they passed through St. Louis. Ironically the shooting took place near the storefront Black Muslim Mosque.

Remarkably, the driver who had been shot in the back of the head by Craz was able to speed away from the scene.

In those days there was an overabundance of cops. The city had over 2700 commissioned officers. It was a cheap army for the little socialist city and entertainment for the democratic politicians to deploy them.

As luck would have it, there was a narcotics crew on surveillance just a block away, and they heard the shots being fired by the Black Liberators and the cops.

The supervisor of the crew was Sergeant Boaz. He was a Chief of Detectives John Doherty disciple. As were most cops in those days, he was brash and demanding.

He was accompanied by two young cops, Detective Danno and Detective Penno. They were both, no doubt, in awe of Detective Sergeant Boaz. It was his job as a supervisor in an investigative unit within the Bureau of Investigation to nurture and guide these young men into positions of cop royalty.

Young cops as they were, they were just in their early twenties and were assigned to the Bureau of Investigation, meant they had prestige and were entitled to one-on-one tutelage.

Detective Danno was an affable guy, easy to like, quick with a smile and a hand shake. He had been a police cadet since shortly out of high school and he knew the way of the St. Louis Police Department. Basically, he grew up in the department. As soon as he reached twenty one years of age, he went into the Police Academy.

After the academy he was assigned to the Ninth District where anyone with a little luck or an influential friend was assigned. He did a minimal amount of time in the Ninth and then was assigned to the Narcotics Division. Some cops go their entire careers trying to get to the Narcotics Division. Detective Danno did it in under two years.

He was proud of his achievement. He would occasionally return to the district station on Lucas decked out in hippy apparel, long stringy hair, and beard. He flaunted his success at the non-prestigious cops who were answering radio calls, fighting drunks, and dope heads, and pulling cars over on North Grand. Guys like Frenchy and Craz.

Detective Sergeant Boaz pulled his detective car up at the scene of the car stop as the Oldsmobile was starting to pull away driven by the guy who shot at Craz and missed and carrying a bullet in his brain fired by Craz. Shots were still being fired by the Liberators inside the Oldsmobile as the car pulled away.

The occupant in the right rear of the Oldsmobile, the one who had fired the first shot that struck Frenchy in the belly button and launched him into the air, was already dead from one of Frenchy's frantic shots as he lay on the sidewalk shooting toward the car's occupants.

The narcotics crew pursued the Oldsmobile to a super market

parking lot at 2501 North Grand where the path of the Oldsmobile was blocked by a fence with barbed wire on top of it. Three of the occupants left the Oldsmobile and attempted to leave the scene by climbing the fence. Two of them dropped off of the fence and took a position behind the Oldsmobile firing shots at the narcotics detectives.

The third suspect made it over the fence. Sergeant Boaz stated he fired five shots at the suspect making it over the fence. He appeared to fall off of the fence landing on the opposite side.

Sergeant Boaz and Detective Danno exchanged gunfire with the two remaining Black Liberators. For some unknown reason Detective Penno did not fire his weapon.

The two remaining Black Liberators were ordered to give it up by Sergeant Boaz. One fell to the ground, and the other suspect ran to the front of the Oldsmobile.

The subject in front of the Oldsmobile stood as if he was surrendering . Detectives Danno and Penno walked toward the subject as Sergeant Boaz walked toward the subject lying on the ground.

As Detectives Danno and Penno came within reach of the subject, he grabbed Detective Danno's revolver and attempted to wrestle it from his grasp.

Detective Danno gained control of his weapon and struck the subject in the head with it. He and Detective Penno then subdued the subject and placed handcuffs on him. Sergeant Boaz handcuffed the other subject.

The third subject was arrested by other detectives walking on a nearby street bleeding profusely.

Luckily for Patrolman Archambault, Doc Cooper was waiting at the hospital when he arrived. He saved Frenchy's life.

The investigation began. The two Black Liberators were questioned at the hospital. They lied about their identity. After fingerprinting them, it was ascertained that their true identities were Thomas McCreary, twenty seven, of Brooklyn, New York. and Ronald Brown, twenty four, of Detroit, Michigan.

One of the guns found at the scene had been stolen from a murdered police officer in New York City. He had been assassinated, shot in the eyes with a thirty eight caliber pistol.

McCreary stated he was in New York at that time but had no connection with the murdered cop. McCreary was the driver of the

Oldsmobile. He had a fractured skull. He was one of the guys Craz shot during the car stop and shootout. Ronald Brown was hospitalized for a broken arm.

Ronald Brown was eventually indicted in New York for the murder of Patrolmen Rocco Laurie and Gregory Foster.
The suspect who escaped was identified as Twyman Meyers twenty one, from Atlanta. The deceased subject was identified as Ronald Carter, twenty eight, from New York. Twynam Meyers was eventually arrested.

Frenchy was gaining his strength and recovering nicely under the care of Doc Cooper. Craz had gotten the national publicity he had sought for his entire life. The case was neatly wrapped up, but the "spin" had begun.

Life and death comes and goes quickly in a district like the ninth. Cases are remembered but not dwelled upon. The local cops hear tales about the interesting cases, but they never dig into the reports and read them. The cops don't have the time for such luxuries. They believe the ever present rumors.

The rumor mill in the ninth was buzzing about one of their own. It wasn't Frenchy or Craz. The mill was producing tales about Detective Danno.

The "official" rumor was that Detective Danno shot and killed the bad guy who had shot Frenchy. It even went into detail about how Detective Danno pursued the assailant on foot and shot him as he was climbing over a barbed wire fence.

The ordinary cops in the ninth were certain Detective Danno was a prestigious guy before the incident with the Black Liberation Army; now he was a bona fide prestigious cop. With this Black Liberation killing Detective, Danno was for sure going to be cop royalty.

But the rumors were untrue. It was cop mythology. It was never substantiated who killed suspect Ronald Carter, the guy riding in the back seat of the Oldsmobile. He had not climbed a fence. He was dead when the detectives opened the door of the Olds. I believed the Detective Danno myth for years.

Frenchy healed quickly. He longed to get back on the street and lock bad guys up with his best buddy, Craz. It wasn't long before they were in a police car patrolling the Ninth District ghetto.

The "spin" plan was working well. Sergeant Boaz was promoted to lieutenant and shortly after that promotion he was promoted to captain.

Detective Danno's friends wanted him awarded and rewarded for his enthusiasm but he was too young to be promoted to sergeant. He was too nice of a guy. He needed to be seasoned a bit.

There was a new unit starting up in the federal system. The Bureau of Narcotics and Dangerous Drugs (later to be called DEA) was forming a task force consisting of federal agents and local police detectives. It was the perfect fit for young cops on their way up in the pecking order of the police department. Detective Danno was one of the lucky ones assigned there.

We would hear tales of Detective Danno's adventures in federal narcotic land, for us, the land of milk and honey. He was making a good wage, driving an undercover vehicle, and dressing like a hippy. All of this freedom and he was barely twenty three years old.

The task force would react to almost any information regarding the illegal sales of narcotics. The unit consisted of federal agents, cops, and some investigators from the Illinois State Police.

There wasn't much investigation. If a location was targeted, they would go there en masse, knock on the door, and enter. While inside, they would search for drugs. Most of this was done without a warrant. They were the feds backed by the United States Department of Justice. They were untouchable and successful.

But there is always a fly in the ointment in the cops and crooks game. On the evening of April 23, 1973, the group had received information from a St. Louis City cop that drugs were being sold at a home in Collinsville, Illinois.

They responded. They went to the home in question but were told by the resident that they had the wrong house. They were directed to the house next door, the alleged suspect's house.

The group of cop hippies surrounded the house. The group in the front knocked on the door and a man came to the door. One of the bearded cops showed him a badge. The resident refused to allow them entry.

A cop standing guard at the rear door, of the house subsequently kicked the door in and entered carrying a rifle. The home owner's wife came out of a bedroom and wanted to know what was going on.

A detective with the Illinois State Police later stated that a City of St. Louis cop handcuffed the male resident, pointed a gun at his head and spoke loudly to both the man, and the woman. The house was searched by the detectives.

After realizing their mistaken raid on the wrong house, they removed the handcuffs from the male resident, apologized to the occupants, and exited the house. It appeared the residents accepted the detective's apology.

Subsequent to this raid in Collinsville, Illinois, the raid victims sued the federal government and the St. Louis Metropolitan Police Department for four million dollars.

None of the Illinois State Police detectives were included in the case. They were used to give testimony against the city cops and the federal agents.

Even in the federal system, it's clannish in southern Illinois. It was a witch hunt for the St. Louis cops. The prosecutors wanted their heads. They were appalled that St. Louis cops had the gall to come to southern Illinois and invade a house without a search warrant issued by them.

Federal agents were suspended, cops were second guessed and ridiculed. The entire task force was in deep trouble. Some of the detectives were singled out and sued individually. It was a time of high emotion for all involved.

The feds turned on their agents. Many of the agents lives were ruined by the accusations. Chief Camp could have brought his city cop detectives back to the police department under a cloud of suspicion, but he chose not to. Chief Camp stood by his men.

The attorney for the victims called the detectives barbarians and vigilantes. Detective Danno was eventually exonerated from the case, but the case dragged on for five years before he was cleared.

These were crucial years for a young cop wanting to become cop royalty. No one knew for certain how long Chief Eugene Camp would continue to be the chief of police.

At least three years is required in grade for a young cop to be promoted in succession. The Honorable Board of Police Commissioners would not approve the promotion of a cop burdened by bad publicity.

Time cures all ills. Detective Danno continued with the federal drug unit, but they stayed in the confines of the state of Missouri.

His ambition did not wane. He saved his money and invested in real estate. He acquired a number of houses, rehabbed them, and turned them into rental property.

He bragged to his friends that when he got one million dollars in property he would leave the police department.

Chief Camp was nearing retirement. He promoted Detective Danno. He went to a district as a supervisor of cops. He eventually went to vice as a supervisor. Detective Danno retired at twenty-five years.

Frenchy and Craz toiled for two more years in a police car. They were finally made detectives in 1974 and rode together in a unit that patrolled the city and targeted street criminals.

At the end of a shift they made a decision to drive to the eastside for a few beers. Alcohol is available on the eastside at all hours of the day and night.

While leaving a liquor store parking lot, a street creature jumped into their car. It was a bad decision on his part. Craz was driving, Frenchy was digging into the six pack; the street creature put a gun on them and demanded their cash.   Frenchy shot and killed the robber. The life of a cop never leaves him. He sees things normal folks don't see. He hears deceit in normal conversation. He feels the urge to react when normal folks do not, and sometimes he draws danger to him like a moth to a flame.

It was the case with Frenchy and Craz. Their lifestyle was peaking. It was coming to a head. They had cheated death far too many times.

Craz recognized this fact. He had dwelled too long at the scene of the crime. His life and Frenchy's was a constant moving crime scene. They had always come up the winners, but you can only tempt fate so many times before the fate sisters win.

Craz resigned from the police department to open a "cop bar" on the south side. He had had enough of street crime and heroism. He just wanted to be a detective with his buddy Frenchy, it's all he ever desired, but an intelligent man occasionally needs to reevaluate.

He wanted Frenchy to quit with him, but Frenchy refused to leave, although he did go into a financial partnership with Craz. The bar failed.

Frenchy was transferred from his detective job. For once the cop royalty made a proper decision. Frenchy was like an old race horse. It was time for him to go to pasture. There are places for cops to go for an easy rest of their career; A place where they can eat free, walk around, and talk to decent folks, businessman, and pedestrians.

Frenchy was walking a beat in downtown St. Louis. It's a good job, one of the best. I did it and I can vouch for it.

But Frenchy still longed for his buddies. They would meet and drink beer together whenever they could. A group of cops were going to the Lake of The Ozarks for a beer bash. Frenchy asked Craz to go with him but Craz had another engagement.

The group rented a houseboat. They anchored in a cove. Frenchy went for a late night swim. He didn't get back onto the boat. The next day they found his body.

Gaslight Square in its heyday.
Photo courtesy Virginia Publishing.

**Black Liberator's clubhouse, Leffingwell and Easton. Courtesy
Mercantile Library.**

Lieutenant Robert F. Scheetz,
Detective John Dolan, Detective James Glasscock shortly after
the Black Liberators shot up
the Ninth District Station.

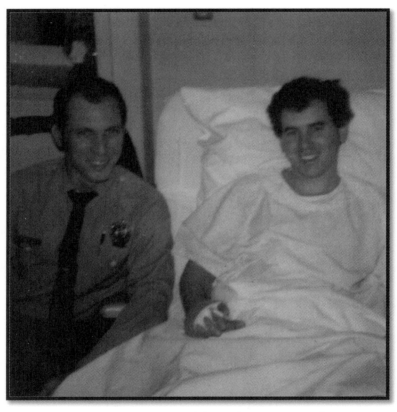

**Patrolman Larry Tinnell (Craz), and
Richard Archaumbault (Frenchy) after the shooting by the
Black Liberation Army at
Grand and Cass.**

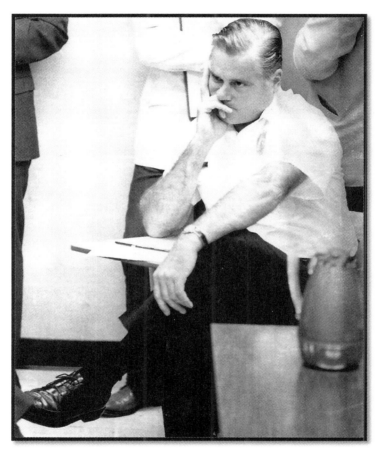

Ninth District Commander Captain Harry Lee. Compliments of the Mercantile Library.

**Ninth District Commander Captain
Bernard (Barney) Mundt. Compliments of
the Mercantile Library.**

**Chief of Detectives Colonel John Doherty.
Compliments of the Mercantile Library.**

Before and after photos of Eastside lawyer and power broker Amiel Cueto.

Detective Glen Lodl.
Compliments of the Mercantile Library.

From left to right----Two unidentified
Customs Agents----Special Agent Steve Stoddard and
Task Force Detective Timothy C. Richards----
Pakistani cooking wok----eight pounds of pure white heroin.
Taken at the DEA Field Office---Clayton, Missouri.

Patrolman/lawyer Mike Williams

Old Ninth District Station---3021 Lucas.

'THE JUNKY COP'

Story four:

On March 16, 1972, the federal government started demolishing the infamous Pruit Igoe Housing Project. It wasn't completely torn down until 1976.

In May of 1972, FBI Director J. Edgar Hoover died. On June 17, 1972, five men were arrested at the Watergate Complex for burglarizing the Democratic National Campaign Headquarters.

President Nixon, was drawn into the burglary of the DNC, and charged with having an illegal slush fund that paid the burglars. He was impeached and resigned the Presidency on August 9, 1974. He was transported to his San Clemente, California, home via military aircraft.

On September 8, 1974, former vice president, now President Gerald Ford issued a full and unconditional pardon of Richard Nixon.

The housing project, these men and their historical events, and the pardon of President Nixon had a great impact on the small/big-city of St. Louis, Missouri, for compared to New York, Chicago, or Los Angeles, St. Louis is small.

When it comes to working the street, FBI agents and city cops are the same. Hoover modernized law enforcement, scientifically, but the streets are the same today as they were back in the 1920's.

After initial academy training, city cops were and are trained by the FBI. We mimic the FBI. When the FBI agents were using Thompson machine guns to shoot down bank robbers in the early 1900's, local cops did the same thing.

It was rumored that FBI agents assassinated criminals. The same rumor applied to city cops. Most cop training comes directly from the FBI, and in most cases FBI agents are conducting the training.

Some fortunate cops are sent to Quantico to go through the FBI National Academy. Federal law enforcement inspires and directs city street cops

As unbelievable as it may seem, the poor folks in the ghettos of the Ninth District were aware of this fact. They learn about the system through churches, rabble rousers, black newspapers. They're poor but not stupid. As long as the monthly government check keeps coming, they are placated, not satisfied.

If a guy pays a group to burglarize someone or something, then he is also a burglar. If a high ranking federal official tells someone to kill someone, then he too is a murderer.

The cops patrolling the black neighborhoods get feedback from the people they come into contact with. We were and are still riders on the same horse.

The black folks knew Pruitt Igoe was a joke which they as a race were the brunt of. Now that it was being demolished and they as a race were being colonized in the old north side neighborhoods, they were the brunt of a new joke.

J. Edgar Hoover was a murderer. Richard Nixon was a burglar. Gerald Ford, in the eyes of the black ghetto dwellers, was an accomplice. They were free men.

The sons, daughters, and friends of the black residents were taken away by the beat cops for possession of a minute amount of marijuana. "Where's the justice?" they would ask.

But the checks kept on coming. The beat cops kept on taking the sick to the hospital. They took the abusive boyfriend to jail, their children to school or to detention. If a family needed food, the beat cop conveyed them to a food pantry. We looked after their everyday needs.

But we were still images of the establishment. When they looked at us driving through their neighborhoods, they saw J. Edgar Hoover and Richard Nixon. Their hatred of the establishment, who in their minds still has them in the chains of slavery, was thrust upon us, the cops patrolling the black communities.

We slowly patrolled at all hours of the day while they glared at us with Marvin Gay "jungle music" pounding in the background. We glared back at them playing the same music on the transistor radios we had to smuggle into our patrol cars. Most days were strange events.

There were smaller political milestones in 1974, closer to the lives of the Ninth District ghetto dwellers and to the hearts and minds of district business owners and cops. For one, Captain Harry Lee was transferred out of the Ninth District.

Harry was transferred to Headquarters. He was an office cop, a guy with nothing to do, with no one to lead. Decisions in headquarters are made by the Office of the Chief of Police. The other high ranking cops were lackies.

Harry finally retired. The city got their money's worth from Harry Lee. He retired after giving the city forty one years of dedication. He did what old cops dream of: they buy land away from the masses.

Harry had a farm in Farmington, Missouri. In July of 1989, he was riding a tractor up a hill and the tractor fell over, killing him. He was sixty eight years old.

Joe Leos, owner of El Sarape Restaurant, was devastated by Harry's death. Joe mourned for him like Harry was a close relative. An out-of-district cop came in for a free meal and said that "Harry was probably drunk when he got killed." Joe asked the cop to leave his restaurant. Harry Lee was a mesmerizing strong personality. Anyone who met him did not forget him.

But all was not lost with the death of the dedicated cop, Harry Lee. His son, Larry Lee, had joined the St. Louis Metropolitan Police Department. He was a lot like his dad, aware and alert. He carried the same pragmatism, had the same look and gait, and was as dedicated.

He made rank quickly, sergeant and then lieutenant and spent most of his time in uniform patrol supervision. It is where the action is. He was assigned to the bloody Ninth District as a sergeant. He was a no nonsense guy.

I had heard a story about a lieutenant in the Seventh District, who had gotten word that the cops on his watch had been buying or confiscating stolen license plate tabs from the local thieves. Missouri is archaic in many ways. One of the strange old fashioned ways was the issuing of yearly or multi-year license plate tabs to show you had paid your taxes and license fees.

The thieves throughout the state stole them on a regular basis. The state would then have to re-issue them. It was and still is a pain for the citizen trying to have mobility in the state of Missouri.

The lieutenant strolled onto the parking lot of the Seventh District station and jotted down the license plate numbers of all of the vehicles on the lot. They were cops personal vehicles.

He went back into the station and entered the plate numbers into the department computer. Over half of them had stolen license plate tabs. He went to roll call and advised his watch that they had two weeks to register their vehicles legally or they would be written up and charged criminally.

I found humor in the lieutenant's revelation. The symbiotic relationship of street creature and cop was alive and well. They depended on one another for survival

This was typical of districts far away from Headquarters. The cop royalty in headquarters didn't care what happened in far northwest St. Louis. It was predominantly black. The districts were dumping grounds for bad attitude cops and commanders who were not politically in tune with the downtown royalty.

The command structure is cyclical. When the political climate changes, cops and commanders from the ethnic trenches get switched for the politicians in headquarters. Few are safe. Every dog has his day.

State Representative Charles Quincy Troupe accused the police department of using the north side as a dumping ground for problem police. He went further stating that homicidal, psychotic police officers were assigned to black neighborhoods.

His comments were sparked by the police shooting of Marilyn Banks who was sitting on her front porch on a summer afternoon in 1983. A police officer fired his weapon at someone else and the bullet struck Miss Banks. The police officer had been involved in nine shootings in six years. Miss Banks was the third person he had shot in the year of 1983.

The police officer started his career in the Ninth District. I knew him, although he wasn't on my watch. He was a likable guy, intelligent and a good cop. He had good insight and good cop vision. He wasn't as good as C.C.Smith, but he was uncanny in spotting criminals and stolen cars.

He wasn't a physical guy. He didn't project the persona of a guy who should have been a cop. When he came to the ninth, he was punched out regularly by street creatures.

Some old cop advised him that he had a gun on his side and that he shouldn't allow himself to be victimized by street folks. The old cop probably laughed up his sleeve as he walked away from the young kid cop.

The cop started pulling his sidearm, and at times using it. He was in several shooting incidents in the ninth. He was desperately seeking recognition from downtown royalty. It wasn't forthcoming in the cop business. There has always been an abundance of police work and a plethora of talent.

He wanted to be referred to as a super cop. He was good but no human is super. He wanted the chief or someone on the police board to make him a detective in the Intelligence Unit, or Homicide.

He was sort of a friend of Chief Camp. He had outside political influence; and he had influential business associates, the Busch family respected him. The demigods will award but they will rarely reward.

He patrolled the bloody ninth during his off hours, using his personal car with a portable red light on the dashboard. Had he been selling life insurance or shoes, or had he been employed by an advertising firm or a construction company, this dedication would have been looked upon favorably. It's the American way, work hard and reap the benefits. His toils got him transferred to the deep north side.

He continued to work the streets on and off duty in his north side district. In his six year career he made 1,750 arrests---650 of them involving felonies----twenty four of those arrests were made off duty.

He was twenty seven years old and was hated by black residents and politicians, but he was also commended for several heroic acts. He was credited for saving the life of a seven month old black child during a snowstorm in 1982.

The "straw that broke the camel's back" was when the officer shot Marilyn Banks. While on duty, the officer was looking for a sixteen year old girl who had threatened him with a knife. They found each other and the officer stated the girl fired three shots at him, causing him to drive his patrol car into a tree.

He chased the girl on foot, fired a warning shot, then took aim and fired at the fleeing sixteen year old girl. He missed the girl but struck Miss Banks, a mother of two small children, who was on her front porch at 5077 Geraldine. She died at square mile hospital.

The officer was placed on desk duty. Representative Troupe and other black leaders called for the officer's suspension. The assistant chief, William Brown countered by stating the officer's suspension could cause protest actions by the Police Officers Association.

Colonel Brown also stated, "It would be unfair to suspend any officer in the same predicament. You can't convict a man before an investigation."

Witnesses said the officer just got out of his police car after wrecking it and began firing at the fleeing sixteen year old. He missed the girl and struck Miss Banks.

The sixteen year old ran home. The father of the girl stated that police officers barged in to his home and demanded he turn his daughter over to them.

He further stated that a police officer placed a gun to his head and told him he was going to blow his brains out if he didn't tell them where his daughter was. He called out for his daughter and she came out of a bedroom. She was turned over to juvenile authorities.

The officer stated he retraced his route and found the twenty five automatic pistol he said was used against him by the girl. The weapon had no ammunition clip. Colonel Brown, assistant chief of police, stated the automatic could not have been fired more than one time without a clip.

The pressure was mounting against the officer and the police department. Circuit Attorney George Peach was forced to prosecute the officer. He was charged with manslaughter and suspended.

The trial was moved to Kansas City, Mo. During the trial a surprise witness testified that he observed the officer drop a gun shortly after the fatal shooting of twenty year old Miss Banks.

The witness stated he heard three shots, ran to the corner of Thekla and Geraldine where he saw a police officer run past him and drop a gun.

The officer was found not guilty and acquitted. The Honorable Board of Police Commissioners held a board hearing into the incident. They ruled that the officer fired his gun carelessly and negligently, falsified a police report, and mishandled evidence in his possession. He was permanently dismissed from the police force.

The officer did what most fired city cops do; he went to Dave Sinclair Ford seeking employment. Dave hired him.

It didn't take Larry Lee long to make sergeant. He was a good test taker and he knew the lay of the land. After his first promotion, he was assigned to the bloody Ninth District.

I had progressed in my cop job and was assigned as a detective in the prestigious Intelligence Unit. My partner was Tom Rangel. The captain of the unit didn't want Tom and me to be partners. We were both laid back and accused of being lazy.

We were under the gun to statistically show arrests, and under pressure from our peers, to have long term investigations. It was what the unit was about. The captain would go to the chief weekly and brag about what his team of crime fighters was doing. But we were not a team. Each crew of two detectives was on its own.

I naturally migrated to the Ninth District looking for someone to lock up. It was home to me. I knew the streets and the crooks. Just like Sergeant Larry Lee.

There was a huge old house in the 2600 block of Howard near the old torn down Pruitt Igoe project. It was an obvious dope crib, people coming, and going and dope being sold on the street in front of the building.

Tom and I set up surveillance on the dope crib and watched it for a couple of weeks, taking down license plate numbers and documenting who the sellers and buyers were.

Heroin had dried up in the city. Some genius pharmacist came up with a recipe: an analgesic and a pain pill that when ground up and injected would give the same feeling of euphoria as heroin. The concoction was called "T's & Blues" and was an instant hit with the heroin seeking junkies.

Tom and I, like the young officer who shot Marilyn Banks, were seeking recognition and awards. We as, a team, had over extended ourselves. We weren't super cops. We were two cops who enjoyed saying that we were detectives in the prestigious Intelligence Unit. It was a huge ego trip for us, and we didn't want to leave the unit so we did foolish and dangerous things.

On a summer day in 1979 we were on surveillance about a block from the house on Howard, parked at the curb nestled in among other ghetto cars, watching through the rear view mirror.

There were approximately twenty dope slingers and buyers standing in the street doing business. There was a dope dealer sitting in a new black Oldsmobile 98. We had previously identified him and knew he was wanted for a felony. He was a disgusting guy who had been arrested previously for rape and robbery and drug dealing. He had just gotten released from the Missouri State Penitentiary.

We were waiting for him to leave the crowd so we could pull him over and arrest him. A car came by our location and observed us. The driver turned the car around and went back to the house on Howard and informed the group of drug dealers they were under surveillance.

Tom and I didn't want to go back to the office without an arrest. I asked Tom if there was a night stick in the car, and he answered "Yes." He had a heavily decorated type night stick, maroon wood with silver tips. Those nightsticks are impressive to look at but are not easily swung because of their weight. The recipient of a head strike can block it or duck away from the blow. They are also difficult to hang on to in a fight because of their weight.

Our captain, George (Bud) Ninteman, didn't like us to use district personnel for assistance. He wanted us to do our own surveillance and make our own unassisted arrests. I figured we were going to need assistance on this arrest, but there was no one for us to call on for help.

Each crew of detectives was in competition with Tom and me and with each other. There was an undercover crew who stalked and documented the mafia types: George Venegoni and Gary Thomlison. They would have helped but their undercover vehicle would be compromised in the ghetto neighborhoods. They never knew where their travels would take them, and good undercover cop cars were hard to come by. Most of the time they were in Illinois or St. Louis County.

A year later Gary Thomlinson was following a Syrian gangster who had wandered in to the Ninth District. Gary stopped his undercover cop car at a red light at Newstead and Delmar. He didn't look like a cop. He looked like a "John". He was skinny, bearded, and wore wire rimmed glasses. The undercover car had trash and a beer can on the dashboard as props.

A prostitute jumped into the undercover cop car, grabbed Gary's revolver, and shot him in the face. It was the end of the police life for Gary. After several surgeries he was put out to pasture with a disability pension.

There was a crew who stayed in the office and wired detectives from other units. Mostly they ran errands for the captain and his lieutenant. They wouldn't have helped us.

Detective Pete Gober and his partner were always in the office doing paper investigations. They would have refused to help us. They thought Tom was okay but despised me behind my back. I get that reaction when I'm in close proximity to groups of my peers. It's a congenital problem.

Pete and his partner were both real good cops. Pete had personality, and he wooed cops from other jurisdictions to give him information on state wide crooks. Their partnership was an office partnership only. They didn't hang out after hours.

Pete rode with me during field training in the ninth. It was just one night but he had his fill of the district, he didn't like it. He was another of the cops who had a relative who dated Chief Gene Camp. Pete got transferred to the Eighth District, a neighboring district to the ninth.

While in Intelligence, Pete and his partner executed a search warrant in the 4700 block of Laclede, Ninth District. He always carried a briefcase with a variety of throw-down pistols, a cache of weed, cocaine and heroin in it, just in case they struck out or had to shoot someone who wasn't armed.

On this bright fall day in 1978 they parked their undercover car on the street and trekked to an apartment complex to execute the warrant. Pete left his briefcase in the car. Someone broke in to it and stole his cache of drugs and throw-down guns.

Pete panicked. He became paranoid and thought the FBI had taken the briefcase. His partner who was pragmatic to a fault calmed him down. I was with them during the execution of the warrant. I would help and assist them.

Pete's partner later got promoted. Pete was never actually seeking a promotion. He was an investigator, and it's what he strived to be. He was transferred to the prestigious DEA Federal Drug Task Force. I was transferred there shortly after Pete. We were never close, but we managed to work together in the drug unit.

Pete started a romantic fling with an employee of DEA, even though he was a married man with a family. Her husband was a federal agent in another agency and most of the cops and agents were friends with the agent. It was an ugly thing to watch, because the civilian employee, wife of the agent was cute, and intelligent. He would bring her to group drinking fests and show her off. We figured her husband/agent was aware of the fling but it caused bad feelings against Pete for infringing on a fellow warrior's wife.

Pete was obese. This worked well for him in DEA, because the dopers didn't suspect him of being a drug agent or even a cop. He carried a Colt revolver in his waistband, and if someone patted him down looking for a gun or a wire, they would miss it. His fat enveloped the weapon or the wire.

Pete, a jealous guy, had another cute, and petite hard-bodied girlfriend. She was a civilian employee in the homicide section. Pete wasn't around a lot. The task force guys are always working, travelling, indisposed, and aloof.

Pete walked into a bar in downtown St. Louis, pulled up a layer of fat, and pulled his pistol on one of his old partners. He put it deeply into the old partner's side and told him he would kill him. What goes around comes around.

When I heard the story I could never figure it out. Pete and this particular partner worked closely together for years. They trusted one another with their lives. I came to the conclusion: "There's no honor among cops." I had studied crooks and I had studied cops, (another congenital problem,) and I came to a realization: "Crooks are the same everywhere. So are the cops." Talk with a cop or a crook from Russia, China, England, Miami, or St. Louis. They mirror one another.

The old partner gained more rank, and with rank comes power. We all have to come back to the police department sooner or later. Cops obtain these cushy assignments because someone of importance likes them. There is always someone with more influential friends than our friends. His old partner, now his arch enemy, was waiting for him. Pete knew life would not be good for him back in the police department.

Pete took a twenty year retirement. He and his hard bodied girlfriend moved to the country. Pete got a job as a country cop in "Sticksville" and made rank. He was still a strong personality, and he was well respected by the cops in and about the little town he was working in. He became ill and had to leave police work. He went to work for a security company as a dispatcher. As luck would have it, the security company offices were in the Ninth District, right down the street from where his briefcase was stolen. Pete eventually had to have a heart transplant. He died a young man.

Each crew was on a mission to get a promotion except Tom and me. We just wanted to investigate organized crooks. The other crews in intelligence were busy guarding dignitaries.

Tom laid the nightstick on the seat as I turned the detective car around. I quickly drove to the dope crib and Tom and I got out. We stood in the street on this bright summer day among the dope slingers. We were outnumbered ten to one. The dope heads cursed us, calling us honky motherfuckers and white pigs. They spat on the blacktop and made aggressive moves toward us, but they did not make contact.

My focus went to the guy sitting in the Oldsmobile. His window was up and the engine was running. I tapped on the window and told him to step out. He was wearing a large brimmed black leather hat. He turned his head to me and said "Fuck you."

I tried the door handle. The Olds was locked up. Tom and I could have shrugged and crawled back to our little detective car with our heads down. It's what the scofflaw dope dealers wanted us to do. It's what they would have done had they been outnumbered.

I had the nightstick in my back pocket out of the sight of the guy in the Olds. I pulled it out and smashed the window of the Olds, unlocked the car, and pulled the wanted subject out in to the street.

My action shocked Tom Rangel, and the drug dealing street vermin. I figured if the dope slingers were going to come to the aid of their compatriot it would be now or never.

I carried a small thirty eight Chief's Special. I had five rounds in the weapon and six more in my pocket. Tom had a six shot Colt. I figured some of the dope slingers were armed. Tom and I were taking things as they came. It was all improvisation.

The guy from the Olds wanted to fight so I hit him up side his head with the nightstick. The stick went flying out of my hand and skidded across the pavement as I brought it back for another whack at his head, and his hat went flying on to the hood of the Olds.

We started fist fighting, exchanging blows, and grappling at the side of the car. He jumped toward his big brimmed hat on the hood. I jumped on the hood after him banging his face with my right fist.

He kept reaching for his hat and he got it. He had a twenty two caliber pistol in his hat liner, and he got it in his hand. I landed a good solid right on his jaw, and he released the hat and the twenty two. They went flying off of the hood. We continued to fist fight off of the hood and back on the street. I finally subdued him and handcuffed him. I figured Tom had the dope slingers at bay, or I would have been attacked from the rear.

I was still in fight mode as I seized the hat and twenty two pistol. I led the wanted dope head to the little detective car. I observed Sergeant Larry Lee with Tom holding their weapons on the group of street dope dealers. Larry Lee had been patrolling and observed us fighting the dopers.

We backed away from the dope mob with guns drawn. They were super excited and wanting revenge for their beaten and arrested compatriot. With our prize handcuffed in the backseat we drove to safety. Larry Lee saved our lives on that fine day. Tom and I would have never won that battle or the war.

Larry Lee was not an office supervisor. He was on the street most of his watch, helping and monitoring his cops, assisting cops in trouble in the bloody Ninth District. He knew what the district was about. He grew up hearing tales about it from his dad. It was a lucky day for Tom Rangel and me.

The new captain in the ninth was Captain Bernard (Barney) Mundt. He had been a John Doherty disciple in the old days of cops and robbers. But he was not like John Doherty or Harry Lee. He was the exact opposite of them.

Barney was a showman. He wore tailored suits and diamond rings. He always had a tan to back up his white head of hair, and he smoked big expensive cigars. His demeanor was that of a guy trying to sell himself. First impressions were a big deal for him. He knew how to schmooze.

Barney associated with union gangsters. He was a gambler, always had at least a $1000 in his pocket, and gambled three times a week; mostly gin rummy card games.

The card games were held at the union officials' offices late at night. There were times when a district cop would get a call to meet the captain at 300 S. Grand, Council Plaza (Union complex), to drive Barney home after an evening of drinking and gambling.

Barney was highly respected, even though most cops knew he was a "spoofer" with a tan in an expensive suit.

A new crazy cop came to the ninth. His dad was a lieutenant on the department, and the crazy cop knew the in's and out's of dealing with the cop bureaucracy. He grew up around the job. It was second nature to him.

Through his family, he knew Barney Mundt. He knew him so well that he disrespected him. I always felt that he would go home to his parents and say something about Captain Mundt, and his parents would react negatively about Barney. Back in the day participants in the cop game knew what dastardly deeds each ranking cop had done in their early years.

It was common knowledge how cops got promoted, who their "ace" was, and what he did to achieve fame and fortune in the "poor folks cop game".

The new crazy cop was apparently on some kind of drug, maybe prescription. He would wander into Barney's office and argue with him over nothing. It rankled Barney but he did nothing about it. The crazy cop apparently had the "goods" on him.

The crazy cop was big time trouble for the district and the police department, but he had the backing of several politicians on the "Hill" area of the city and would soon be promoted, given a personal cop detective car, and moved to an office in headquarters to spend the rest of his life.

A Second District cop was on patrol on the south side. It was the night watch, and the area he was patrolling had been hit hard by a burglar who kicked open business doors and walked out with whatever he wanted.

The patrolling cop observed a guy get out of a car at a strip mall, walk up to a Singer Sewing Machine store, and kick the door open.

The cop drove to the front of the store and observed the burglar walking out carrying a sewing machine. The cop drew his revolver and arrested the burglar. The burglar was the crazy Ninth District cop with the influential dad. He was fired and prosecuted. Barney Mundt was a happy man.

Barney was always looking for an aide, someone to do his typing, organizing of reports, lengthy administration and allegations of misconduct memorandums.

He transferred a guy into the district who was good at office work. Patrolman Bruce Highley was in my academy class. He was a different kind of a cop.

His dad was a lifer cop. Bruce was a civilian aide, meaning he assisted the commanders of the bureau where he worked. He was an office "pinky" and good at it.

Bruce had been assigned to the homicide section for most of his career as a civilian. The reports in homicide are long and tedious to put together. Several detectives write on different portions of the investigations. Bruce would piece the report together and then type it for the homicide dicks. He was appreciated and well respected.

The problem with being a civilian employee in the city is the pension. It is weak. The cop pension is strong. The basis of police work is pension and discretion. Remove one of them and cops will leave for greener pastures.

The most hated form of police work is paper work. Many cops aren't good at it. All of them hate it. That's how Bruce came to being in my academy class.

His dad had a brain storm that Bruce should be a cop instead of an office "pinky" so he advised Bruce to apply for the academy.

Bruce did, and with the support of many of the commanders on the fourth floor (Bureau of Investigation) he was accepted as a cop candidate.

Bruce was treated with "kid gloves" in the academy. High ranking cops checked on him periodically. A group of detectives in "Vice" took him out of class so he could pose as a "john" in a prostitution sting. He got "beat up" by a hooker. He was in a hotel room when the hooker asked him if he was a cop. He apparently did not convince her so she grabbed a house phone and bashed him in the face with it. The detectives had to rush in and save him. Bruce was cop royalty and he hadn't yet graduated from the Police Academy.

Bruce stayed away from most of the Viet Nam veterans in the class. We were rude and crude, smoked cigarettes, and were hung over most of the time. Even during physical training or at shower time, Bruce kept to himself. He would not shower with the class.

He was a married guy, but there were rumors swirling around the academy about him. Most of us didn't care. Even though he was a class mate, none of us knew him.

After we all went to a district, I would see Bruce occasionally while on duty. He always wore the dress uniform, full blouse with Sam Brown Belt across his chest. It was a strange way to dress, and I never could figure what kind of a message he was trying to send. Having that much clothing on was uncomfortable and dangerous. It gave a crazy ghetto creature something to hang on to when he was fighting for control for your revolver.

Brucie showed up at the ninth with his dress uniform, bleached blonde hair, and a smile. He was Barney's main aide. That meant he got weekends off and good hours during the week. He didn't have court, didn't have to fight crazy people or haul bloated dead bodies to the morgue.

It was all a plan by his dad. He knew that it wouldn't take long for Brucie to land a clerical job within the department. But now, but he would carry a badge and a gun and have a good pension. "The best laid plans of mice and men."

But Brucie had a blot on his name. He had been in the Third District. On an afternoon watch late in his shift he went into a vacant building without notifying the dispatcher of his location.

We had gotten portable radios from a generous government grant and every cop had one. He later told investigators that he tried to contact the dispatcher, but the radio would not transmit.

The alleged reason for entering the vacant building was to pursue a burglar. While inside, in the dark, he allegedly confronted the burglar and attempted to arrest him. After a daring fight, Brucie was shot with his own revolver.

It was a slight wound to his side, but it caused a firestorm in the Third District. The on duty cops sped to Brucie's aid after he eventually got on the radio waves and advised the dispatcher that he had been shot.

Brucie was rushed to the hospital and admitted. He was out in days with no lasting damage. In his mind, he was now a hero. He had been wounded in-the-line-of-duty.

The story line didn't add up. Investigators checked the radio transmissions for Brucie's radio. He had never keyed up to speak. Why would the radio work after the shooting but not before? The incident was swept under the carpet. No one really cared.

A police captain's phone is always ringing. In many instances it is a citizen snitching on a cop for something that the cop did off-duty. We couldn't be private citizens. Our families aren't private citizens. In many ways our lives were open books.

Someone telephoned Barney Mundt about Brucie. The caller advised Barney that Brucie was having sexual relations with a Catholic priest, and that the two of them were sexually involved with some Ninth District children.

Barney was known for having couth, but he couldn't contain himself after this revelation. He confronted Brucie with the allegation. Brucie didn't deny it. Barney ordered him to resign and walked out of the office.

Brucie took Barney's police command car keys from his desk, walked to the garage, and drove off with it. He drove to the Cathedral at Taylor and Lindell, parked the car, and walked inside. He wandered in to the rectory and shot himself in the head.

The cop answering the call for Brucie's death almost went into shock seeing him lying there with his brains blown out, wearing his dress uniform, his bleached blonde hair matted with blood.

Brucie was dead and that should have been the end of the story, but it wasn't. Brucie's dad heard the sexual abuse allegation, and that his son had committed suicide. He was hurt, but more than hurt he was furious. He drove home where he and Brucie and Brucie's wife lived. He shot Brucie's wife and then shot himself to death. Brucie's wife survived.

The government had, for decades, been rebuilding the slum property in north St. Louis. The Jeff Vander Lou neighborhoods, which were within the confines of Jefferson, Vandeventer, Natural Bridge, and St. Louis Avenues, were called the "Negro neighborhoods" at the beginning of the overhaul.

The housing was of brick structure which meant it met the government criteria for rehabbing. The fed contracted with outside developers to rehab entire neighborhoods at the same time. It gave work to the tradesman and housing to the poor.

The St. Louis Metropolitan Police Department was actively searching for eligible minorities to become police officers. "Minorities" meant black men and women. I could never understand why they were referred to as minorities. Black folks were not in the minority in the City of St. Louis, Missouri.

Many of the applicants came from the north side and specifically from Jeff Vander Lou neighborhoods. Several were hired, and after training in the police academy, were sent back to their neighborhoods to patrol.

The transition from "street kid" to cop isn't easy. Most kids are "street kids" no matter where they grow up. Kids in Ladue are "street kids" just like in Jeff Vander Lou. Almost every kid is a scofflaw and most kids hate cops.

In order to survive in the cop business, the cop must sever his ties with his childhood friends. In their eyes you have gone to the other side. They want you back as their compatriot. You are blood to them, and they will resort to anything to get you back to their level of existence.

Patrolman Marvin Allen was a Jeff Vander Lou kid. He joined the cops in the early 1970's and fell into the routine of a cop street warrior.

Shortly after he became a cop, he accidentally shot himself with his cop revolver. There is always an explanation for an accidental shooting. Rookie cops are in love with their new cop revolvers. It means the end of being bullied for life.

Usually when someone involuntarily shoots oneself it is because they are intoxicated and playing with their gun. Cops don't put much faith in accidents, but the case wasn't delved in to and it went away.

Shortly after the shooting fiasco, Patrolman Allen was found in a residence when a drug raid was conducted by city narcotics' detectives. He was on sick leave at the time. He was not arrested but he was demoted to probationary patrolman.

Chief Camp had favors to fill. He couldn't promote all of the friends of the politicians who had befriended him along the way to chiefdom. It was almost impossible. So Chief Camp invented a new unit. He called it TACT, an acronym for Tactical Anti-Crime Team.

Chief Camp told the press that this unit was comprised of the best officers the city police department had to offer. His comment was a kick in the gut to the hard working beat cops in the black neighborhoods. The cops I worked with weren't asked to join TACT. Neither was I.

Someone with influence liked Marvin Allen. He was appointed to a position in TACT. A friend of a friend asked Chief Camp to help Marvin Allen out in the department. It worked.

In contrast to Marvin Allen was Steve Jacobsmeyer. Steve wasn't a street kid. He had the best of everything. He grew up in a cop family. His dad was cop royalty, a Lieutenant Colonel, Assistant Chief of Police. His uncle was the commander of homicide.

There was no doubt that Steve Jacobsmeyer would become a cop and would rise to the top of the cop totem pole. He was the all American boy, studious, reverent and groomed to St. Louis greatness. He knew the way of the police department before he ever set foot in the Personnel Division to fill out an application. Steve Jacobsmeyer and Marvin Allen became partners in the prestigious TACT unit.

The chief manned the unit with cronies and placed it in the basement of Headquarters. "Frenchy" Richard Archaumbault and "Craz" Larry Tinnell were assigned to TACT several years after the Black Liberation Army shootout. It was away from the eyes and ears of almost anyone in or outside of the police department.

There is a grand scheme in the St. Louis Metropolitan Police Department just like there is in big-business, for law enforcement in a city like St. Louis is big-business. More than a third of the city's revenue goes toward the police department.

The leaders of the St. Louis Police Department are constantly trying to justify their existence. They don't want the citizens of their fair city to ask themselves an obvious question; "What has a big-city-cop ever done for me?"

The folks who didn't pay taxes could reflect on the services they demanded and are receiving from local beat cops in a positive note, but they wouldn't.

For the average tax-paying citizen, the only contact they have with a cop is when they are on the receiving end of a speeding ticket and a lecture.

If a citizen is stranded on a city street and seeks assistance by waving to a passing city cop, he or she will get a return wave and a police car speeding away from them. Cop philosophy is that, if you really need a cop, you will dial 911. They don't take into consideration that, when you were just robbed, the robber also stole your cell phone and all of your money.

Specialized units like TACT (Tactical Anti-Crime Team) are experiments in police/community relations. They are formed to show the citizens of the city that the police department really cares about their plight, their unsafe feeling walking to their vehicles after a dinner date, their broken car window, their stolen vehicle, their burglarized home.

The chief tosses a group of cops into a unit, gives it an acronym, and turns them loose on the street. The cops, now detectives, aren't given assignments. They aren't told to go to location A and follow a crook to location B so that you can arrest him.

The new detectives are on their own to glorify their names so that somewhere down the line they will be promoted by their aces. It's kind of like selling life insurance. The detectives ask friends, relatives, and enemies for clues about criminals.

It takes a certain kind of supervisor to get results in a unit like TACT. He/she must have the ability to shame the detectives into obtaining information for the unit. Arrests and warrants issued are the life blood of the newly formed unit.

The common "Buzz phrase" of newly formed investigative units is: "The chief went out on a limb for you guys. He brought you all here so you could prove yourselves to him and to your family and friends. Do not embarrass the chief."

The stats are checked monthly. Existence must be justified to City Hall, the Honorable Board of Police Commissioners, and the local newspaper. The new detectives react to any clue. They are doing it for the Chief of Police. They are doing it for themselves. Nothing else matters.

As a team, TACT Detectives Steve Jacobsmeyer and Marvin Allen received information that heroin was being sold at 2505 North Market. Without fanfare, they responded to that address.

White heroin junkies frequented north St.Louis, travelling from one dope house to another looking for a fix. They come from Illinois, Jefferson County, St. Charles County, West County, South County, and North County.

If one dope house was sold out, they would be directed to another one nearby. It was a cooperative venture for the neighborhood heroin dealers. It was not uncommon for a white boy to come to the door of a ghetto house and ask for dope.

In the summer of 1976 at approximately 10:30 p.m. Detectives Steve Jacobsmeyer and Marvin Allen parked their undercover cop car in front of the dope house on North Market and devised a plan. Steve would go to the door and ask for some "caps," and Marvin would back him up out of sight.

They initiated their plan. Steve walked to the front porch and banged on the door. Willie Grady McCurry came to the door. Steve advised him he wanted to buy two caps, and Willie told him, "Okay, I'll be right back."

Willie left, then returned with a gun and some dope. In the meantime Detective Marvin Allen joined Steve Jacobsmeyer on the porch in plain view.

When Willie observed Detective Allen, he started shooting. Steve Jacobsmeyer was shot in the neck. Marvin Allen was shot in the shoulder.

Willie McCurry slammed and locked the door. After Steve got on the air and told the dispatcher he and Marvin Allen had been shot, another crew of detectives arrived on the scene.

TACT detectives converged on the house. Willie shouted out that he was giving up, but instead he fled out the back door. He was arrested in his backyard.

Steve Jacobsmeyer's wound was serious. Any gunshot wound can be a death sentence, but a neck wound by the carotid artery is more serious than most.

The arriving cops rushed Steve and Marvin Allen into a cruiser and sped to Firmin Desloge Hospital. Their lives were spared.

The house was searched, three grams of heroin and eighteen grams of marijuana were found.

Willie McCurry went to trial and was convicted of "Possession of Heroin" and "Assault to Kill". He was sentenced to ninety five years in the Missouri State Penitentiary.

McCurry later filed a suit against Steve Jacobsmeyer, Marvin Allen, unknown police officers, and the police department claiming he was beaten by police and that officers illegally searched his home without a warrant. The suit was dismissed.

Steve Jacobsmeyer filed a counterclaim against Willie McCurry and was awarded $105,000. Of course Steve didn't collect any money from the incarcerated heroin dealer. The suit was symbolic. If crooks can sue cops, then cops can sue crooks.

Steve Jacobsmeyer was born with the name. Now he had the fame. Being shot in the line-of-duty brought more attention to him. He also was now a bona fide cop hero.

Steve filed a workman's compensation lawsuit against the police department for his injuries incurred in the shooting. There are lawyers who specialize in these suits, but Steve decided to go it alone. Lawyers get twenty five percent of the cash award. It's a racket for the lawyers.

The Workers comp suits are cut and dried. Steve knew that all the lawyer does is file the suit and then wait for a judge to make the award. He received one hundred percent of his award for being shot in the line-of-duty. He invested in real estate and went into the real estate business, part time.

The TACT unit clambered on. Steve Jacobsmeyer got promoted to sergeant. He was now a supervisor of cops which meant he sat in an office and studied the statistics of his men and tried to figure out ways to motivate and manipulate them.

Marvin Allen eventually went back to a district in uniform. He was a radio call "shagger" going from one ghetto home to another one, asking and answering the same questions, making the same threats, telling the same lies and solving nothing. A meager attempt at keeping the peace.

Things were changing in the police department. Guys who went to college now had degrees. Most elected to stay with the police department. It was a rational choice. Our moniker was changed. We were now referred to as Police Officer instead of Patrolman.

Chief Camp turned sixty five and was forced to retire. He petitioned the Honorable Board of Police Commissioners for an extension but it was denied. He then presented thousands of hours of overtime he stated he had worked and requested he be paid for it. That request was denied.

Chief John Berner was now the chief of police. He was a pro-cop, hands-off chief of police. He loved the guys answering the radios and wrestling the drunks. Entitlements were on the wane.

On July third 1979, Police Officer John Leo Rice, assigned to the Sixth District, on the north side, was riding his bicycle home from the afternoon watch. He rode his ten speed bicycle frequently, it was his primary mode of transportation.

John was a sight to all who knew him. Cops as a group were not bikers. As far as most cops were concerned bikes were for kids. John rode his to work, to court, or for anything else he needed to do.

When John rode to and from work, he wore civilian clothing. He didn't look like a cop. He was spectacled, stone faced, and different looking. He looked like a victim.

At approximately 1:05 a.m. John was riding south on Jefferson just inside the Ninth District boundaries at about Delmar, close to the center of the street trying to avoid debris in the roadway.

Just north of Delmar, a dark Pontiac passed John on the right, cut in front of him and stopped about ten or fifteen feet in front of him. John stopped his bike and waited for the vehicle to move.

A black guy, passenger (Larry King), got out of the Pontiac. He had a nickel plated Colt Python .357 magnum in his hand. John looked at the guy and the gun and made some instantaneous decisions.

John figured the gun belonged to a cop. It was the kind of gun cops carried. The guy flourishing the Python at him was definitely not a cop. He had a corn rows haircut. "He's got a cop gun but he's not a cop," John surmised.

John slipped his hand under his vest and grabbed his model ten Smith and Wesson cop revolver out of his shoulder holster. John was a gun guy. He had mentally trained himself for a confrontation like the one presenting itself to him.

He was indecisive at this point in the confrontation; Larry King made John's decision for him. He fired the Python at John, ghetto style, pistol canted horizontally, wrist bent.

John felt Larry King was surprised at the recoil of the Python, and he knew he had to seriously wound Larry King before he recovered control of the Python and shot at him again.

John fired six times with the Smith and Wesson cop gun, using both hands, waist level, without aiming, at a distance of twelve to fifteen feet, just like we are trained to do at the pistol range

John hit Larry King three out of the six times, once in the stomach, once in the right shoulder, and once in the right hand. He collapsed in a heap. The Python fell to the pavement.

The driver of the vehicle got out and stared at John as John stared at him, then they both looked at Larry King lying in the street clutching his gut. John realized he had fired all of his six shots from the six shot revolver.

John dropped the cop revolver on the pavement and rushed to the Python. The driver realized that John was going to get to the Python before he could so he jumped back into the Pontiac and sped east on Delmar.

John fired the last five shots from the Python into the Pontiac as it drove away. He fired two double action and as the vehicle got farther away he cocked the weapon and slowly aimed and squeezed the trigger. The car, riddled with bullet holes, was abandoned a couple of blocks away.

John had more bullets in his left pocket, but they were mixed with change, keys, and a roll of lifesavers. John advised me the incident was a learning experience and that now, if he carries a revolver he always has two speed loaders. If he carries an automatic he always has two magazines and they are always carried in a pocket with nothing else.

John approached the subject he had shot who was lying on his stomach. The suspect, (Larry King) advised John that he was uncomfortable and that his stomach was "on fire."

John told him he would call an ambulance for him. A taxi cab came by and stopped. John asked the cabbie to call the police. Larry King asked John to roll him over onto his back. John complied. The police arrived.

Homicide arrived and took over the crime scene. John was questioned about the driver, the one who got away. John advised that the driver was a black guy, twenty seven years of age, six feet tall and about 180 pounds. John said he could identify him if he ever saw him again.

The car that the two robbers used was stolen at gunpoint (car

jacked) from an elderly female. It had been used in other street rob-
beries in the city. The investigation began. A police officer (David
Wilmering) was detailed at City Hospital Number One Emergency
Room to guard Larry King prior to his surgery to remove the bullet
from his stomach.

A person entered the room Larry King and Police Officer Wilmering were in. He advised he was a cousin to Larry King and that
King was like a brother to him. He was cordial to both of them then
advised the officer that he was a city cop, and showed his badge. He
identified himself as Marvin Allen of the Eighth District.

Officer Marvin Allen walked to Larry King and stated, "Fish,
what's goin on?" The two began a conversation of whispers, getting
close to each other's ears so Officer Wilmering could not hear what
they were saying.

During the whispered conversation, a doctor came in to the room
and requested that Marvin Allen leave the room so Larry King could
be prepared for surgery. He was asked several times to leave the room
but he remained. Officer Wilmering ordered Marvin Allen to leave the
room, and he finally did.

After Larry King was prepped for surgery, he was wheeled out of
the Emergency Room and past the waiting Marvin Allen. Marvin Allen walked next to the gurney whispering in Larry King's ear.

They got on an elevator to the operating room and Marvin Allen
got on with them, whispering with Larry King. They got off on the
operating room floor; Marvin Allen followed them. Officer Wilmering
ordered him off of the operating room floor. Marvin Allen took the
elevator down.

Homicide ran a computer check on the Colt Python .357 magnum
Larry King used to shoot at Officer John Rice. It came back issued to
Marvin Allen, a police officer in the Eighth District. He had reported
it stolen shortly after the shooting/robbery incident with John Rice.

A photo lineup of Marvin Allen, in civilian attire, and two other
subjects was shown to Officer John Rice. He was asked to try and
identify the subject who had gotten out of the car and then rushed
back to it and fled the scene. John Rice chose Marvin Allen. It wasn't
a positive identification, but John was almost certain Marvin Allen was
the driver of the car.

Police Officer Marvin Allen was brought into the homicide offices
and placed in an interview room. The detectives began the interview

by talking about Marvin Allen's visit of suspect Larry King at City Hospital Number One.

Officer Allen stated that he and Larry King were old friends and that he had heard he had gotten shot and had decided to visit him.

He was asked how he heard about the shooting. Officer Allen said his girlfriend, Gwen Sampson told him Larry King had been shot and was at City Hospital Number One. He stated he did not know how Gwen Sampson found out.

Officer Allen further stated that at the time of the shooting he was at his mother's house at 5461 Arlington. Also present at that time was his mother, Wilma Bailey, her boyfriend Cassius Bailey, and his sister Belinda Allen. He refused to answer any more questions from the detectives.

Marvin Allen was escorted to Prisoner Processing and booked for "Assault First Degree, Attempt Robbery, Robbery, and making a false report of a crime (stolen Python .357). All charges were issued except the false report charge.

The detectives responded to 4803 Fountain to interview Officer Allen's girlfriend, Gwen Sampson. She corroborated Officer Allen's statement and stated she heard of the shooting of Larry King from a friend of hers named Sheana. She declined to make any other statement.

The detectives responded to City Hospital Number One to interview suspect Larry King who had just gotten out of surgery to remove the bullets from his body, placed there by Officer John Rice.

They read him his constitutional rights and asked him about the night of the shooting and robbery.

Larry King stated that he and Marvin Allen were riding around the city and needed some money for liquor. Marvin was driving and they were at about Jefferson and Delmar when they saw a white guy on a bicycle.

"Since we had no money, we decided to take the bike. I got out of the car with Marvin's gun and walked down the street with it in my hand. I got within three feet of the guy and found myself lying in the street shot."

Officer Marvin Allen eventually pled out and was sentenced to seventy five years in the Missouri State Penitentiary. He did five years and was released on parole. He was killed in an alley near Union and Harney trying to buy a ten dollar button of heroin.

Larry King was released at about the same time. He was killed by a knife to his chest by his girlfriend when he tried to take her food stamps to trade for drugs.

Police Officer John Rice was awarded the "Medal of Valor" (the highest award offered by the city of St. Louis) and remained a district cop for thirty years. He retired and took a job with the City of St. Louis Sheriff's Office.

I asked John why he retired; "I got tired of shagging calls," he replied.

Chief John Berner retired and Robert Scheetz was promoted to chief of police. Chief Scheetz was respectful to the Jacobsmeyer family and to Steve Jacobsmeyer.

Chief Scheetz had a plan: do three years as chief and then move to Florida with his new wife. As time went on he relinquished most of his chief duties to his aides. His mind wasn't in St. Louis, it was in Naples, Florida.

As Chief Scheetz neared retirement he had some decisions to make concerning his future in St. Louis. He owned two houses in south city, and he needed to sell them. They had been on the market for some time and were not moving.

Chief Scheetz was an entitlement guy. One of the cop royalty ploys was to identify talented cops without rank or prestige and use them to better the royalty cops' stature in life. Quid pro quo was and is a way of life in the St. Louis Metropolitan Police Department.

Patrolman Carpenter, a guy who had been a district cop for his entire career, was introduced to the chief and was mesmerized by him. He was good with a hammer and a saw, and he was in awe of Chief Scheetz. The chief smiled and joked with Patrolman Carpenter, drank beer with him, and invited him to his residence.

The house needed carpentry work, a lot of it, before it could be sold. Patrolman Carpenter volunteered to do the work.

The chief decided the house also needed a wood burning fireplace. It was a large two story home. Patrolman Carpenter got started on the massive remodeling job immediately.

Building materials are expensive. Patrolman Horowitz, a Ninth District graduate, another cultivated friend of the chief whose wife had a good paying job, volunteered to pay for the building materials. He knew business people, hardware, and lumber yard people.

The remodeling job dragged on. Patrolman Carpenter labored day and night knowing after he finished the remodeling job, he would be rewarded by his idol. Patrolman Horowitz kept signing checks at the hardware store.

Both officers were later assigned to the prestigious Drug Enforcement Administration Task Force. I was there with them. Patrolman Horowitz was assigned with me. Patrolman Carpenter came later.

Detective Horowitz relished being a pawn in the quid- pro-quo system. While at DEA, he regularly had expensive floral arrangements sent to the federal supervisors. They did not refuse them. In return Detective Horowitz got his pick of the seized government cars made available to us.

My desk at DEA was right next to Detective Horowitz. I heard most of his telephone conversations. I soon figured out his path to power within the drug unit. I asked him why he was spending his hard earned money on the mini federal bureaucrats. I didn't know his past with the chief at the time. His method of persuasion had gotten him detached to the feds. It's what most cops desired.

I was older than Detective Horowitz and had been in the cop game a lot longer. I tried to counsel him. "St. Louis cops aren't supposed to send gifts to their supervisors," I advised him. He laughed at me.

I later found out that he had been successful in the past with his barrage of gifts. I watched and listened to the phone calls to supervisors past and present. It amazed me how he could manipulate his targets. Had I been a supervisor I would have turned down any gifts, flowers or tickets or anything else. Detective Horowitz was able to read his bosses. He knew they were vulnerable and were lacking the one thing that made them vulnerable to his gift giving: character. None of them had any. He amazed me.

For a pair of Cardinals baseball tickets, he got to travel to warm places in the winter and cool places in the summer doing drug investigations for the federal government. Quid- pro- quo is alive and well in the federal system also. Patrolman Carpenter was eventually promoted to Sergeant and remained in the drug unit. When he was eventually reassigned to the street, Chief Scheetz had retired and left the area.

The new chief, Ron (Bubba) Henderson, waited for his chance to bushwhack Sergeant Carpenter. The department personnel had heard the stories about Carpenter and Horowitz. Most of the cop royalty partook of the talents of their personnel. The rank and file cops desired to be friends with the demigods. It was a way of life, a way to get ahead.

The new chief was probably angry because Sergeant Carpenter and Detective Horowitz didn't do any carpentry work on his house. He got Sergeant Carpenter by having his aides scrutinize Sergeant Carpenter's squad of officers. Some were found congregating in a service station, a violation of the cop manual.

It was duly noted by the chief, and Sergeant Carpenter was accused in an official allegation for failure to supervise his officers.

After years of special treatment, the beneficiary becomes spoiled. Scrutiny is the kiss of death. The special cop can't live with it. Sergeant Carpenter was hounded by the new chief and left the department early without a full pension. But things got worse for Sergeant Carpenter. His wife left him for another man. He was divorced and the wife took fifty percent of his savings and the value of his home.

Patrolman Horowitz came back to the police department and landed a good job in Headquarters. He became good friends with another new police chief, He retired at twenty years and took a city job managing the city tow lot.

He was indicted federally for a scheme concerning the selling of towed cars, pled guilty, and was sent to a federal penitentiary. It was big news in the city and the police department. The new chief's daughter had been driving a towed vehicle, a BMW, one that belonged to someone else. High ranking officers were buying towed vehicles for next to nothing. His chief buddy retired under a veil of corruption because of the towing lot scandal.

.

Chief Scheetz was in need of someone trustworthy to list and sell his houses. Steve Jacobsmeyer was the cop who could do the job. He listed his houses and sold them for the chief.

Steve Jacobsmeyer, the cop with a pedigree, was promoted to lieutenant and then to captain. He was in a hotel room in Chicago, Illinois, with his girlfriend. They loudly argued and scuffled. The Chicago police were called.

They handled the incident like most cops do; they placed the girlfriend on a bus back to St. Louis and advised Steve he should leave town.

He returned to a firestorm of controversy. Chief Scheetz had retired and the new chief was Clarence Harmon. Clarence wasn't mesmerized by the Jacobsmeyer name. Steve had only been a cop for twenty two years and he was already a captain. He was a junior VP in the cop corporation.

Steve was charged by the Honorable Board of Police Commissioners for allegedly beating his girlfriend and his wife.

A hearing officer at a police board trial concluded that Steve was guilty of the internal charges of bringing discredit on the department and lying to investigators regarding the allegations. Steve was never charged criminally.

Steve denied the abuse charges. He said his ex-wife and girlfriend were vindictive and trying to discredit him. He also said that Chief Clarence Harmon wanted to demote him in order to fill the captain's vacancy with another officer.

Leaders of counseling and advocacy agencies for abused women wrote letters to the police board urging that Steve Jacobsmeyer be fired.

About twenty five of those leaders picketed police headquarters while the board wrestled with the Jacobsmeyer decision. Steve turned in his badge and gun and took early retirement. He wanted to spare family and friends any more turmoil. "The only thing abused here is the truth," was Steve's only comment.

Steve dove full time into his real estate business. He now owns and operates his own firm, Jacobsmeyer Realty, and sells and manages real estate throughout the St. Louis area. He has rental property and salesmen working for his firm.

I visited Steve several months ago. He sits in his big office in front of a messy desk, smoking big cigars, and talking on the phone. He assured me he was a happy man.

Bob Scheetz, living the good life in Naples, was out of sight but not out of mind. Folks who knew him well were naturally curious about him. He was now a high profile guy.

A couple of his kids became St. Louis cops and they would keep his friends back home informed about his life in paradise.

'THE PURSUIT'

Story five:

When Bob Scheetz would preach to us, all of us young energetic cops sitting in the basement of the slum station house in the slum Ninth District, wondering what the day or night would bring to us, he would hit us with various topics hoping to influence us in our daily lives. Just like a real preacher would do from the pulpit. There were usually forty or so cops at roll call silently wondering what they had done in their lives to deserve such a fate.

Manpower was cheap during those ancient days. The department didn't pay overtime, any work done after eight hours was comp time. The compensation slips were kept behind the duty desk in a file cabinet. Whenever a cop filled one out, the watch commander would sign it.

If a cop screwed up real bad, the watch commander could and would go behind the desk, dive in to the comp files, obtain the officer's comp records, and hold them up for the cop to look at. Some of them had 1000's of hours of comp time. Cops would tack them on to their vacations and get months off instead of weeks. It was an incentive to work overtime.

As the cop in trouble and his peers watched, the watch commander would tear up the compensation files of the bad boy cop. We rationalized the treatment as mild. If a cop screwed up bad and often, he would be placed under allegation and sent to Internal Affairs. That usually meant being fired or at least suspended.

As much as the cops moaned and groaned about the city cop job, few really wanted to leave it. Discretion was what made the job neat. Discretion gave us power and a feeling of belonging. It made us feel important. We could do whatever we wanted as long as we could explain it. Most cops are good writers. We could explain our way out of trouble.

I had the privilege of working on almost all of the different platoons and working for all of the watch commanders. I went to college during the day so I worked the night watch often. Cops didn't mind switching shifts with me. An afternoon watch for a night watch was an easy decision. Cops hate the night watch. It is unnatural to be up all night and sleep all day. You never feel rested. And if you are up all night, sit in a classroom most of the day, and then try and get some sleep before you come to work, it's even worse.

In the summer the night watch never slows down. It's the busiest watch to be assigned to. It's dead in the winter, so winter is when I tried to stay on nights.

A watch commander, Bob Truetken who I worked for briefly during the night watch, was beside himself with the night burglaries that were plaguing the district.

Lieutenant Truetken was a young and sharp cop. He took care of himself, and he looked neat and military in his uniform. He quickly made friends with a police commissioner and he was promoted to sergeant and then lieutenant in under eight years.

The commissioner's tenure is four years. After the commissioner left the department Bob Truetken was exiled to the Ninth District.

Bob tried hard to gain the admiration of his troops and his supervisors, but it wasn't working for him. The troops could care less about rank or how it was gotten. Most were assured that they were never going to be on the receiving end of a promotion. They were mired in to the Ninth District soil and they accepted their fate.

The supervisors (sergeants) had jumped through hoops, befriended any state legislator they could find, and eventually paid the $3500 fee to get promoted, so they weren't impressed with an eight year lieutenant.

The end result was at least one big business burglary a night on the night watch. Business people would flock to the station and complain to the captain about the burglaries. The captain would put out special patrols, set up surveillance with detectives, and place cops inside of businesses but they kept on happening.

McHenry Metal, a truck fabricating business in the district and a company who did work for the police department and the city, was being hit regularly. The guy who owned it was a VIP and wired in to city politics. He had clout.

Clout was what Bob Truetken was searching for. It was what he was accustomed to. If he could make captain then he might be able to run for the office of chief when Gene Camp retired. It seemed like most cops with rank desired to be the chief of police.

He made friends with the businessman, and he promised him that he would have his men stake out McHenry Metal for the entire night while his watch was on nights. He preached to us nightly about the burglaries. He was almost as good as Bob Scheetz in getting his opinion out to the troops but not quite.

The troops referred to Bob Truetken as "Burglar Bob", and they made fun of him behind his back. They would imitate him standing at the pulpit preaching before roll call, and when "Burglar Bob" took the pulpit, some of the down and out, exiled for life Ninth District quagmire cops would laugh in his face. Bob didn't know why. I felt it hurt his feelings, and I felt distress for him.

The preaching about the burglaries, and the promises to the owner of McHenry metals was in vain. The business still was burglarized. Bob came to roll call after the latest burglary. He was carrying a sub machine gun, probably taken as a prop from Harry Lee's closet.

"If you see an open door, or if you think there is a burglary in progress, don't take any action. Call me and I will respond. We're going to get those bastards tonight. I will eliminate them once and for all." He held the machine gun high in the air with his right hand like a Black Panther guerrilla.

In his left hand he held a compensation slip. All eyes went to the blue compensation slip. "This is a 1000 hour comp slip. All I have to do is to fill in the officer's name and DSN. I've already signed it. You know what you have to do.

It didn't work. There was another burglary. McHenry metal finally spent the money it needed to spend on an alarm system. The burglaries stopped. Their theory had been, "Why should I have to spend money on an alarm system when I have cops on duty to protect my business."

Victims eventually realize that cops aren't there to personally protect them. If a cop sees a crime in progress, he will stop and assist the good citizen, but it seldom happens that way. You have to protect yourself. Cops show up at a crime scene after the crime has been committed.

Bob Truetken became disengaged with the St. Louis Metropolitan Police Department. Most cops do at some point in their careers. But for someone like Bob, or hundreds others who come to the department with outside influence, or who gain influence when they arrive here, the slightest downfall is disastrous to them. They want to run and hide. Things aren't going their way, and it's time to move on.

The cop on the wane feels that the next place they go will have someone there who will recognize them as a special person and treat them accordingly. It drives them to seek another position, preferably one with more stature.

Bob made friends with the Mayor of Florissant, Missouri. The mayors of municipalities have the power to name chiefs of police at will.

The mayor of Florissant, James J. Eagan, offered Lieutenant Bob Truetken the job of police chief for Florissant, Missouri, which at the time was the third largest city in the state. Bob jumped at it. The system was again working for him. Someone recognized his pure talent in the field of law enforcement. He was going to be a special person again. He left without fanfare and without a pension. It was a gamble, and as the saying goes, "you gamble, you lose."

Bob's tenure at Florissant was short and not sweet. He was scrutinized at every turn and was soon ousted as chief. He was now a special guy without a job. I had seen it dozens of times as a young cop. Guys can't wait to leave, and then they can't wait to return. There was no returning for "Burglar Bob" Truetken.

Semi-important guys like "Burglar Bob" are on their own as far as the St. Metropolitan Police Department is concerned. He obtained two promotions and approximately ten years of experience. He had a grand resume, compliments of the St. Louis Metropolitan Police Department. It was up to him to cultivate what he had gained there.

Bob experienced what every St. Louis cop comes to realize: rank or not, quit or retire; when you aren't here, carrying the badge and gun, using your discretion, taking your big vacations, working two part time jobs to survive, driving fast and flashing your badge to get off, fighting and drinking on duty, it comes to you like an Epiphany; you are just another face in the crowd. It isn't a good feeling.

Burglar Bob Truetken went into hospital security. He was a supervisor. That means you sit in a windowless office, usually in the basement of some stinking hospital, and make schedules all day.

Other people of self-importance call you on the phone and threaten you for something one of your guards did or said to them. Hospital administrators nit-pick your records for expenditures and payroll. They force you to lay off security personnel.

The security chief is the sounding board for trouble that occurs in the hospital. It makes the bloody Ninth District look like a rose garden. And to add insult to injury, you don't have what you so direly need: discretion. Only St. Louis cops have it.

Bob Scheetz had set the standard for roll call sermons. Other commanders wanted to influence their men and make friends with them. The sermon appeared to be the answer. The problem with their rationale was that in order to impress and influence, the preacher must be sincere. Bob Scheetz was; the other watch commanders in the ninth were not.

There was a fat, small minded little fellow by the name of Lieutenant Russell Taylor. He was a politician and the brother of the Coroner of the City of St. Louis, Helen Taylor. He was not respected by his group of guys. All of the troops knew where he had come from. He was a political appointee who wanted to be a great policeman and leader of men. He fell short.

His group of guys didn't trust him because of his background in the department. He had been an investigator in Internal Affairs. Most cops are summoned to Internal Affairs at some point in the career. Their only thought when they go through that door on the sixth floor is to try and save their job.

The Internal Affairs investigators know this, and they use it as a tool to make them snitch on a fellow cop. It takes skill not to snitch on your partner, and during the interrogation, the investigators double team the cop and treat him like a prime suspect in a murder investigation.

If the cop is lucky enough to walk out of the internal affairs offices with his job still intact, he takes a big breath and says to himself, "I'll get those dirty bastards someday." But there will be no revenge and the cop knows it.

The beat cops hated Lieutenant Taylor. The lieutenant would try to act like a good guy at roll call, even cracking jokes and smiling at his troops. It didn't work. They nick- named him "Fat Albert" from the animated television series.

Before roll call at least one of the cops would get in front of the troops and imitate "Fat Albert" saying, "Hey, hey, hey, I'm Fat Albert from the Inspectors Office, I want to be your friend."

When the footsteps from the stairway echoed into the roll call room, the imitator would rush to his chair and wait. "Fat Albert" would walk in, and all of the cops would stare at him with a smile. The lieutenant would think that he had won his troops over and that they liked him.

Someone told him he was being ridiculed behind his back and that his nickname was "Fat Albert" from a cartoon. He was crushed. Rumor has it that he asked his sister to get him transferred. He went back to Internal Affairs and joined the "goon" squad. He rode around in the Ninth District and made allegations against cops who didn't have their hats on. He was convinced he was an important fellow.

The roll call sermon is a lost art form. Shifts and relief changes are staggered now. Roll calls are small groups of guys and gals, sometimes just two or three officers. A desk officer reads the desk book; the lieutenant reads the faces of his troops and they go to their patrol cars.

Every minute of every shift is documented. If a cop is late for roll call, the minutes of his tardiness is deducted from his paycheck.

The department pays overtime now. There are no more compensation slips. No hanging out or congregating. When a cop gets into the patrol car the radio starts spitting out assignments, and it doesn't stop until the shift ends.

The patrol cop cars have computers in them and the cops write their reports from their cars in most instances. The cops wear microphones and cameras to document their communication between the caller, or bad guy, during their confrontations. Manpower is way down, so is morale. The cops hardly know one another compared to the way it once was.

The modern cops are sad robots riding the rail of crime going from house to business back to house and telling the callers what they want to hear. And the saddest part of this tale: the radio calls are scrutinized. Discretion, the art of doing what you want to do during your eight hour shift----using judgment instead of general orders, is getting weaker. New cops are afraid to use it. The cop job has been gutted by a book of rules and regulations.

In the old ninth driving to work was an experience in itself. There was an entire five square mile corridor that was completely slummed.

Black folks were loitering, fighting, begging, shooting, and crashing before your eyes as you drove to the station house. The station was surrounded by slums and its people. The slum tenements were owned by wealthy heirs who had offices in the slum buildings and collected the rents from the government welfare checks.

These rich old landlords were the original "rent men" of the city. The slums had been handed down from generation to generation and patched when needed to make them barely livable.

So when Bob Scheetz took the pulpit to give us his sermon for the day, we were skeptical of anything coming from management, city, county, state or federal.

Most watch commanders instructed their men, because we were all men at roll call in those days. There were no women street cops.

Will Gooden, a watch commander in the Eighth District would preach from the pulpit with is hands in his pockets, rocking melodically from side to side, advising his men to "simonize" their watches so they were certain what time it was when they received radio assignments. He whistled and was referred to as Lieutenant Whistling Will.

He was a strangely built individual, big on top and skinny at the bottom. He had a large belly which made his pants sag under the weight of a gun and cop radio. His pockets were deep because of trouser tailoring, and he always had his hands in his pockets almost up to his forearms.

One day Will was preaching, hands in pockets, when he attempted to place his foot on the bar holding the steel table the pulpit was set upon. His foot missed the bar, and Will tumbled onto his face in front of his group of guys. His hat fell off and a couple of candy bars fell out of it.

To add insult to injury, he couldn't get his hands out of his pockets. He rolled around on the floor cursing and moaning until a couple of the front row cops got up and assisted him.

But no commander could preach like Bob Scheetz. He would use his good guy demeanor, crack jokes, laugh and do a stand-up comedy act wearing his tattered commander uniform, blouse unbuttoned showing his dingy white shirt. When he finished you would almost think he was a trusting individual instead of cop management who would read you your constitutional rights in a heartbeat (it happened to me) and fire you in two beats. The guy was in dire need of more promotions.

One of Bob's speeches hit home with me and stuck with me my entire career. He came to roll call loaded for bear. He was serious as a heart attack, no smiling, joke cracking, or standup comedy routine.

He looked all of us in the face and said, "Here's a question for all of you. What causes cops more harm, women, booze, corruption or your big mouths?"

Most of the cops shouted women and booze. It's what I said. "No," he replied. "It's your damn big mouths."

Sergeant Larry Land shouted, "Attention to roll call." We stood and pulled our revolvers and Larry with his stinking cigar breath would come by each of us and try to smell our breath to see if we were wasted. If a cop was drunk he would be placed in an office and fed coffee and doughnuts until he was sober enough to go on the street.

As we were being inspected, we all had time to assimilate Bob's question and his answer. I knew he was correct in his assumption. I had a big mouth. Most of the cops did. The cop job in those ancient days was a place where you went to work and did and said anything you wished.

We were working poor serving non-working poor. Who cared what was said or what was done? Apparently Bob cared. His riddle worked on my psyche. I tried to curb my big mouth. I was never a "snitch" and I disliked "snitches' in and out of the cop job, but Bob meant more than snitching. We were all wise-assed cops, and I didn't want to fit that mold, so I worked at not being a wise ass. It wasn't easy. I had been a big mouthed wise ass for most of my life.

The afternoon watch cops drank in the parking lot at the rear of the station on mild fall and summer nights when they got off duty. I had done it a couple of times, but the drinking tended to get out of control with so many adrenaline juiced cops reliving the last eight hours of beating slum dwellers for the City of St. Louis.

As the years went on the watch commanders would make the off-duty cops leave the cop parking lot, but that did not quell them. They would move to a business parking lot that had closed and continue to drink themselves in to a coma. It was cop overkill but then everything was.

On a night watch I received a radio call sending me to a parking lot where the off-duty cops were drinking. I didn't know they were there--- the call was to investigate a group of men on the lot near Vandeventer and West Pine.

When I saw the guys were Ninth District cops in uniform, I smiled and got out to talk to them. It was going to be a long night for me and talking with a bunch of drunk cops was always good for a laugh.

One of the cops pulled his service revolver on me and pointed it at my forehead. He had the look of a zombie, and I felt he was mentally prepared to shoot me. I backed away, got back in my cop car, and drove off. I figured I would let them eventually go home, sober up, and tomorrow I would confront the drunk cop and, at the least get an apology from him. Drunk cops with guns are dangerous. Sober cops with guns are dangerous.

My sarge at that time was Al Parton, a good guy and a caring supervisor. I was riding around hoping I didn't get an accident call where a DWI was involved when Al called for my location. I was still in the vicinity of Vandeventer and Lindell, but on Lindell so I advised the dispatcher. Al rolled up to speak with me.

Al had serious health problems. He was terminally ill, but he loved the St. Louis Metropolitan Police Department, and he stayed until almost the last days of his life.

"What happened on that last call, the one for a group of guys on the lot?" he asked.

Bob Scheetz' words were haunting me. I could visualize him saying, "Your damn big mouths" as my good supervisor Al Parton waited for a reply. I wasn't going to snitch on another cop, and I wasn't going to be a wise ass to Al Parton so I said, "Oh, it was nothing, just a group of guys drinking."

"Afternoon watch cops?" he asked.

"Yes," I replied.

"One of them pulled a gun on you, didn't he?"

I stared at him, wondering how he knew. Did he have me under surveillance? Someone had to have called the station and relayed the information to him. The watch commander's phone never stops ringing about cops and their special problems. But who could have seen the flourishing of the weapon? It was nighttime dark and there were only cops in the group. Cell phones hadn't yet been invented.

"How did you know?" I asked.

"Never mind that. Which one flourished you?"

I reluctantly told him and I felt bad about being an informer.

"We're going over there. Follow me," Al said.

We pulled on to the lot and the cops were drunk out of control, hooping and hollering and dancing in the lot to a blaring car radio. It was about 1:00 a.m.

We parked and got out. Al went to the drunk cop who had pulled the gun on me. He took his revolver and then handcuffed him behind his back. He placed him in the backseat of his cop car and turned to the group of cops. "Party's over. Go home," he shouted.

We entered our cop cars, and I followed Al to the station. The drunk wasn't saying anything. His head was down and he was just like other drunks I had seen in handcuffs, surly but non-resistant.

Al took him in to the holdover and shoved him in to a cell. The cop backed up to the bars and Al removed the handcuffs. "Sleep it off," Al said as we walked out of the holdover.

This would usually be the end of the story, but it wasn't. The drunk cop didn't sleep it off. He had a knife in his pocket. He got it out and tried to jimmy the lock on the cell door. He got the knife in the lock and turned it thinking he would unlock the door and gain his freedom. The knife blade broke off inside the lock.

Several hours passed; Al went to the cell to unlock it so the cop could go home, but the busted knife blade prevented him from getting the key in the lock. Al figured out what had happened. The drunk cop spent the night in jail and part of the next day. The department locksmith does not work nights. He got there when he could.

There was more trouble for the cop. His wife called the station wondering where her husband was. Cop wives are always leery of spouses who don't come home after their shift. It usually means disaster. She was advised of the incident by desk personnel.

Word got around the police department that a cop pulled a gun on an on-duty cop answering a radio assignment. It didn't play well for the drunk cop. He had had other alcohol/gun events in his past.

He was a couple of months short of a ten year anniversary. Cops bundle their years on the department in groups of ten. In their minds, two or three bundles and they are retired, living on a beach or some other imaginary dreamland. The demigods allowed this cop to do his last couple of months and then he quit. His wife left him and subsequently divorced him. I never heard what ever happened to him.

I wonder if Bob Scheetz' sermons would affect the modern cop the way they affected me. As I wound my way through the department, working organized criminals (Mafia types) in the Intelligence Unit I noted that most of the violent crimes occurred because someone said something he should not have said.

John Paul Spica (a convicted professional hit man) was blown to smithereens by Ray Flynn. Spica was in contention for the leadership of Laborers Local number forty two. His opponent was Ray Flynn (a convicted burglar).

Spica made the fatal mistake of trusting a hood Anthony Leisure. Spica didn't know that Flynn and Leisure were partners in a lucrative nation-wide home invasion business that netted millions in diamonds and cash.

Spica bragged to Anthony Leisure that he was going to "whack" Ray Flynn so he could gain leadership of Local number Forty Two. The next day Spica walked out of his house, started his Caddy and was blown up. Ray Flynn gained the leadership position.

When I was assigned to DEA, there was always an informant who said the wrong thing to the wrong person. The informant would come to us begging for federal witness protection. DEA would lead them on. Many were never heard from again.

It was the same experience while I was assigned to the Homicide Section. The gang bangers would spout off about killing a rival over nothing, maybe a girl or a drug debt. There would be a killing and then a retaliation killing and then maybe two or three more.

On a winter afternoon roll call Bob Scheetz came to the pulpit. He was ashen, and haggard looking. His dingy white shirt looked dingier than normal. I figured he hadn't slept in days, working any extra job he could get to make ends meet. I had seen him in this state many times. It was his sign to stay clear of him. I heeded his signals.

In another district on the night watch, a cop pursued a car for a traffic offense. The streets were mostly bare and the pursuit went on for about ten minutes. The cop was losing the race, for that's what a pursuit is really about; who can win. It's a pissing contest between the cop and the pursued.

The pursued "T"- boned a car at an intersection killing the driver of the struck car. The cop couldn't stop in time, and he struck the pursued car. The young cop was seriously injured. As is the case most of the time, the guy being pursued was hardly injured. He was arrested and he was still laughing when they put him in the back of the paddy wagon for conveyance to the district station.

The desk officer read from the desk book while we all studied Bob Scheetz. "This is going to be a doozy," I said to myself.

Bob cleared his throat, "Why do we pursue cars?" He stared at us waiting for a response.

A couple of guys shouted out, "To get the bad guy off of the streets."

Some more shouted, "Because they have broken the law and are running from the police."

Some said, "Because they are violators and it is our job to bring them to justice."

"Wrong," Bob loudly shouted. "We do it because we are stupid. A license number would eventually bring the culprits to justice. Am I wrong?" He continued his rant. No one answered.

"Of all the things we are paid to do, what is the most dangerous?" he asked.

"Domestic peace disturbances," some shouted.

"Alarm soundings," some said.

"Auto accidents on highway forty," a few said.

"Wrong," Bob again shouted. "The most dangerous part of our job is self-initiated police work. Pursuits are self- initiated. They never have a good ending. Someone is always hurt or killed. Most of the time it's the cop and an innocent bystander. Use your brains while you are out there. Go home to your families when your shift is ended. Stay safe. Dismissed!"

Needless to say, there weren't many pursuits on our watch for a while. Nobody wanted to cross Der Fuehrer. I agreed with Bob Scheetz. I hated pursuits. I had been in many and, unlike most of my counterparts, I had been on both sides of the spectrum.

I grew up on the eastside. I didn't go to private schools, and I was not a good student. Luckily I left the eastside at the tender age of seventeen but I wasn't tender.

While I pursued cars in the bloody ninth I would think about the driver of the vehicle I was pursing. I knew what was going on in his mind.

The running from authority starts out as a lark. It's like a rabbit running from a dog. The rabbit knows the dog can't catch it so it bobs and weaves, jumps and changes directions, taunts the stupid dog and laughs as it dives in to its hole, safe and out of harm's way.

It's the same with most car chases. The pissing contest starts fool heartedly with an "I can outdrive that cop," or "my car is quicker and handles better than the damn cop car." The pursued turns from rabbit to primate and during the chase goes from primate to a similar sub-human species called "Zog". He is not rational like a human, but he tries to think and make rational decisions, like speeding through an intersection at eighty.

In his primate condition his brain tells him there is a leopard chasing him in the canopy of the jungle. He uses his small brain and long arms to brachiate from limb to limb, tree to tree with flowing movements while the leopard crashes through the branches trying to get its claws and eventually his fangs in to the primate's flesh.

The primate knows he is on his turf, not the leopard's in the canopy, and the leopard cannot catch him, but he goes into panic mode, listening to the growls of the savage beast as it grows nearer to him. He trusts the strength of the branch he is reaching for. If a branch breaks and he goes to the ground, the leopard will pounce and devour him.

As the pursuit continues, the primate smoothly swings away from his personal jungle. He finds himself in a strange land with strange limbs he hasn't tried before. He continues on in mild panic mode, watching for strong limbs and monitoring the leopard gaining on him.

As the panic worsens, the primate isn't concentrating on the strength of the branches. He gets reckless and swings to a weak limb. It breaks and he goes to the ground. It's the same as "Zog", the sub-human species, wrecking at an intersection. The leopard pounces and the contest is over.

On the other side of the spectrum, the cop is pumped up and angry. He wants to catch the guy driving the car running away from him, drag him out, and beat him with his nightstick. Nothing is more insulting to a cop than to have someone run from him, on foot or in a car. The cop takes it personally. It's a slap in the face to the reasoning behind law enforcement. No one should question the authority of the police, and if they do, it is because they are criminals, not traffic violators. The pursuer has the same mindset as the pursued. Pursue until you can't pursue any more.

The pursued changes from his primate condition to his sub-human "Zog" form and is thinking, "How can I get out of this? If I pull over I will be beaten, arrested, and probably sent to prison. It was just a game. How did it escalate in to this?"

The cop continues to wonder why the pursuit happened. "The pursued must be wanted for a heinous crime. He has to be a career criminal that needs to be taken off of the streets forever. He is a danger to the community."

The pursued is as dangerous to himself as the big-mouthed wise-assed cop is to himself. As the pursuit continues, both the pursued and the pursuer swear to themselves, they will never engage in this activity again. They are praying to God to get them out of this predicament.

The "Zog" species can only be changed back into a rational being through the administration of a powerful medication called "nightstick." It must be applied by a large wised-assed cop, and when bounced off of the head of "Zog" it instantly turns him in to a rational being, even a victim and at the same instant it turns the wise-assed big mouthed cop into a criminal.

Luckily for the eastside kid, in a car and on a motorcycle, the cop ended the pursuit. It doesn't always play out that way in the City of St. Louis.

In March of 1977 on a rainy cold afternoon watch a conscientious St. Louis County Police Officer, Patrolman Richard Weinweber, patrolling in south St. Louis County, attempted to pull a car over for a traffic violation.

The car was driven by Johnny Lewis, twenty who resided in Cahokia, Illinois. A passenger in the car was Rickie Rall, twenty one who resided on Courtois Street in St. Louis. The pursuit began on Lemay Ferry Road and continued on to Gravois to Twelfth Boulevard to Tenth street and onto Highway Forty.

Before getting to Highway Forty, two conscientious Third District officers, not wiseasses, Patrolman Ron Oldani and Mike Marshall observed the pursued car and joined in on the pursuit. Their police car was in front of the pack closely behind the pursued car with approximately twenty other police cars behind them.

The pursuit was being broadcast by the county and city police to all points which meant all on-duty law enforcement officers could listen to it on their police radios. The wail of the sirens on the cop radios while the passenger in the cop car is "keying" up to tell the dispatcher their location is like a dinner bell to a captive carnivore. The excitement is insurmountable.

The lead car has the responsibility of keeping the pursued vehicle in sight and calling out the direction the pursued is travelling. Usually the passenger in the cop car will say, "south on Gravois" or north on Tenth street," etc.

This banter is mesmerizing to the cops in the other nine police districts listening to the pursuit. It is like a Buddhist monk chanting for his flock to come to prayer services.

The cops listening to pursuits hanker to get involved in it. It's the dog chasing the rabbit syndrome. Most cops can't resist the urge. It's why there were twenty or more city and county police cars chasing the vehicle driven by traffic violator Johnny Lewis.

The chase continued on and had been successful for the pursued. They hadn't crashed yet and they hadn't been caught. If their luck continued, they might make it to Illinois, hide out in a corn field, and successfully elude capture.

But they weren't going to make it to the safety of Illinois; they were going directly toward the bloody Ninth District. A group of un-supervised Ninth District cops took it upon themselves to set up a road block on the Highway Forty overpass at Vandeventer.

Their supervisor rarely left the district station. His method of su-pervision was to write down on the back of a hot sheet the times and location of each one of his officer's radio assignments and then note on the same hot sheet the disposition of the assignment.

For the supervisor this was a safe and efficient way to document his actions in case something went awry while he was safe and sound in the station house. If summoned to Internal Affairs, he could doc-ument that he knew where his men were at all times.

But there was playtime between radio assignments in those ancient times. Cops congregated, drank beer, held cookouts, told stories, and day dreamed about roadblocks and nightsticks.

As the pursued vehicle came over the rise on Highway Forty they observed the roadblock of about ten police cars. They stopped, they had no other choice. It must have been a surreal experience for every-one involved. The cold light rain added to the cop's misery. The yel-low streetlights caused thing's to look distorted in the rain. The faces of the cops at the roadblock glaring at the two "Zog" scofflaws in the pursued car had to be terrifying.

Ron Oldani, the driver of the lead pursuing police car, came to a stop behind the pursued vehicle. Johnny Lewis put the pursued vehi-cle in reverse and rammed the police car. It was a senseless response. There was no place for them to go. They were caught with no hope of escape. The leopard was going to devour them.

Oldani exited his police vehicle and went to the driver's side of the pursued car. He ordered Johnny Lewis out of the car. Lewis refused. It was his last defiant act of the evening.

Mike Marshall went to the passenger's side and ordered Ricky Rall to exit the vehicle. Rall came out swinging. He ran toward Mike Marshall and head butted him in the solar plexus while he flailed at him with his fists. They went to the ground and several Ninth District cops came to Marshall's defense with nightsticks.

Ron Oldani pulled Johnny Lewis from the car. They were fist fighting along the side of the vehicle. An unknown Ninth District officer climbed onto the trunk of the pursued car and bashed Johnny Lewis in the head several times with a six cell steel flashlight. A couple of the glancing blows hit Officer Ron Oldani. The striking cop then melted back into the crowd of cops. Johnny Lewis stopped fighting.

There were approximately sixty cops in uniform milling around inflicting damage to the arrested "Zogs." As the carnage played out, there were citizens coming and going on the overpass, being directed around the cops and the "Zogs". Many were appalled at what they observed.

The supervisor, who had been safely ensconced in the station house came on to the scene. He quickly dispersed the cops, telling the majority of Ninth District cops to go back in service and patrol their assigned areas, and advising the other district cops to go back to their districts. A few Ninth District cops were assigned to assist Ron Oldani and Mike Marshall. An old timer from the ninth, Officer Walter Otten was recruited to write the police report.

Johnny Lewis and Ricky Rall instantly morphed from "Zog" to victim. They were taken to City Hospital and listed in critical condition in the Intensive-Care Unit with severe head and face injuries. None of the cops were injured. Johnny Lewis stated he didn't stop for the county police because his driver's license was suspended. He and Rall stated that they offered no resistance after their car was stopped at the roadblock.

They further stated that, as they got out of their car, several officers started hitting them with nightsticks. They said the beating continued after they were handcuffed and in the police wagon. They estimated that at least ten officers struck them.

Lewis fell unconscious in the paddy wagon. Rall said the cops dragged them into the hospital by the collars of their shirts. As Rall was awaiting treatment, an officer grabbed him by the hair, called him an obscenity, and said, "Die, die."

Lewis was hospitalized for nine days with a concussion, ear injuries, internal bleeding in his head and other injuries. Rall was hospital-ized for three days with head and face injuries, abrasions of two ribs, two broken fingers and four broken knuckles.

Ron Oldani, Mike Marshall, and Walter Otten worked on the po-lice report until 3:00 p.m. the next day. Lewis was charged with nu-merous traffic violations, driving without a license, resisting arrest, and destruction of city property (police car). Rall was charged with resisting arrest and interfering with a police officer.

Both Lewis and Rall denied they backed into the police car. They stated the police car rammed them from behind. In addition, both stated they opened their own doors to get out of the car. In fact, they contended, police could not have opened Lewis's door because it is broken and can only be opened from the inside.

It was determined that both Lewis and Rall were suspects in three jewelry store burglaries in St. Louis County. County Patrolman Wein-weber, who began the chase, stated that when he arrived at the scene of the arrest, Lewis was struggling with two city policeman. "He was fighting with them, and they were trying to control him. It was dark and I couldn't tell who was doing what."

Problems started arising for Ron Oldani and Mike Marshall. In most large police departments the cops don't really know one another unless they have worked with them. Cops in the Third District don't know cops in the Ninth District. They know cops in the districts to which they are assigned.

Ricky Rall's mother filed a complaint with Internal Affairs stating that officers physically abused Rall and Lewis. Concerned citizens who witnessed the beatings while travelling on Highway Forty also con-tacted Internal Affairs and lodged complaints against officers at the scene.

Internal Affairs (IAD) started interviewing witnesses. They esti-mated there were four St. Louis County police cars at the scene of the arrest and twenty one city police cars. They interviewed eighteen po-lice officers, City Hospital employees and at least five citizens who witnessed the incident.

George Peach, Circuit Attorney for the City of St. Louis, launched his own investigation. He publicly asked for anyone with information concerning the beatings of two men by St. Louis Police Officers to contact him or his chief warrant officer.

The City Counselors' Office dismissed the charges of resisting arrest and interfering with a police officer against Lewis and Rall. George Peach was incensed by their action. George Peach was a pro-police prosecutor.

The City Counselors office stated that the dismissal was simply a "technical legal device and that it doesn't mean they believe the witnesses in the report of the officers."

Peach stated he was "extremely disappointed that the cases didn't go to trial because I'm interested in hearing what the officers have to say." He stated he believes the officers involved have maintained a conspiracy of silence through which they have avoided prosecution.

Ron Oldani and Mike Marshall spent a lot of time at IAD. The focus of the IAD investigation was on the cop who jumped on the trunk of the car and bashed Johnny Lewis in the head with the steel flashlight. Oldani and Marshall didn't know who he was.

Oldani stated he would have gladly told them who the mystery cop with the killer flashlight was, but he had never seen him before.

About two weeks after the incident Oldani and Marshall were summoned to IAD to stand in a line-up. They recruited a bunch of Third District cops of their general physical makeup to stand with them. The people who viewed the line-up were not able to pick anybody out as being at the scene. Oldani and Marshall were ushered out of the room.

Oldani was again taken into the viewing room at the line-up. There were police officers in the line-up, the same police officers Oldani and Marshall had hand-picked to stand in a line-up with them. IAD instructed Oldani to pick out the guy who was on the trunk of Lewis's vehicle bashing him in the head with the steel flashlight.

There was one cop in the line-up who Oldani didn't know. He was a big raw boned young cop. Ron Oldani was and is a smart cookie. He put it together quickly that this young cop was probably the one he was supposed to identify as the cop who jumped onto the trunk of Johnny Lewis's car and bashed his head in with the steel flashlight while Oldani was fist fighting with him.

Oldani asked the IAD investigator if the big kid cop was the one he was being compelled to identify. The investigator became enraged, and that was the end of the line-up.

The big raw boned young cop was Robert Worley. He was indeed the cop who bashed Johnny Lewis. Ron Oldani didn't know him. He honestly could not identify him. IAD knew Robert Worley was the cop they were looking for.

Worley was as stupid as he was big and violent. He trusted his fellow colleagues and the Ninth District supervisors. There are no secrets in the St. Louis Metropolitan Police Department. A colleague advised a supervisor and the supervisor informed the lieutenant and the lieutenant informed the captain and the captain informed IAD. Robert Worley was doomed. He just didn't know it.

George Peach, the Circuit Attorney, IAD, the press, and the chief's office were enraged that there was a code of silence hindering the successful investigation of the Highway Forty overpass incident. All were zeroing in on Patrolman Robert Worley.

I was writing a long report in the old ninth report room. It was a gathering place for cops, writing or gossiping. There was a group of guys sitting down, and Robert Worley was standing and addressing them. The guys sitting looked concerned. Robert Worley was cocky and sure of himself. His claim to fame was that he was personal friends of influential St. Louis hierarchy. He felt invincible.

He had just been summoned to IAD. A supervisor was waiting to drive him downtown. Before he walked out of the little report room, he said to the group of worried cops, "I want all of you to know and to rest assured that I won't tell those motherfuckers anything."

I had been on the department for about eight years and I had heard such false bravado from numerous cops in the past. It was a prime example of "famous last words".

I continued writing my report. The group of cops wandered away. I was alone in the room with the spring sunshine pouring in. I wrote and daydreamed. I glanced out into the parking lot. Robert Worley was wandering around in the lot looking for his personal car. He was crying, sobbing uncontrollably. His badge and gun were gone, his head was down. He located his car, entered it, and drove away. They fired him at IAD for refusing to answer questions regarding the Highway Forty incident. His influential friends could not save him.

IAD, George Peach, and the press still had not gotten to the bottom of the incident. They still blamed their failure to solve the case on the alleged "code of silence" among the cops at the scene. None of the cops would make an accurate statement. Most said they were not there at the time of the incident. The rest stated they were directing traffic and didn't see anything. There was no way to prove they were lying. There was no record of what cops were at the roadblock.

So George Peach and IAD took the next step. They were going to railroad Ron Oldani and Mike Marshall. George Peach sent the facts to a Grand Jury. Ron Oldani and Mike Marshall were indicted, arrested, suspended, and booked for "Assault with the Intent to Maim with Malice." They had gone from "street warriors" to criminals. They were looking at three years to life in prison.

The bottom line was and still is, that cops love to beat and abuse other cops' prisoners. After doing the dastardly deed, they disappear leaving the arresting cop with the job explaining the injuries inflicted upon their prisoner.

Oldani and Marshall were suspended for about a month and then were transferred to Prisoner Processing. They were getting a paycheck which is all that can be said about working in the jail. Going to work there is hell.

They hired attorney's. Oldani spoke to his lawyer about trying to get some of the cops who were at the scene to come forward and tell what had happened. The lawyer frankly told them that there was just a fifty/fifty chance that he could keep them out of prison. It was Johnny Lewis' word against Ron Oldani's and Ricky Rall's word against Mike Marshall. They were on their own.

Their lawyer asked for and was given a change of venue for the trial. It went to Cole County, Missouri. The trial lasted for four days. Several officers who admitted they were at the scene were subpoenaed to testify, some for the prosecution and some for the defense.

Ron Oldani never denied striking Johnny Lewis. They were fighting at the side of Johnny Lewis's car. It's what city cops did in those days. They fight the bad guy and try to get him under control. But it was a fist fight. Oldani could not have severely injured Johnny Lewis with his fists or even with a wooden nightstick.

Most fights between cops and crooks are scrambles with hardly anyone getting a damaging punch or strike on the other. The fight usually stops because the arrestee hasn't the heart to finish. He has made his point; he fought the cops. He doesn't want to do anything else except quit.

The cop then does his thing: handcuffs the nut, takes him to the hospital, and then to jail and then works hours of overtime to write the report. But it's not over then. The cop has to go to the City Counselor's Office and or the Circuit Attorney's Office and apply for a warrant. It's time consuming and the cop usually hasn't been asleep in days. It's torture.

Ron Oldani and Mike Marshall were acquitted. During testimony, Ron acknowledged the assault by the unidentified officer and testified that due to the confusion at the scene, he was unable to identify anyone there. The jury believed him.

They weren't going to prison, but they still had police department charges against them. They were hated and hounded by IAD. The powers still believed there was a code of silence conspiracy. The police department still desired to make examples of Ron Oldani and Mike Marshall.

Almost daily the commander of IAD would call Ron to his office and toss a resignation form in front of him. Ron kept tossing them back at him. Ron started using his sick days. He figured he was going to be fired so he might as well take the days. Police Board trials are a farce, a kangaroo court where the officer has only a slim chance of saving his job. Ron had twenty department charges against him.

About three years had passed and Ron and Mike Marshall still had their jobs. The Police board trial was nearing. In their minds the end of employment was near.

In the spring of 1980 Johnny Lewis was again pursued by the police. He had mutated into the sub-human species "Zog" and had made it to Sunset Hills. He hit a bridge abutment. He never made it back to human form. Maybe it's the way he wanted to go out: fleeing from the cops. It might have been a hobby for him, the ultimate excitement, the thrill of a lifetime. It may have even been sexual for him.

The problem on this "Zog" adventure was that he had his wife and young daughter in the car with him. Everyone in the car was killed. It was a tragedy of monumental proportions. I attempted to put it into perspective but I couldn't.

This is usually the way it is when someone flees. Someone is going to get killed. Bob Scheetz had insight. He didn't want to see any of his work children maimed or going to prison for someone's kinky "Zog" fetish. The cops and the bystanders usually end up as the victim. This time family members suffered the consequences. There's never a winner.

Ron Oldani and Mike Marshall were dreading the police board trial, but there would be no trial. Johnny Lewis was the complaining witness. He was the "Zog" turned victim. Dead men can't testify against street warriors.

Ron Oldani and Mike Marshall, the conscientious cops from an adjoining district to the bloody ninth recovered from the Highway Forty incident. Ron was promoted two times, to the rank of lieutenant. He became the president of the Police Officers Association. He retired after thirty seven years on the job. He drove the train at the St.Louis Zoo then took a job as a bailiff at the St. Louis County Courts. Mike Marshall stayed on and collected a good pension.

The cop supervisor who didn't stray far from the station house had come under scrutiny. It's a terrifying situation for low-level management. They convince themselves that they are members of the demigod totem pole. They aren't. They aren't even on the totem pole's lowest level.

When the scrutiny monster turns its evil eye on members of the St. Louis Metropolitan Police Department, the recipient wants to turn and run, hide and shiver, depend on his political cronies to protect him. But there is no place to run and nowhere to hide.

The station house supervisor was being snitched on by his fellow supervisors. They had all sat in the warm and safe station for years, gossiping, evaluating, managing working cops and drinking coffee. But when one of them is threatened by the scrutiny monster the majority will quickly turn on the minority. The odd man is always on the outs.

The problem arose that his co-supervisors knew everything about him. And they conveyed it to a friend of a friend of an IAD investigator who would use the information against him.

The supervisor eventually retired. He had a stroke and then he went blind. He is cared for by friends and relatives. I spoke with him recently. I asked him about Robert Worley. He told me he didn't remember much because of his stroke, but he said he wished he'd never met Robert Worley. The cop destroyed the supervisor. Robert Worley put several good cops through hell with his irresponsible action.

I watched the incident play out. It was a learning experience for me. I always guarded my prisoners like my life depended on it because in reality it did. There was always a cop waiting to let his frustration out on any handcuffed scofflaw prisoner. It isn't just an old time cop game. It still goes on in this modern day game of crook and cop.

After the firing, Robert Worley bopped around in different jobs trying to make a living. His heart was in the bloody Ninth District. It's where he was a "somebody" instead of just another face in the crowd.

He was observed riding around in the district in his personal vehicle. He didn't keep in touch with any of his old co-workers. It wouldn't have done any good if he'd tried. Once you're gone you are forgotten. There's too much turmoil in a cop's life to dwell on the faces of the past.

Robert Worley shot himself in the head. His brains were blown out. There's no "going home" and he realized it. There's freedom and power in the lowly district cop's job. Add to that-- excitement, camaraderie, discretion, pension, vacation and a feeling of family, and the job can't be replaced by anything.

George Peach, the prosecutor who loved cops and didn't want to see any harm come to them, had his own personal problems. He hated the local newspaper, and he wrote scathing "letters to the editor" which were publicized for readers to peruse.

George Peach had an appetite for young beautiful prostitutes, not the kind a john picks up on the street. Mr. Peach desired the call girl type of a hooker.

His exploits took him to St. Louis County. He had an alias and he would routinely pay for the talents of these beautiful women. In doing so he made himself vulnerable.

Beautiful hookers get arrested just like street hookers. When arrested, they will do or say anything to get them- selves in to a bargaining position. Somewhere along the propositioning, hiring, and being arrested stage, a hooker advised St. Louis County Vice detectives that George Peach was a frequent customer.

St. Louis County cops, politicians and prosecutors, and St. Louis City cops, politicians and prosecutors are just okay with each other. There's no love lost between them, and little honor among them. Someone in the St. Louis County police department or the prosecutor's office had ties with the local liberal newspaper. They carefully initiated the sex sting against George Peach. It was done with perfection.

St. Louis County has beautiful female police officers. George was steered to one of them through another prostitute. A date was made and George went to the location to consummate his deal. He was arrested.

The local newspaper had a field day with George Peach. He was destroyed, lost his law license and his position as the lead prosecutor. He went to work for a national moving company. It was a great loss for the cops of the city.

I often thought about Bob Scheetz. He was the supervisor who truly cared about his band of crime fighters. I listened for rumors about him living the good life in Naples, Florida.

A rumor was circling that he was a bagger in a grocery store in Naples. I found that hard to believe, but I couldn't see him sitting around the house with nothing to do. He didn't golf or fish or have any hobbies. What else is there to do in Florida?

Another rumor was that he was having one of his famous temper tantrums, and he slipped on the slick floor of his kitchen and severely injured himself.

I bumped in to one of his cop kids, Bob Scheetz, Jr., and asked him. He told me Chief Scheetz was in a nursing home. He was being fed by a feeding tube inserted in his stomach and confined to a wheelchair. I read his obit shortly thereafter.

'BLOODY OAK LEAVES'

Story six:

Most cops have a plan, a personal itinerary on where their career will lead them within the police department. In the Bloody Ninth, through my perceptions, only about fifty percent of the cops wished to further themselves in their given mode of employment.

I figured that approximately twenty five percent wanted to be promoted and would do anything within their power to do so. But promotions were sparse. Most of the guys in the ninth who really wished to be promoted didn't have the $3500 it took to pay a state legislator.

There were other ways to get a promotion to sergeant. One was making a perfect score on the promotional test. That meant studying special and general orders and legal decisions; city, state, and federal. Cops use these laws daily, but when given a multiple guess test it is hard to pick out the right answer unless you actually know it. Out of the twenty five percent who are intent with promotion only about one percent actually follow through with the whole process of getting promoted.

As time went "on" the state passed term limits on state legislators which basically put an end to the pay-for- promotion system.

The other twenty five percent just desires to get into a good investigative position within the department and to stay there until retirement comes around. A soft clothes job with a car weekends and holidays off and an office with a view of downtown St. Louis is what most cops dream of.

If a cop is lucky enough to land such an appointment, he or she guards the position with their life. In their mind nothing is going to jeopardize their hard fought for position. But supervisors change within specialized units. New supervisors desire to have their friends working for them. They are hounded by friends of friends to make a place for a fellow friend in the specialized job.

Cops are trying to make it to the twenty year mark. If they can make twenty years, they are vested and will get a pension whenever they want to take it. It's like a football player catching the ball on the one yard line and trying to make it to the end zone ninety nine yards away. He has gigantic athletes coming after him. He bobs and weaves and slips tackles as the opposition charges after him. He must be quick and sure footed, strong and agile, with stamina and finesse. But most of all he must be slick. Very few make it while assigned to a specialized unit.

Investigative cops don't feel like they are on the management path. They feel talented and special, almost professional in their demeanor. In their minds no one can do their job they way they can. In reality anybody can do the investigator's job. It is more work ethic than knowledge or talent, something I lacked.

What cops in investigative positions don't realize is that those specialized jobs are there as a primer to promotion. The demigods look for talent in those units so they can promote them. The investigator/cop is management.

In the itinerary they have imprinted in their minds, they have an escape plan. If things go awry in their current dream job, they have a secondary position they will covertly slide into, with the help of outside influence. Like animals they seek escape. There are federal task force jobs: FBI, IRS, ATF and DEA. It appears to be a new lease on life and the investigator on the wane pursues them with zeal.

As the department attempted to modernize, a demigod thought there should be a yearly list of choices for transfers to specialized units. The "dream list" was a requirement for transfer. If a cop didn't wish to participate, he had the option of marking, "stay in present assignment."

The Catch 22 of the dream list was the definition of the word "transfer" compared to the word "detached." If a commander had enough power to request a person to come to work for him in a specialized unit, and if the cop had not specified that unit on his dream list, he/she would be detached and told to put that particular unit on the list for the next go around.

I had eight years in the ninth. I had learned a lot seen a lot and figured I was prepared for the next step. I put in for Intelligence and with the help of a friend/cop who worked in the Chief's Office (Mike Williams), I got it. My colleagues and I were amazed.

My plan was to hold on to the neat investigative position for twelve years, get a twenty year retirement and get on with my life.

Planning seldom comes to fruition. I had eight years in the Intelligence Unit, and I thought I was slick, but I wasn't slick enough. It was time for me to move on. Luckily, for me, I had placed DEA Task Force on my "dream list". I got it, with inside influence.

I had worked with DEA special agents while assigned to Intelligence. In my opinion they were just like any other cops, but they had the backing of the federal government and the U'S. Attorney's Office, and they had federal funds to pay informants.

I wasn't thrilled to be going there. It was away from the police department, which at the time I felt was a positive point; in fact it was in another city. There was travel, weirder hours than I had been accustomed to, and the task force consisted of young city and county cops as well as special agents. I wasn't a young cop. I was a family man with young children.

I wasn't expecting a warm welcome. Pete Gober, my non-friend from my Intelligence Unit days had been assigned to DEA for approximately three years. He was still my nemesis, and I figured he had laid the ground work for my demise, if possible.

The first drug deal was a disaster. It was a raid of a party. We barged in without a warrant, without nightsticks or backup or shotguns, and we were outnumbered five to one. There were several DEA special agents and approximately eight city and county cops. The special agents and the county cops had big semi-automatic pistols. The pistols had extended oversized ammunition magazines sticking out from the grips, the way cocaine cowboys in the movies used.

The big guns with their protruding magazines were impressive, and they were being pointed at the partiers in the massive suite. The partiers were all stoned on booze, weed, and cocaine. There were business people, union people, working class folks, all partaking of the coke and weed.

They were all North County white folks and most of them had known each other since grade school. In a town like St. Louis, city and county, that meant they were closer than cousins and would be friends until death.

The cops and the agents were screaming at the partiers to get on the ground. Some of them were shouting, "get on the wall" and the stoned group didn't know what to do. They finally figured out that we were cops and agents, and several went to the floor while some just stood and glared at us.

I pulled my "pea shooter" snub nosed thirty eight and pointed it at a large man who was refusing to either get on the wall or go to the floor. His name was Paul Wayne King, and I had had dealings with him before.

He grabbed my little gun and tried to take it away from me. Luckily for me, the police department forbade us from carrying any weapon but the issued revolver or a smaller version like mine. If my gun had been large and impressive like the other cops, Paul Wayne King would have had it and killed several of us with it. He was a fighter, a Teamster enforcer, and he was completely under the influence of cocaine.

I wrestled with him, jerked the gun out of his hand, and stuck it in my jeans pocket. I had no intention of shooting anyone at the drug party. He finally gave in and allowed me to place handcuffs on him behind his back. He was surly and cursing at us.

The special agent in charge of the raid was Steve Stoddard. He was my age, early forty's, small in stature and cocky. He was referred to as "Little Stevie Wonder," by his DEA peers. Asset forfeiture (the seizing of drug dealer funds) is the life blood of the Drug Enforcement Administration, and Special Agent Steve Stoddard was an expert in the field. He always had a forfeiture case pending. He also had the respect of the young St. Louis County and City cops. He had been a special agent with DEA for as long as I had been a cop with the city. Our lives were a lot alike.

If I learned anything from my DEA experiences prior to going to DEA, it was that there were no rules and cops working for or with DEA usually got hurt or killed. In most cases, the U.S. Attorney stood by the agents who worked there. The cops were mostly on their own.

As the stoned partiers stood and lay waiting for the next command by the agents, Steve Stoddard and a young St. Louis County cop, whose dad was a high ranking city cop, and who himself is now a high ranking St. Louis city cop demigod, dragged Paul Wayne King back to the adjoining bedroom. They beat him with their fists and kicked him in his gut. Paul Wayne King took the abuse. He was unable to defend himself so he absorbed the blows to his face and body with dignity. He had been around the criminal justice system for most of his life and he was aware there was no recourse for him in the federal system. Federal agents get away with murder. The solution? Don't commit federal drug crimes. Apparently there is an unwritten law that nobody is allowed to resist arrest during a federal drug raid without being beaten after being handcuffed.

I flashbacked to the ninth: Ron Oldani, Mike Marshall, and Robert Worley. I had seen it dozens of times, I had always protected my prisoners from cop abuse; usually when the cuffs go on, the beating stops. They beat Paul Wayne King badly in the bedroom where none of the other partiers could see what was going on. For a massive man like Paul Wayne King the beating was the equivalent of an insane man shaking a hornet's nest. He was enraged.

There was also an unwritten rule that the person who handcuffs a prisoner is the one who will un-cuff the prisoner. He is the property and responsibility of the cuffing cop. After the beating, Steve Stoddard removed my handcuffs and he and the county cop with a pedigree, shoved the monster man toward me. I didn't know the drill, but apparently this was an initiation. It was up to me to fight him all over again and get him re-cuffed. It was a bloody battle and I lost. It took four cops and agents to finally subdue him. Paul Wayne King almost died. He was admitted to the Federal Prison Hospital in Springfield, Missouri.

The incident was another learning experience for me. The agents were showing me that they were in charge no matter what. I was interviewed several days after the beating by the Group Supervisor. "You have to be one of the boys if you want to stay here," he advised. I had burned my bridges in the police department and I had four years left for a meager pension.

I quickly learned that being one of the boys meant drinking with the boys. DEA not only stood for Drug Enforcement Administration; it also stood for Drunk Every Afternoon.

We were housed in a Clayton high rise office building. There was a restaurant/bar just ten short steps from our office. It was the focal point of our work day. We ate lunch there, as a group, and we drank there, as a group, before and after drug deals.

Little Stevie Wonder (Special Agent Steve Stoddard)
Was in need of a partner, preferably a cop partner, someone to travel with and to do the heavy lifting and police work for the federal deity. He chose me.

We travelled a lot. Whenever someone would telephone the DEA offices in Clayton about a possible drug conspiracy from an outlying state, Iowa, North or South Dakota or outstate Missouri, Steve and I would get the assignment.

We travelled in undercover government cars and communicated by two way secure DEA car radios. Surveillance was what we mostly did. After enough surveillance to satisfy federal probable cause guidelines, we would get a search warrant and Steve and I would execute the warrant.

We traveled to Burlington, Iowa, several times. At first I was stumped why DEA would go to Iowa. It was in the sticks, and I couldn't imagine any major drug gangs operating out of the state. I soon found out that Burlington has a commuter airport with hourly flights to and from Chicago. It was a twenty minute flight. There was big dope and big money coming through the little berg of Burlington, Iowa.

As a group we had a big drug deal in Cedar Rapids, Iowa. I came to work one morning and was advised I was going to New York City. I always had a bag packed. It was a requirement of the job. Whenever the phone rang in the group supervisor's office we were compelled to react.

Customs in New York had a large Pakistani cooking "wok" in their possession. A drug dog hit on it and they opened it. Inside was eight pounds of pure white heroin. It was addressed to a Pakistani fellow in Cedar Rapids. I flew commercial to JFK, seized the wok and the heroin, and flew back to St. Louis the same day.

The next day we removed most of the heroin and replaced it with white powder. The package was wired so that when it was opened it would set off a silent alarm which would register on one of our radios. The package was re-sealed, delivered to customs in St. Louis, and the addressee was contacted and advised that his package had cleared customs and was ready to be picked up.

We sat on surveillance for days at the airport. We all had packed bags and anything else we felt we needed. I would leave home in the morning and tell my wife I probably would not be home for a week or so and then I was back home that night.

There was surveillance around the airport. The person picking up the package would have to go to the East Terminal and then be directed to customs. We had a description and license number of the vehicle we thought the Pakistani would be driving, and we had a surveillance plane waiting for our command that the package and the Pakistani were on the road back to Cedar Rapids.

The guy finally arrived at the East Terminal. He had a Mid-Eastern woman and some kids in the car with him. He parked his junky car and walked inside. We chatted on the radio assuring each other that this was indeed the target heroin smuggler.

The young county cop who helped "Little Stevie Wonder" initiate me with the Paul Wayne King beating, and my beating, was issued a neat government undercover car. It was a bright red Nissan 360Z Turbo sports car. It stood out wherever it was parked, and at this point in time it was parked, illegally, in the turnaround in front of the East Terminal.

The Pakistani heroin smuggler stopped and admired the Nissan then walked inside. He admired it again as he left to go to customs. We didn't think anything about it. It was a neat car; people admired it. The weather was cool and bright and about to change into the winter season. Clean and shiny cars wouldn't be available for six months or so. Car guys look at cars and girls. It's the American way.

The heroin smuggler took possession of the package and headed north. The young county cop was still inside the terminal. He didn't have a radio (we were all undercover), and the line of DEA cars, assisted by the airplane, was following the smuggler from a safe distance.

Finally the county cop with the Nissan got on the air and asked for our location. He was advised and quickly caught up with us. The airplane observer kept us apprised of the target's location. The target would periodically pull over to the side of the road. The observer would tell us, and we would pull over and wait until we were advised the target was on the move again.

The problem with air surveillance is that the small single engine aircraft is loud. Add the noise to the fact that it never leaves the general area of the target (it constantly circles), and it makes it suspicious to the savvy heroin smuggler.

About half way to Cedar Rapids the heroin smuggler pulled into a restaurant/gas station. The airplane observer advised us, and we all pulled over to wait him out. It was over an hour and nothing was happening. We were told to stay put and wait for the airplane observer to direct us.

The young county cop with the Nissan drove up to the restaurant just as the heroin smuggler and his Mid-Eastern occupants were walking to their car. The cop drove back and told us that they were about to start driving again. We followed them into Cedar Rapids to a clean little neighborhood with small but neat houses. He parked his junky car in the driveway but didn't retrieve the heroin wok from the trunk.

It was dark and getting cold and it was surveillance time. The Cedar Rapids' police were asked for assistance, mostly with overnight surveillance while most of us headed for a downtown hotel and cold beer.

Cedar Rapids supplied an old surveillance van, and somebody gave the order to park it about a block from the target house. It was to be manned twenty four hours a day until the smuggler retrieved the wok from the trunk of the car.

A Cedar Rapids cop was assigned to my DEA vehicle and was showing us TFD's some of the drug dealer sights of the city. As was normal for DEA, we had a cooler of beer, and we started to drink it as we drove around town. The Cedar Rapids cop freaked out at our behavior.

"You guys can't drink and drive in Iowa or in Cedar Rapids," he advised us. We ignored him and continued to guzzle beer. He repeated what he previously told us.

"Hey man," someone told him, "We're DEA and we can do anything we damn well please."

"Fine," he said. "Take me back to my station. I'm not working with you guys, DEA or not." We dropped him off.

After about an hour our group supervisor contacted us. "Stay away from the Cedar Rapids cops. They aren't our friends. Understand?"

"Yeah, boss," I replied.

The surveillance van was a joke. We staggered shifts every four hours and the guys relieving the on-duty shift just walked up to the van and knocked on the door. Neighbors and the smuggler were eyeballing us. The Pakistani never did go to the trunk of his car and retrieve the dope laden wok.

Somebody obtained a search warrant, and finally after days of surveillance, we executed a search warrant on the neat little house in the clean neighborhood.

It was a daytime only search warrant. Most federal search warrants specify that they be executed in the daytime. We went to the front porch en masse, and before we could knock on the door, it came open and the smiling and friendly Pakistani heroin smuggler walked out.

"Hi, guys," he began. "Are you wanting to come into my little home? Please, come in," he motioned with his arms and backed into the house with us following him. "Feel free to search my home, and if there is anything I can get for you, please tell me. Can I get you something to drink? Or to eat?"

He was smiling like a carpet salesman, and he and his family stayed out of our way while we searched.

There were several more woks, just like the one he had in his car trunk in plain view in the attic of the house. Someone asked him about them.

"Oh, those. They belong to my uncle in Pakistan. He mails those here so when he gets a visa, he can open a Mid-Eastern style restaurant here in Cedar Rapids. I pick them up for him and place them in my attic." He stared at us triumphantly, continuing his smile.

"The one I picked up yesterday is still in the trunk of my car. Do you guys want it? Here are my keys; take it with you when you leave."

A TFD got his keys and removed the wok. It had never been opened. It was tossed into the trunk of a DEA car. The DEA group supervisor took him by the arm and walked him into the kitchen. We all stopped and listened.

"How did you know we had you under surveillance?" the supervisor asked.

"I'm a cautious man," he began. "I'm also a car guy. I love cars. I saw this beautiful Nissan 360Z Turbo parked in front of the terminal. I see the same car half way home to Cedar Rapids. It didn't take a genius to figure out what was going on. The airplane was loud and obvious. Your surveillance was embarrassing. I have committed no violations of the law. You want to arrest somebody, arrest my uncle."

We walked out of the house and headed back to St. Louis. There wasn't much radio chatter. It was a somber time, a sobering experience, and an eye opener. The Pakistani heroin smuggler was smarter than DEA or the United States Government. An international federal arrest warrant was placed on the uncle. Years later he was arrested, prosecuted and sent to prison.

In most rural areas there aren't any federal courthouses or assistant United States Attorneys, but the fed has attorneys under contract with the Department of Justice to serve as Assistant United States Attorneys. Steve Stoddard and I would go to their offices and request they approve an affidavit and issue a federal search warrant. Most of the attorneys were shocked that we would use them. They had been under contract for years, and no one had ever asked them for assistance.

In some cases we would request the assistance of the local sheriff's office, but most of the time Steve and I would execute the warrant. We never had any big drug seizures. We mostly seized cash for the United States Government. It made our Group Supervisor happy. He was on the "fast track" to promotion, and any statistic he could glam on to was important to him.

We had another assignment in Burlington, Iowa. The owner of a new fancy hotel (P'zzazz) called our office seeking help with a hotel guest who had paid for a room and wouldn't allow anyone to enter the room to clean it. He had been in the room with a female companion. It was the "newlywed suite" complete with a hot tub and bar. The owner advised Steve that the guy was a New York drug dealer with a briefcase full of cash. We left immediately.

The ride up was enjoyable. It was early fall and the colors were bright and spectacular. Steve had a new big government car, a Buick four door. I drove a Chrysler LeBaron Turbo My car was a seized vehicle. Steve got a new "G" car every two years.

The motel owner treated us like cop royalty. He gave us two rooms perpendicular to the alleged dope dealer's room. We ate in the hotel restaurant gratis, and we had access to the owner's minor league baseball team box-seats.

We conducted surveillance from our rooms and communicated by DEA two way radios. The female companion made several trips to Chicago via commuter airlines returning in about four hours. We figured she was carrying heroin to Chicago and cash back. We ran a criminal background check on the guy in the room and found out he was a convicted drug felon out of New York State.

Steve had the idea for the motel owner to somehow cut the electricity to the room so a maintenance man could go in and inspect a circuit. I was the maintenance man's assistant. We went inside and I perused the room. It was filthy with roaches in the ash trays and empty beer cans and trash strewn around. I eyeballed the briefcase with the supposed cash in it. It was closed but in plain sight.

The New York suspect was surly and unfriendly, and he looked the part of a gangster: dark and wiry like someone who had just gotten out of prison.

The maintenance man fiddled around with some electrical outlet and then we left. The owner returned electrical power to the room. Steve and I located a lawyer working for the government and went to his office. Steve wrote out the affidavit, and the lawyer had actual search warrants hidden away in his office. He had to look for them.

Based on what I observed in the room and what the owner and some hotel maids advised us, we were given a search warrant to be executed the next day.

That night we had a great meal in the hotel restaurant and then headed for the ball game. The problem with working undercover in a town like Burlington, Iowa, is that the populace knows you are there. The whole town was talking about us. They knew our descriptions and we were the "strangers" sitting in the owner's box seats.

Locals wanted to get to know us. People would wave to us, buy us beer, and try to engage us in conversation. At the ballpark the beer never stopped coming. I thanked so many locals for their hospitality that I couldn't keep track of them.

The next day we woke up with hangovers and a search warrant to execute. Steve didn't want to implicate the owner so we had to devise a plan of entry to the room. We waited the entire morning and finally the female companion left the room. I told Steve I would follow her. She went to the hotel restaurant. I went back to the room and advised Steve that she was eating. Our plan was that when she came back up to the room, we would barge in with our guns drawn before she could close the door, get the drop on the male drug dealer, and make sure he doesn't go for his gun. We felt certain he was armed.

We waited for about thirty minutes and then I went out in to the hallway near the elevators leaning against the wall reading a newspaper. I felt stupid and out of place. I asked myself, "Why would someone be standing in the hotel hallway reading a newspaper?" But I did it anyway.

The female room occupant walked right by me and stuck the key in the door. As soon as she opened it, I knocked her out of the way and barged into the room, thinking that Steve was behind me. He wasn't.

The female occupant hit the floor and the male was sitting in the hot tub, naked and stoned. I pointed my little pea shooter thirty eight snub at him and told him not to move. He said, "Please don't kill me."

Steve strolled in with his big DEA gun and pointed it at the male drug dealer. He had the guy climb out and get dressed, and then we handcuffed both of them. We searched the room and didn't find any hard drugs, but we opened the briefcase and seized it and the cash that was inside of it.

We marched the pair out of the hotel and to the local jail. They were held for a while and then released. The federal government didn't care anything about a little dope. The fed wanted dope dealer cash.

The hotel owner was elated that we got rid of his problem tenant for him. We ate at a restaurant called Autumn Winds near Burlington that evening. Great food and then we went to another baseball game. The owner joined us and the beer flowed like water. I was becoming mesmerized by the DEA lifestyle.

Steve was hosting a Christmas party at his house in Chesterfield, Mo. We were advised by our group supervisor that our attendance was mandatory and that we must bring our spouses. It was a big new expensive home, modern with high cathedral ceilings, designer furniture, and custom kitchen, and there was an expensive flower arrangement, compliments of TFD Horowitz.

The St. Louis Field Office DEA Special Agent in Charge (SAC) was in attendance with his wife, as well as other high ranking DEA officials. The city and county cops (Task Force Detectives) with their wives were not allowed to enter the living room area where Steve and his wife our group supervisor and his wife and the other DEA brass were drinking and talking.

The TFD's were sequestered in the kitchen. It was like two different parties under the same roof. Most of the city and county cops had been in investigative positions in their departments before coming to DEA and were treated with a little respect. It's something a cop gets used to, being respected by their peers. We were all being disrespected by DEA, and there was nothing we could do about it. It was a good gig being detached so we accepted the DEA insult and drank beer in the kitchen like hired servants.

But there were other instances of disrespect on our minds. Whenever some office furniture needed moving, or any other kind of labor needed doing, the other groups would call the SAC's office and request some TFD's to do the chore. We were whores for the federal government.

Steve's house had acoustic problems. Anything said in the kitchen echoed off of the cathedral ceilings in the living room where the DEA brass sat.

Guys like the SAC, who is black and came to St. Louis expecting to be treated like he would be treated in New York or Chicago, became incensed at unfriendly neighbors. The master plan with all federal law enforcement officials is to buy a house in a neighborhood you can't afford because the house will always go up in value, and you will always make money on it. They are usually transferred after five years. It keeps them house poor.

For guys like Steve Stoddard" St. Louis was home and it always would be. He wasn't on the federal fast track to promotion. He was a journeyman grade special agent which meant he was in place for as long as he wished to be.

He seemed to be the guy who had it all: big expensive home, classic sports car in his garage, wife with wealthy parents, and a job with power and prestige. He loved St. Louis, the Cardinals, The Blues, and the climate.

In neighborhoods in St. Louis County where they buy these monstrously expensive homes, their neighbors have moved to those neighborhoods to escape the black race. The people living in those neighborhoods look down their noses at government servants. The big time DEA employees get their feelings hurt quickly in places like St.Louis, and they become distrusting and hateful to anyone who is white and has grown up in the area.

The West County neighbors weren't friendly to the white federal executives either. A white agent was transferred to St. Louis from the deep-south. After moving in he threw a neighborhood party at his home for all of his new neighbors. It's a common practice in the south but not even thought of in trendy West County. The party was a bust. No one showed up. The agent immediately classified residents he met in the general area as "damn Yankees", and he sought revenge for the embarrassment of his doomed party on almost every city or county cop he came in to contact with.

We had a drug deal in southeast Missouri where the natives talk like southerners. They say, "ya'll and no-ma'am and yes sir and fixin," and they eat southern food. The southern agent was incensed that these people would dare talk like southerners. "Who do these hicks think they are talking like a southerner? They're north of the Mason

Dixon Line."

The SAC (Special Agent in Charge), was distrustful of all of the Task Force Detectives (cops detached to DEA). In the minds of most of the high ranking black DEA Agents we, as TFD's were mostly red necks from the Missouri woods. They had opinions of themselves as being worldly and sophisticated, educated and wise. When addressing them, we had to refer to them as Mr. or sir. The difference between them and us was that we kicked in drug dealer's doors for a living and they sat behind a desk.

But we were all loose cannons who were required to drink too much, be on call twenty four hours a day and to be the first person through the door with a sledge hammer for the Drug Enforcement Administration. But we weren't kitchen help, and most of us were outraged at being relegated to the kitchen.

The TFD's started getting loud as the party dragged on. Our group supervisor would periodically come in to the kitchen and tell us to keep our voices down. He was afraid we would offend the SAC or his wife. In order for our boss to get a promotion that would send him to DEA Headquarters in Washington, D.C., he needed the SAC's support. If he could get us to work like dogs for him and if he could keep us as a group in check, he had a good chance at promotion. It was all that mattered to him.

As a group we wandered into the master bedroom which was off of the kitchen. We figured we could be a little louder without offending anyone. Most of the group respected our group supervisor and would do anything to please him.

The coats of the DEA brass were laying on the king-sized bed. The SAC and his wife were large people, larger than any of the TFD's. There was a gigantic full length mink coat on the bed that belonged to the SAC's wife.

A St. Louis County Cop, who was a certified hero and had been awarded by his department for saving lives above and beyond the call of duty, eyeballed the coat. He dragged it on and walked around the bedroom making primate sounds. The group laughed uncontrollably. Our boss came into the room to quiet us down and observed the county cop hero wearing the SAC's wife's $10,000 mink.

Our boss was beside himself. We had done what he had asked us not to do. We had disrespected the SAC and his wife. "Take it off," he quietly said. The hero cop removed the coat and placed it back on the bed. "It's time for all of you to go. Please leave." We left en masse.

As in most corporations, schools, street gangs, police departments, and drug task force units, a lose lip usually sinks the ship. Something was allegedly said by "Little Stevie Wonder" about our group supervisor and his now estranged wife. Steve left the task force and was placed in another group of special agents.

Our group supervisor got his wish and was transferred to DEA Headquarters Washington, D.C. The drug deals slowed down, city and county cops came and went, and it was now my turn to rotate back to the police department.

It was a bitter sweet moment for me. I was never able to easily conform to any group's morays, but I did conform to the task force golden rule, "be one of the boys". I fought it and it won. I was at a point in my life where I was one hundred percent DEA. I didn't even question my culpability. Leaving the task force was like leaving home. I didn't want to go back to the police department.

Being a fed became cool and exciting. Working with the United States Attorney's office and the assistant USA's was unique and satisfying. I couldn't fathom going back to state court. The judges in state court allow the defense attorneys to abuse and attempt to humiliate the police officers while giving testimony. This behavior makes the defendant feel like his lawyer is doing a good job for him. The defense lawyer knows that most of the people on the jury hate cops so he puts on a show for the jury. It isn't that way in federal court. The federal judges are straight business.

The transfer came through. I reported to homicide. I didn't want to go there. One of the guys I had had problems with in Intelligence was now a lieutenant in homicide. Another guy who wasn't my friend was an aide to the chief of police. The aides basically run the police department.

I was just a couple of months shy of my twenty year retirement mark. It's an important milestone in most cops' lives. I looked upon the pension as something no one in my family had ever achieved.

I was placed in a three man service crew; a supervisor and two detectives. If there is any way that there is a third man out situation, I will play into it. I was the odd man in the group. I wasn't friends with the supervisor or my partner detective. It was a miserable existence.

The cops in the task force drank too much; this is a fact. We all told ourselves that we would "dry out" when we went back to the police department. It doesn't work. Cops drink in most bureaus. In homicide I either sat in the police car waiting for my partner to come out of a bar or I went in with him. I was compelled to be one of the boys again, and I didn't like the feeling.

I kept in touch with some of my DEA friends. Our group supervisor was now a real big shot in DEA headquarters. I also heard that Steve Stoddard" had been transferred out of the St. Louis Field Office and was now stationed in San Francisco, California. I couldn't figure this out, unless Steve decided to get on the fast track to promotion. It was almost etched in stone that he would finish his time with DEA in his beloved St. Louis.

He had just purchased another huge modern home in Grover, Missouri, sitting on a championship golf course. It's where people with big money lived. He would be playing golf with millionaires, bankers, business executives, and the like, if he were still living in good old St. Louis.

I did some checking. Steve's wife was living in the home. Steve was living above a garage at another agent's home in San Francisco. Somebody in DEA headquarters had gotten even with Steve. He was not a happy man. He missed St. Louis, his wife and family, and his million-dollar home. His life of power and prestige was unraveling. So was mine.

Steve was in a dilemma; he was fighting to get back to St. Louis, but his requests were being blocked by his enemy in headquarters. He didn't have enough time at DEA to take a retirement. He hated San Francisco but he had no choice but to stay in the garage apartment, arrest San Francisco dope weirdos instead of St. Louis dope weirdos, and await his chance to return home. It was a strange phenomenon for I was going through the same ordeal. I wanted to go back to the DEA Task Force. The police department was foreign to me. DEA had become my home.

Homicide was busy in the year I was assigned there. One month my three man service crew handled sixteen homicides. The service crew is the on-call crew who goes to the scene and investigates directly after the murder. In those days we would be investigating one crime scene and receive a call for another murder. It was hectic.

I heard through the grapevine that Steve Stoddard's wife contracted a terminal disease. I could imagine how Steve felt being sequestered in San Francisco while his wife was battling for her life in St. Louis. I again thought back to Bob Scheetz and his sermon on cops "big mouths." The mouth is more lethal than poison. It causes never ending repercussions for all involved. It's what caused this rift between Steve and our old supervisor. The supervisor gained power at headquarters, and he used it against Steve. He was being tortured for his past behavior, and it had affected his wife and his family.

It is remarkable how corporate enemies tactfully study one another to find the one spot to insert the thinly bladed knife. For Steve Stoddard leaving St. Louis was a fate worse than death. He lived like a wealthy man here. His life was glamorous compared to the other special agents; even the supervisors did not have the lifestyle of Steve Stoddard. St. Louis was Steve's Achilles heel. Remove him from his home and he will self-destruct.

The homicides we worked were mostly ethnic. There were shootings or cuttings for what someone said. They were boring; the witnesses were like aliens from another planet. Their descriptions of what happened and who had killed who was stupid.

The suspects all had nick names like Poo Poo or Kee Kee, or some other stupid slang name. The witnesses didn't know the real names of the shooters or cutters. They would say, "Boo Boo and Ree Ree got into an fight, you dig, and Ram Ram told them they had better stop or he was gonna off both of dem, you dig, so Pee Pee came ove to the crib, you dig, and offed all of dem, you dig? Then his play momma and my play grand momma said." It was ludicrous. I was used to interviewing millionaire drug dealers. Instead I was rolling over stinking dead bodies, searching them and conveying them to the morgue. I felt like a Haitian mortician. And to add insult to injury: I never asked to be a homicide dick. If fact I specified that I did not want to go to homicide. There was no investigation for the service crew. Just bodies and ethnic witnesses. No satisfaction, just sadness and pity.

There are indoor crime scenes and outdoor crime scenes. Crowds gather at both types of scenes. A beat cop usually gets the first call to a crime scene; he contacts his supervisor and the supervisor contacts homicide if the case is a death of a suspicious manner.

The neighbor inhabitants know what is going on in their neighborhood. If someone has $100 in loose bills in a nightstand drawer, the rumors in the neighborhood say there is $1000's.

When homicide arrives on a crime scene, the crowds lowly moan in fear of the unknown, death. If the scene is outdoors they can watch and make sighs of fear and despair.

If the scene is indoors, they are left in suspense. After a crime scene investigation, the medical examiner calls for the conveyance for the ride to the morgue for the victim.

When the "meat wagon" arrives, the crowds go berserk, moaning and exclaiming, signifying and chanting as if they just witnessed the culmination of a voodoo curse.

The homicide detectives scan the crowd as they exit the scene. The chances are strong that the perpetrator is among the voodoo voyeurs. It is a scene from south Florida or back country Louisiana.

City homicide was not my cup of tea. It was time for me to reassess my life. I was not thinking properly. I attributed it to the beating I received from Paul Wayne King and the boozing I did at DEA. I had difficulty focusing and I couldn't stay on track when I started a homicide report. I was failing miserably with no place to go but out the door with a measly twenty year pension.

I had acquired attributes that I despised; I had a short temper, pride, no humility, and I felt I was important. I had become "one of them". I was extremely disappointed in myself.

I had a young family, a mortgage, and bills. I could not have survived on forty percent of my pay. I was having trouble surviving on one hundred percent of it.

The cool fall evenings in the Central West End (the garden spot of the bloody ninth) was often on my mind. On the private streets off Euclid, where the mansions were, the ones built for the 1904 World's Fair, the pin oak trees were dropping their leaves.

I had occasionally walked a beat on Euclid, and I would walk the private streets and admire the grand old homes. I had been inside many of them. Victims call cops. The residents were victimized frequently. The homes were so large that someone could break in at night, and the resident wouldn't hear the turmoil. One guy got up in the middle of the night to use the bathroom and bumped in to a burglar in the hallway.

The shopkeepers and the restaurant owners liked to see a cop in their businesses. The beat cop ate well. Some of the residents would invite the beat cop inside for a cool glass of iced tea. I can't see that happening in any other major city. The CWE is mid-west urban paradise.

I kept trudging through the turmoil of service crew homicide. Every day was an unthinkable chore. We were always on call; the telephone would go off at 0300, and I would have to trudge in and handle an ethnic murder. There was no getting away from it.

On October 24, we received a call for service at 4611 McPherson. It was in the CWE and I knew the area well. I visualized the location as we drove there. It was late evening, 2108 hours, and the streets were lighted by dim street lights. It was "fall quiet" with hardly a breeze. We arrived and took charge of the crime scene.

EMS was already there and had been for some time. They had tried to save the victim's life, but their labor was to no avail.

The victim, Peter Maguire, a guy about thirty five was lying on his back toward the rear of his car in an area between the street and the sidewalk. His face was covered in blood, and he was lying on a bed of oak leaves about one foot thick. I could see his face, and I commented to my partner that he was a "white guy".

There was a lot of blood, not regular blood but thick inner-organ type blood, and it had covered the oak leaves in coagulating blobs. There was blood on the hood of his car, a late model Mustang, and there was blood on the door and around the driver's side of the car.

The blood on the hood appeared to be hand prints. We later found out that the hand prints were Peter Maguire's. I glanced around the neighborhood, a place I was familiar with and comfortable in. I felt like I was home after a long adventurous voyage.

The cool and the quiet were comfortable and calming to me. The giant trees and mansions were warm remembrances, like seeing old friends. We searched the scene for evidence. There was a twenty five caliber shell casing in the bloody leaves, a paper bag containing a paperback book, "The Magic in Your Mind," a cigarette, a book of matches, a photo negative, and seven-keys on a ring.

We continued with our preliminary investigation by knocking on doors and interviewing possible witnesses. Most of the possible witnesses stated they had heard what they thought was a shot, looked out, and saw nothing.

My partner tried to interview a juvenile, but his mother refused to allow him to be interviewed. She told the detective that if he wanted to question her son he would have to go through her attorney. The juvenile witness had seen more than most of the people interviewed.

After some prodding by our supervisor, the mother allowed the interview. The juvenile stated that he was doing his homework in front of the second floor South West window of his home when he heard what he thought was a firecracker.

He looked outside and saw two black guys, both approximately five foot, ten. One of them ran toward the east on McPherson, one of them stayed by the car and looked at his hands, then ran east. After they left the sight of the witness, he heard a car door slam.

The witness went to the first floor front door and looked out through the window. He saw the victim staggering near a car to the west of his home. He called 911.

My supervisor, my partner, and I were trying to visualize what had transpired. I figured the victim, who was out of his element being alone in the CWE at night, had just purchased the book at the bookstore at McPherson and Euclid, was walking to his car, and was killed during a botched street robbery.

The victim was white and soft. He emitted a vibe, smell and demeanor of a person who is a victim. Predators pick up on the slightest variance of a possible victim. Maybe it's the gait, just one step too many or maybe a stumble. It might be the movement of the head showing insecurity or lack of confidence that triggers the predator. But fear is the trigger that puts it all together for the street killer. It's like a tiger shark smelling blood in the water. If there is fear then the predator has the upper hand. If a victim emits fear, it's all over for him.

To me the scene read like a book; the victim was accosted, tried to run, was shot, and then left to die. He knew the nasty little twenty five caliber slug had gone deep in to his soft white body. He probably felt it severing one of his main arteries.

He felt the blood gushing from his mouth and knew that when that happens there's no coming back. He wanted to help himself but he couldn't. He was angry at himself for being killed by a deranged street predator who just wanted to rob him.

He staggered around in the street, banged his hands on the hood of his beloved Mustang, staggered over to the soft bed of oak leaves, fell out and bled out. That's the way I saw it. My partner and my supervisor agreed with me.

We wrapped up the scene. Peter Maguire went to the morgue. His car went to the police garage for a complete forensic investigation. We went to police headquarters to sort this out, contact his next of kin, and write the reports. It was going to be a long night.

I wondered if I would be able to do any investigating in the case. It had perked my interest. I loved a long and intricate investigation. It's what I had been trained to do and I missed it.

The victim's dad came to our offices. It was another sad experience to add to the scores of bad homicide interviews. He talked about his son the way most survivors of the dead do. He said the same thing, "the parent isn't supposed to outlive the child."

The dad advised me that Peter had a Gold American Express credit card. He asked me if he could have it. Peter Maguire's property was still at the morgue. I was going to the morgue and retrieve it from his property and was advised by my supervisor that I would be breaking protocol if I did so. The property would be turned over to the next of kin when the medical examiner deemed it necessary. Mr. Maguire heard my supervisor and didn't ask for anything else. He left and I never saw him again.

We wrote the report between homicides. It took about a week but the Peter Maguire scene report was finished. There was another report floating around the office pertaining to the murder of Peter Maguire. A morgue attendant stole Peter Maguire's gold credit card and went on a shopping spree. He was arrested by some detectives in homicide. There's no honor anywhere in the judicial system.

Time marched on and I was still rolling over dead bodies and conveying them to the morgue. Things hadn't gotten any better for me in the homicide section.

I kept contact with some old associates in DEA. I was advised that Steve Stoddard had taken "family leave," had left San Francisco, and was caring for his terminally ill wife in Grover, Missouri. Apparently he had enough sick leave on the books that he could retire when it ran out and would never have to return to San Francisco or DEA.

His nemesis in DEA headquarters wasn't able to hinder his "family leave" request. I bumped in to Steve and his wife at a Cardinals' ballgame. She looked like she was on the mend. Steve looked stressed and heavy.

The ethnic murders kept on coming. There were so many that I couldn't keep track of them. They all just ran together in my mind. The crime scenes, the method of attack, and the witnesses were mostly the same. It was as if murder didn't matter. It was a cultural phenomenon that society would never stop.

We had a murder in the west end. A victim was lying on some steps of a neatly kept old home, stabbed to death in broad daylight. EMS showed up and pronounced him dead on the scene (DOS), and the area supervisor contacted homicide.

As we were investigating at the scene, moving the body, and trying to locate any witnesses; a man came up to me and announced that he was the guy I was looking for. I asked him why I would be looking for him, and he told me he was the one who had knifed the victim.

I handcuffed him and my supervisor came over to us. I advised the supervisor of the spontaneous statement given by the neighbor man. He read him his constitutional rights, and we had him conveyed to the homicide offices.

We continued to do our preliminary investigation at the scene, had the body conveyed to the morgue, and then went to our offices. I interviewed the confessor.

He advised me that the neighbor (victim) had brutally raped his thirteen year old daughter. The victim was in his fifties. The confessor told me he was having trouble living with the crime and that his daughter cried a lot, and it pained him to watch her go through this turmoil in her life. He advised that his daughter was a good girl and didn't deserve to be raped by the monster next door who had tricked her in- to coming into his house.

The confessor stated that he just snapped when he observed the neighbor sitting on his porch steps as if he had done nothing wrong. He walked over to confront the victim and the rapist laughed at him.

The rapist didn't know it but the confessor had a large knife concealed in his waistband. The confessor grabbed the knife and thrust it in to the rapist gut, then walked back home and had dinner with his family.

I mentally fought with his actions. I was having trouble with the killing, not because of the death but because I deeply felt that he was justified in doing it. I was still an eastside person, and I believed in "street justice." The courts are a joke in the same manner society is a joke.

The problem with killing someone, justified or not, is that the crime does not fall within the parameters of discretion. The justified killer would be going to prison.

We booked the confessor for murder first, wrote the reports, and I took the reports to the Circuit Attorney's Office. The assistant circuit attorney did not issue a warrant. The suspect was released. I felt that justice had been served twice in the same case.

As a crew, we went on with our homicide lives. I was advised by my supervisor that the case would probably be sent to a Grand Jury. I would have to testify at that preceding. I didn't forget the confessor's demeanor at the time of his arrest or the case. I wondered if he would be sent to prison for defending the honor of his daughter. It bothered me even more because it was an ethnic murder with a twist. I had tried to harden myself against any personal feelings toward ethnic murders. I swore to myself I wouldn't get involved in any of them, except to convey the bodies and write the reports, but the frankness of the confessor and the brutality of the rapist haunted me.

I had been to many Grand Juries. There are times during the secret court hearings when the jurors want to talk to the cop giving testimony. It is usually a friendly event with the assistant circuit attorney asking the cop questions and moderating the preceding.

I enjoyed Grand Juries because they were made up of citizens trying to make the correct decisions concerning the lives of the victims and the state. In reality the state is always the victim.

I wondered if they would ask for my opinion. I felt deeply that the victim was the confessor and his daughter. But if I offered any information concerning my feelings, I could be considered an advocate of the arrested subject. I had decided that I was going to offer my opinion and see where it got me. I kept watching for the Grand Jury subpoena but I never saw it.

I heard that Steve Stoddard's wife had died. I envisioned him in his large fashionable home alone. To me being alone would be a fate worse than death. I wondered about his alcohol consumption. If it wasn't under control, he would kill himself with booze. I knew my own consumption was not under control.

I kept my ear peeled for any information in the Peter Maguire murder. I was extremely interested in it, and I longed to work the case. His murder was what homicide cops refer to as "wide open" meaning there was little evidence and "shaky" witnesses.

Homicide Detective Sergeant Joe Burgoon, a legend in his own time and a cop who is known worldwide for solving difficult murders, was contacted by the police department firearms examiner about a gun that was sent to his laboratory by a Third District officer. The gun was a twenty five automatic, and it was the weapon used in the murder of Peter Maguire.

Every gun that is seized by St. Louis police officers and sent to the laboratory is test fired by a firearms examiner. The projectile (slug) from the fired weapon is then compared with the bullets taken from victims of homicides that have not been solved and the ballistics compared. The slug test fired from the seized twenty five was positively the weapon used to murder Peter Maguire.

Sergeant Burgoon advised two of his detectives, Sal Chrum and Joe McCullough, to contact the firearms examiner and find out where the gun came from. I knew both of these detectives. They were top notch investigators. Joe McCullough's dad was a city cop. He was murdered on duty in the Pruitt Igoe Housing Project in the 1960's.

He was a canine cop giving backup to another cop when someone in a crowd shot him. He died at the scene. His canine partner tore the police car up trying to get out to assist him. I heard the story years earlier and I never forgot it. Joe's brother is the St. Louis County prosecuting attorney.

There is an age-old saying in the cop business: "crooks will never let you down". Criminals are basically stupid. Even intelligent criminals commit blunders that get them caught. It's why cops make bad criminals. They think they know the in's and out's of the crime game, and they get confident. When that happens they make the one mistake that gets them incarcerated.

I obtained a copy of the gun report and read it. The Third District is larger and busier than the ninth, but it isn't referred to as "bloody." Mike Bowman and Joe O'Brien, two hard charging Third District officers had information there was a dice game being held at 4029 Blaine.

The cops staked the house out and observed the "crap" game through a window. The front door was open so they walked in and raided it. One of the gamblers tossed the gun as the cops rushed in. It was found on the floor, seized and conveyed to the department laboratory.

The big question now was who did the gun belong to? It was a crappy gun, held together with electricians tape and only capable of being fired one time. I had seen twenty five automatics many times. They were small but deadly. Even in the condition of this junk gun it, was capable of killing Peter Maguire. But it and the person pointing and pulling the trigger didn't just kill him, they made him suffer, vomit blood, panic, run around his car, and bleed out until he died on a soft bed of oak leaves across the street from a million dollar, hundred year old mansion.

Detectives Joe McCullough and Sal Chrum went to 4029 Blaine and spoke to the lady who lived there, Mary Riley. When asked about the owner of the gun she advised that she was the owner and that she was holding the gun for a neighbor who owed her $40.00.

She stated that the person who actually owned the gun was named Walter Conner and he lived in the downstairs apartment at 4035 Blaine.

They proceeded to 4035 Blair and interviewed Walter. He advised that he did not give the gun to Mary Riley but that she received the gun from an acquaintance of his by the name of Al.

The returned to 4029 Blair and re-interviewed Mary Riley. After some thought she advised that she indeed had received the gun from Al, but had seen Walter with the gun on several occasions prior to her coming in possession of the gun. Mary stated that Al works at the Truman Center on Arsenal.

The detectives identified Al as Alf Taylor. They interviewed him. He stated that he knew both Conner and Riley. He recalled giving a twenty five semi-automatic to Riley for a debt that he owed her. He stated that the gun was a piece of junk with one of the handles broken and the trigger missing. He gave the gun to Mary Riley on the same day he got it from Walter Conner.

Detectives Chrum and McCullough continued their investigation going from one lead to another----from one witness/suspect with strange nick names to another until they finally pinpointed their suspects.

Detectives Chrum an McCullough interviewed a suspect named Timothy Hollins and asked him about the twenty five automatic and his whereabouts on the evening of October 24, 1989. Hollins paused and then told the detectives he wanted to talk to them about that evening.

He stated he was at home when Harold Hayden (suspect), called him and wanted to come down and visit. He did not have a ride so he and Ivory Jones (suspect), drove out to the Charvel Apartments at Lucas & Hunt and Halls Ferry to pick him up.

As they were driving back toward the city Harold showed him the twenty five automatic with the electrical tape on the handle. He advised them that he didn't have any money, and he needed to get some money. Tim knew this meant they needed to rob somebody to get some money.

Harold told Tim to drive to the Central West End as there were always people there with money. Tim drove to Kingshighway and Maryland, around the fountain, and then turned left on Euclid to McPherson. He turned right on McPherson, and as they were driving, Harold pointed out a white guy walking west on McPherson and said, "He looks like an easy mark". The guy was Peter Maguire. He had parked his car a city block from the Left Bank Book Store and was walking toward it on the north side of McPherson.

He exhibited the telltale signs of a victim and the pack of street predators picked up on it. They stalked him, watching him as he entered the bookstore. They waited patiently like a pack of jackals and followed him as he walked back to his car.

Tim parked the car east bound on McPherson while Harold and Ivory climbed out of the car to intercept their prey. About five minutes later he heard a shot and he looked around. He saw Harold running east on McPherson toward him. Harold jumped into the car. Ivory then came running and entered the car. Tim sped off turning north on Taylor and eventually going home where they stayed for the rest of the night.

Tim stated he asked Harold why he shot the guy. Harold replied the guy had tried to run from him and he shot him. He further stated he had shot the guy in the leg. The next day Ivory sold the gun. He stated as far as he knew they did not get any money from the guy (Peter Maguire) on McPherson.

As I heard the homicide section banter, and as I examined the case and the investigation, I realized that these were the type of murder investigations that redeem the credibility of any big city police department.

The victim was a real victim. He wasn't a guy trying to buy sex or dope. He was a guy shopping for a book to read. The neighborhood was a first class venue for homes and businesses.

The assailants were real criminals, not misguided youths, or mentally ill street people. They stalked and murdered their victim. I felt good about the case, but I was trying to get up enough nerve to ask to be transferred back to the Ninth District. I felt it was where I belonged.

My supervisor, Lieutenant Steve Jacobsmeyer, a friend to the underdog cop, came to my desk. "Why didn't you go to the grand jury on the confessor case?" he sternly asked.

I was in a mental fog as I looked at him. "The confessor case?" I mumbled. "I didn't see the subpoena."

"Yes you did. It's still in the subpoena box." He walked toward the subpoena box hanging on the wall. He dug in to it and handed me the subpoena. It had been smashed down to the bottom of the pile.

Embarrassment hit me hard. I stood dumbfounded with no reasonable excuse. It was almost a cardinal sin to miss court. Grand Juries aren't rescheduled. The confessor went free. "Justice is served," I muttered to myself.

Steve walked away from me. I could tell he was miffed so I followed him. I felt he was a friend and I trusted him. He turned and looked at me as he got to his desk. "I'm going to have to write you up, and I don't want to do it. Do you know how much trouble it is going to be for me to write you up? I don't have time for it. It's going to be a pain in the ass."

"I've got an idea," I replied. "How about you send me back to uniform? That should be punishment enough, right? I'd like to go back to the bloody ninth, but I'll go anywhere. Would that be considered enough punishment?"

Steve didn't give me an answer. He looked down to his desk and read murder reports. I walked out wondering what was going to happen to me.

About a month went by. I had heard that Steve Stoddard had been introduced to a lady through some DEA friends and that they were now cohabitating. I asked about his drinking and was told it had gotten worse.

Transfers came out and my name was on the list. I went back to the bloody Ninth District. I didn't have any uniforms so I showed up at roll call in civilian attire. When the uniform office opened I went there and got a full set of new uniforms.

To my surprise the ninth hadn't changed much. There was a new station and new cars and computers inside the cars, but the street was the same. The street creatures cops dealt with were the same. Different faces and names but the same people.

It was the same with the cops. Different faces and names but basically the same bunch of guys. It dawned on me that I was destined to be back in the ninth. It's like I was a migratory animal seeking home, and there was nothing I could do about it. I always felt I would be back, but I dismissed the feeling because I felt I was good at playing the game of being special. I had a special assignment, and I acted the part that I needed to act in order to survive. I wasn't a special guy.

The pressure of the cop job was lifted from me. I had twenty years on and could get a retirement anytime I wished. I could show up for work and then tell them, "I quit," if I wanted to and walk out. I was vested.

I didn't worry about cases, informants, court appearance, or anything else. I was just an old street cop plying my trade and letting time speed by.

I heard that Steve Stoddard got married; then I heard they split up but didn't get divorced. I heard he was drinking a lot, and it was affecting his life in negative ways.

Several years went by and I read Steve's obit. I had a friend in the St. Louis County Medical Examiner's office. I called her and she read me the medical examiner's report over the phone.

She told me Steve was alone in his home and had called his estranged wife and told her he was feeling badly. She went to the house, entered, and found Steve dead in a hallway.

Because of his stature the St. Louis County Police arrived. The estranged wife told them that Steve was an alcoholic. The local cops knew of Steve's drinking problems. There were empty vodka bottles and beer cans scattered throughout the house. Steve had drunk himself to death.

I thought about Steve and I compared our lives. I had an out, an escape route, a place to go, and re-group. It was an insane place with a bloody reputation, but it was there waiting for me in my time of trouble.

I was able to break the cops' golden rule, "Be one of the boys." Steve was a special guy. His title, awarded to him by the United States Government, was "special agent" and he and most special agents live up to their title. It means they can do almost anything at any time and get away with it.

In their minds they are licensed to kill, licensed to lie, and licensed to drink themselves to death. It's the curse of the special person.

'INDEX'

The diversity of the cop business never ceases to amaze me. Just a mere sixteen days ago I was going to my office in a one-hundred year old building in the downtown area. There was no place to park the stinking, dilapidated detective-car. My little desk was ancient: the drawers didn't lock, the surface was pock marked, and the walls were coated with nicotine and cheap paint. The typewriters were ancient. The office was thick with smoke and the windows didn't open. It had to be that way so the murder suspects couldn't toss contraband, or themselves out of them.

I dealt daily with desperate damaged people; victims who were dead, victims who were left behind to try to piece their lives back together after losing a loved one. There was never a happy moment. Murder quickly became mediocre and there was no escape from it.

I had been trying to escape mediocrity for the entirety of my life, but despite my efforts, I dug myself deeper into it. I had a mediocre name, Ray Arnold. I was born and raised in a mediocre and infamous town, East St. Louis, Illinois. I had a dangerous job with mediocre pay, so I reluctantly accepted mediocrity, but I still continued to fight it from within by constantly trying to better myself. I worked at being fit and well read and semi-educated. It was the East side curse, a cur dog, and it followed me across the Mississippi to the big city.

I wondered if the mediocrity cur would follow me to Clayton, the county seat and business hub of the metropolitan area. I had a new assignment: a federal appointment, a federal supervisor, a seized Corvette to drive, a parking spot inside a tiered garage, an open modern office with computers, and a great view of a bustling business street from four stories up. The flea-bitten monster-hound hadn't found me yet, but I had brought something else with me, a dossier. The feds knew my demeanor, authority and conformation, I had problems in both fields. I was beaten up on my first drug deal. Set up by some Feds. Now I was being lectured by a Fed while my damaged brain played tricks on me. The humility was overbearing.

I never liked Feds. I could sometimes muster up a little respect for FBI agents but not very often. I had worked with them, on and off for fifteen years, having been a detective with the P.D., but I could never say, you know, I like that FBI agent.

But when it came to narcotics Feds, the most I could dole out was a total lack of respect. I could never say I liked any of them. They were intense to the extent of being annoying. As far back as I can remember, I have been able to read people and know their intentions. For most folks, especially cops, it's a skill they acquire and then polish. But it was pure bred in me. I believe I was born with it.

DEA Feds are just like us cops, but they feel they are superior. They aren't overly educated like FBI agents. They aren't smooth and smart like Treasury agents, and they aren't sophisticated like CIA agents. They present a false persona, that they are the top of the food chain in Federal Law Enforcement. This causes distrust amongst local law enforcement because we as cops read people for a living. We know what we see. It is one of our most revered traits.

Cops know nuts when we see them. We can walk into a room and without fanfare, spot a troubled individual. It is what keeps us alive, because mostly what cops do is go into people's homes and try to help them solve their problems.

We don't go uninvited. We answer our police radio when someone calls to report a domestic dispute. When we walk in we nonchalantly look around and we catalogue, subconsciously, who and what the dangers are to us.

So when we come into contact with a federal drug agent, with their winking eyes, and toothy smiles, we local cops put up our guard. And when you get to know the agent, and maybe drink a beer with him, after two beers he or she starts talking you and your department down, and talking themselves and the Drug Enforcement Administration up. They start by talking about pay.

Feds make more money than local cops. That's a fact, but who cares? The local cops don't care. We can work overtime, or a second job and make federal-type cash. And drug agents are always acting like they want to sell you something. They are used car dealers with federal credentials and a gun.

It sends up an alert for a local cop. "Danger, nut in presence. Take precaution." It's just like going into a domestic disturbance home where the male is drunk and the female has a mouse under her eye. You know you're going to have to fight the drunk.

DEA guys and gals are part of the Department of Justice, just like the FBI, but they, as agents, are fearful of that agency. They are the little brothers of the FBI. They fear the FBI is constantly monitoring them: listening to their telephone calls, reading their reports, auditing their cash seizures, interviewing their informants, placing agents under surveillance, and they have reason for their paranoia. The FBI is monitoring them, constantly.

Cops have names for the people they hate. Internal Affairs Division investigators are referred to as creeps, snitches, back-stabbers. DEA folks refer to FBI folks as Feebs, and they usually spit on the ground when the say it.

This morning was lecture time for Detective Ray Arnold and it reminded me of junior high school. I had the same numb feeling in my gut telling me I had to conform and do what I was told or the new infraction would be stacked upon my East side curse dossier and used against me in this life and the next one.

About The Author

Timothy C. Richards is a former St. Louis Police Detective. he held several highly sensitive investigative positions during his tenure: Intelligence Unit (investigating organized crime groups), U.S. Department of Justice Drug Enforcement Task Force, and a stint as a homicide detective. he is highly decorated by local and federal jurisdictions.

Superman's Eyes is his second non-fiction cop/detective book. He is author of *Crooks Kill, Cops Lie* (5-star book on Amazon.com) and novels *Steal Today, Die Tomorrow,* and *Dope is a D.E.A.d Man's Game,* cop/detective murder mysteries featuring Homicide Detective Ray Arnold. He writes them like he lived them. His writing is in-your-face, true and shocking.

Superman's Eyes is a revealing look into the psyche of every police officer who ever slid into the seat of a cop car. A purely satisfying read for the cop voyeur.